HUNGRY FOR HOME

STORIES OF FOOD FROM ACROSS THE CAROLINAS
WITH MORE THAN 200 FAVORITE RECIPES

AMY ROGERS

FOREWORD BY JOHN EGERTON

JOHN F. BLAIR,
PUBLISHER

First John F. Blair, Publisher, edition
    published in 2004
First published by
NOVELLO FESTIVAL PRESS,
an imprint of the Public Library of Charlotte
and Mecklenburg County, 310 N. Tryon St.,
Charlotte, North Carolina 28202.

Printed in the United States of America

Several of the author's pieces are adapted from
those that appeared in print or were broadcast pre-
viously. Grateful acknowledgment is made to
Down Home Press, publisher of *Red Pepper Fudge
and Blue Ribbon Biscuits: Favorite Stories and
Recipes from N.C. State Fair Winners* for "Edna's
Old Fashioned Pound Cake," "Dee Pufpaff: A Ca-
jun Cook Comes to North Carolina," "Blue Rib-
bon Biscuits: Made by Hand"; to *Creative Loafing*
magazine for "The Kitchen at Wildacres," "Work-
ing Poor but Rich in Blessings," and "Happily
Ever After"; and WFAE-FM for "All-American
Food," "Life Without Sugar," "The Passover
Table" and "Gift Food." A version of "Happy
Chanukah, Y'all," originally appeared in *Gaston
Seasons* magazine and was broadcast on WFAE-
FM. "Dori Sanders, Peach Farmer" originally ap-
peared in *Gaston Seasons* magazine and later in
*Cornbread Nation I: The Best of Southern Food
Writing*, published by University of North Car-
olina Press in association with the Southern Food-
ways Alliance, Center for the Study of Southern
Culture, University of Mississippi.

For an extension of this copyright page,
    see page 404
Book design by Bonnie Campbell
Cover design by Leslie B. Rindoks
Cover illustration by David Wilgus

Library of Congress Cataloging-in-
    Publication Data
Rogers, Amy T.
    Hungry for home : stories of food from
    across the Carolinas with more than 200
    favorite recipes / Amy Rogers ; foreword by
    John Egerton. — 1st John F. Blair ed.
        p.   cm.
Includes index.
ISBN 0-89587-301-X (alk. paper)
    1. Cookery. 2. Cookery—North Carolina.
    3. Cookery--South Carolina. I. Title.

TX714.R612 2004
641.59756--dc22

2004002188

Dedicated to the countless men and women
whose hunger leads them to seek a better life

TABLE OF CONTENTS

FOREWORD

Now here's a combo that takes both hands to handle: Southern cooking and Southern wordsmiths—sublime food elegantly described.

Take the wordsmiths first. How many times have you picked up a novel or a book of short stories, or listened to a speaker on stage (that could be anywhere from a coliseum to a front porch), and said to yourself, "Who is this silver-throated devil?" The best of them are long-winded, deep-dipped masters of the mother tongue, tale-spinners with an accent and an attitude. I can spot them as soon as I'm within earshot. When they're on a roll, they can sculpt a phrase, paint a picture, bend you double or give you chills.

Now let's talk about cooks, Southern cooks. They come in all sizes, shapes and colors. Some can talk a blue streak while others seem to have taken a vow of silence. Some guard their culinary secrets like the crown jewels, others give them away like Mardi Gras trinkets. They may be super-organized recipe wonks or improvisers who cook by their senses, the way Ray Charles plays piano. But whatever their approach, all of them know from experience and intuition how to blend the staples and seasonings of the South into a distinctly delicious cuisine.

Pair these two genius types in the same kitchen, and *bam!* you get a chemical reaction comparable to nitrogen and oxygen, Rhett and Scarlett, Tarheels and Gamecocks, lime juice and honey.

That's where Amy Rogers is leading us when we get *Hungry for Home*, her enticing collection of food memories from the Carolinas. She has mined the mother lode for North and South Carolina writers and storytellers with tales to tell about the dishes and beverages that draw them home to momma. It would be hard to imagine a more ideal conductor for this medley than Amy, a cook and writer of surpassing talent herself—and a founding editor of Novello Festival Press, the excitingly successful new publishing venture of the Public Library of Charlotte and Mecklenburg County.

I could go on in deeper detail, but you get the point: If the food you grew up on still resonates within your soul, this is the book that will give you satisfaction. It's like play-by-play with your favorite announcer, or reality TV with a country ham or a heaping platter of fried chicken shimmering grail-like in the distance. You have no choice but to press on and devour *Hungry for Home* word for word, dish by dish, until you reach the end. And then you can start over.

May you enjoy each page in the peak of health.

—JOHN EGERTON

INTRODUCTION

It was a late winter Tuesday when Hattie Ann Frazier and some of her classmates took a break from their schoolwork and went downtown. They stopped at a local Charlotte lunch place, sat down and looked at the menus. But when it came time to order, the waitresses left their stations, turned their backs on the students, and walked out.

It was 1960 in North Carolina and Hattie Ann Frazier was black. So were the other well-dressed young men and women who sat on the chrome-backed stools that ran the length of the F.W. Woolworth lunch counter. There would be no food served to black patrons that day.

It had started in Greensboro, just eight days earlier on February 1, when four freshmen from North Carolina A&T sat down at the whites-only Woolworth lunch counter in their city and politely asked to be served. They were refused. A waitress told them to leave, but they insisted on staying, even when the police came. The store manager closed the lunch counter rather than serve a meal to Franklin McCain, Joe McNeill, David Richmond and Ezell Blair, Jr.

On February 12, the movement came to Rock Hill, South Carolina, where a reported 100 students sat in at Woolworth and McCrory stores. Already sit-ins were taking place across North Carolina, in Fayetteville, and in Raleigh, the state's capital. Throughout February and March the movement swept across South Carolina, from the tiny village of Denmark near the Lowcountry, to Orangeburg and Greenville, and to the capital city of Columbia in the Midlands.

Just twenty years old, Hattie Ann was one of several hundred protesters in Charlotte who took part in the sit-ins. Her parents back home in Lancaster, South Carolina, were worried. "I know I'm doing the right thing," their daughter said. Fellow Johnson C. Smith University students B.B. DeLaine, J. Charles Jones and Edith Strickland had organized meetings on campus, asking only for volunteers who would adhere to the tenets of non-violence.

What the black students wanted was the right to sit, be served, and eat as paying customers in the establishments where whites were welcome.

And they fought the battle to win that right, not with violent confrontations, but with polite and orderly, yet unrelenting pressure through sit-ins and picket lines. Still, sometimes it got ugly. Many students were arrested; some even refused bail and served jail time in a campaign they called "Jail, No Bail."

Then two other Smith students did the unthinkable. Betty Houchins and Thomas Wright were light-skinned blacks—so light that many thought they were white. The pair went downtown to Ivey's, a Charlotte department store where the fine ladies shopped. They crossed the picket line and approached the roped-off area in front of the store. To their astonishment, the white man standing guard opened the entrance and allowed them inside. They quietly made their way to the restaurant, where they ordered chicken salad sandwiches. The waitress was pleasant as she served them. "We were so nervous our hands were shaking," remembers the woman with skin the color of caramel. The couple paid the bill. Then they went outside and joined the picket line.

As the sit-ins spread from the Carolinas to the rest of the South, the nation couldn't ignore the protests and pickets. Organized bus boycotts had begun in 1955; the March on Washington was still three years in the future. But when African Americans in 1960 united over the right to sit and eat in the presence of whites who were doing the same, the Civil Rights movement coalesced across the South in a way it hadn't before.

Putting food at the center of the debate not only made the issue concrete, it made it universal. Within a matter of months, lunch counter owners who were losing money, along with civic leaders who had begun to comprehend the protestors' resolve, finally relented. By the summer of 1960, the lunch counters began to integrate, one by one.

That Southern society became a sort of civic melting pot in this way opens a window into the region's culture, and its cuisine. Whether we recognize it or not, events such as the Civil Rights sit-ins have influenced how, where and what we eat. The 1960s were a cultural snapshot of a time and place in the Carolinas, and food was an important component. But neither that time nor that place were unique; you could make the same statement about the 1860s, the 1760s, or almost any other time in history.

For this book, I asked current and former Carolinians to share with me, and with you, their stories about the foods, people and places that are meaningful to them. The vignettes, essays, profiles and recipes you are about to read comprise a cultural and culinary portrait as complex as any you can imagine. This book isn't meant to be a reference source, except in the sense that it contains good writing and recipes for good food. Think of it as a sampler that offers a variety of flavors, with something for every taste.

Among the men and women who tell their stories here are descendants of slaves, colonists, immigrants, and the native first people who lived in the Carolinas long ago; the recipes are as diverse as the backgrounds and beliefs of the contributors. Through times of strife and celebration, of poverty and plenty, food connects us to those people whose traditions we want to uphold.

After graduation, activist Betty Houchins moved north and married John Lundy; they made their home in Ohio where today, the children and grandchildren like to hear Betty tell and retell her stories.

Hattie Ann Frazier married Joseph Walker and stayed in North Carolina. Forty-three years after the first lunch counter sit-in, she still remembers her thirst for "that fountain Coke" she was denied. "When integration finally happened, we went to Woolworth's and had hot dogs," she remembers today. "They looked so good." And she did one other thing. She took her mother downtown to the Kress store where they liked to shop and went to the dining room. Then the two women sat down to eat.

—AMY ROGERS

1

From the Start:

APPETIZERS,

SOUPS AND SALADS

"ALL-AMERICAN FOOD"

Amy Rogers

What makes you who you are? Is it your family name, the place you come from, what you believe? In one way, the food you eat defines you. Few of us eat exactly the way we did growing up, and fewer of us cook those foods today as they were prepared for us back then. What we choose to eat reveals something about us, even if it's unintentional.

When it comes to food, nearly all of us are mongrels. We are people whose culinary origins, no matter how noble, have crossbred with others over the years to produce the hybrid mix of who we are today. If you disagree, consider this: Let's say you're a Southerner, born and bred in Dixie, and faithful to your heritage. Your favorite foods are fried chicken, rice and gravy, fried okra, and peach pie, all washed down with sweet tea. All American, and more to the point, all Southern, right?

Wrong.

Early European traders brought chickens to the Americas, from their home countries and from Africa. Traders also brought rice from Asia. While the crop took hold in the colonies, it never flourished until slaves, captured from rice-growing countries in western Africa, arrived in the South. It was slaves and their ability to plant, harvest, and store rice that not only re-energized Southern cooking, but the Southern economy as well.

Okra came from Africa, peaches from Spain, tea from Asia. Sugar, traded around the globe for more than 400 years, eventually made its way to the Caribbean, where it bolstered that region's economy as well.

Are you Italian? You probably don't know that your tomatoes and peppers are native to the Americas. Maybe you're Irish, and faithful to your country's culinary history. Your potatoes, or at least their ancestors, are American, too.

Explorers and immigrants, slaves and royalty; it may not seem that these long-gone people could have had such a lasting impact on the way we eat today. But history, geography, economics, and politics are exactly the forces that determine what we find on our supermarket shelves, in restaurants and on our plates.

You can think of it as a tree. No matter how solid and firmly rooted you may be, geographically and in your food habits, once you look up the tree there are too many branches to count, and they reach in every direction. What's more, the way we eat will continue to change, even subtly, influenced by unseen forces and the evolution of human culture. This is well documented in academic research, and in ambitious cookbooks and other food-themed books that not only offer recipes, but culinary context for the dishes as well. Such research investigates and interprets the complicated interminglings of food and culture that are known as foodways.

These days, as they have for generations, deli counters still sell meat and cheese by the pound, but now they also tempt their customers with wild-rice-and-cranberry salads, sushi and barbecue. You can get a pizza topped with pineapple and jalapeños delivered right to your door. And on Chinese restaurant buffets, near the spare ribs and wontons, you can often help yourself to soft-serve ice cream with candy toppings to sprinkle on top.

This trend toward overlapping and combining foods into before-unimagined combinations is going to continue, especially as travel and communication become easier and faster. If a clever chef can create an adapted version of a favorite regional food, that too can help define a particular time and place.

But purists will still visit Italy for a taste of Tuscan cooking, just as lobster fans will make a pilgrimage to Maine. Traditionalists who complain that food isn't as good as it used to be ought to do their part—by baking biscuits, growing heirloom vegetables, and writing down recipes—to uphold the culinary customs they're afraid of losing.

Imagine what would happen if we tried to limit ourselves to the foods and cooking methods that were native to the places we live. An attempt to go back to a style of food that we perceive as historically and culturally "pure" might make for an interesting experiment, but for some rather dull cuisine. As Americans, we'd have no bacon and no beef. No stir-fry, no curry, no tropical fruits. No croissants, no bagels; no pasta, no rice.

We'd have no coffee and no spices—in short: No flavor.

AMY'S AROUND THE WORLD SALAD

FOR THE DRESSING:

1 ½ cups oil

¼ cup tahini (can substitute peanut butter)

½ cup soy sauce

½ cup vinegar

¾ cup water, or more to taste

1 tablespoon fresh basil

1 teaspoon dill weed

1 tablespoon mustard or ginger powder

1 tablespoon honey

Salt and pepper

FOR THE SALAD:

1 pound mixed fresh salad greens: romaine, radicchio, arugula, Boston or Bibb lettuce, red or green leaf, oak leaf, spinach, in any combination

Fresh snow peas, cleaned and sliced

Fresh mushrooms, cleaned and sliced

Grape tomatoes (can substitute cherry tomatoes)

Scallions, finely diced

Almonds, slivered and toasted, or pine nuts

In a deep bowl, combine ½ cup of the oil and the tahini and mix until well blended. With a whisk, blend in the rest of the oil, soy sauce, vinegar, water; then add the basil, dill, mustard or ginger, and honey. Taste and correct the seasonings with salt and pepper; add a little more water if the dressing is too thick. Set aside.

Carefully wash and dry the greens, taking care to inspect spinach for grit.

You can combine the other salad ingredients in any amount you wish, or make substitutions. Place the greens in a large bowl and top with the remaining ingredients. Give the dressing another stir before drizzling over the greens, then serve.

YIELD: About 3 cups dressing; 10 to 12 servings of salad

HINT
If you're in a hurry, you can throw all the dressing ingredients in the blender and whirl for a minute or two.

BEST PIMIENTO CHEESE

JANET CULLEY OYLER

Years ago, when I was a young girl in South Carolina, my mother hosted a party and served pimiento cheese sandwiches. She asked my aunt to make her delicious and somewhat different pimiento cheese.

Years later, I still remembered how good it was and set out to duplicate it from memory. After a few tries, I developed the following recipe that recaptured the taste I remembered from so long ago. I now prepare it for events and always receive compliments. Serving this Southern specialty always reminds me of family from that time many years ago.

  1 pound extra-sharp cheddar cheese, shredded
  3 hard-boiled eggs, peeled and diced finely
  3 to 4 tablespoons grated onion
  A 4-ounce jar diced pimientos, drained
  ¼ cup sweet pickle relish
  1 cup mayonnaise, or enough to blend mixture smoothly

Mix all ingredients together in a large bowl. Adjust amount of mayonnaise to make mixture spread easily. This recipe tastes best if prepared a day in advance, allowing time for flavors to blend. The spread may be used as a sandwich filling, with crackers, or as a filling for celery sticks.

YIELD: 1 quart

Many cheese straw recipes have been handed down from generation to generation. Here are two favorites.

RACHEL AND OPAL'S CHEESE STRAWS

ANN WICKER

My mother, Opal Wicker, has been making cheese straws since the early 1950s. Cheese straws are not cookies, as my Chicago-raised husband found out when he tasted his first one. Since they look like cookies, he was startled to find they are not remotely sweet. They're really kind of tangy and spicy. I figured out many years later that they are probably called "straws" because the original ones were stretched out on the cookie sheet in strips, like, well, straws.

My mom makes cheese straws for every occasion—in the shape of Christmas trees for the holidays and such. Her favorite general shape is a "wreath" (cookie presses have different discs for the different patterns). Once she says she made 70 dozen for a friend's wedding reception. She has tried variations on the recipe, including a stuffed version with an olive in the middle.

Opal, now retired, was a beautician for many years. She got the original recipe from Rachel Evans, one of her customers, who became a dear and close friend. My parents even rented a house next door to Rachel and her husband, a postman known as Mr. Glenn. Rachel and Mr. Glenn became my adopted grandparents—and I spent many happy hours as a child at their house.

Opal is a cook in the grand old Southern tradition. She taught me not only how to make cheese straws but pound cake, potato salad, coleslaw (with less mayo and just a touch of sugar), slow-cooked beans like pintos and much more. With her beauty shop at one end of the house and the kitchen at the other, she reigned over both with equal skill.

½ pound extra sharp cheddar cheese, grated
2 cups plain flour
1 ½ sticks of butter, melted
¼ teaspoon red pepper
½ tablespoon salt

Preheat oven to 400 degrees.
Combine all ingredients and work dough until completely mixed. Put dough in cookie press. Press out cookies onto an ungreased cookie sheet. Bake for 8 to 10 minutes.

YIELD: 2 to 2½ dozen, depending on the press design

CHEESE STRAWS

LIANE CROWE DAVENPORT

As a little girl, I liked to help my mother make these cheese straws for parties. This is her mother's recipe that she made using an old metal cookie press. That cookie press is still cranking out tasty treats, all these years later.

1 pound New York sharp cheddar cheese, grated
4 cups all-purpose flour
1 teaspoon salt
½ teaspoon ground red pepper
1 pound unsalted butter

Preheat oven to 300 degrees.

In a large bowl, combine grated cheese, flour, salt, and red pepper. Blend well and set aside.

Melt butter over boiling water in a double boiler. Add to the dry ingredients. Press through a cookie press, using a wafer disk or your preference.

Place on an ungreased cookie sheet and bake for 7 to 10 minutes, or until they begin to turn brown. Lift immediately from pan and cool on racks. Store in covered container. These also freeze well.

YIELD: 25 appetizer servings

CRAB MELT-A-WAYS

KATHLEEN H. FALIN

HINT
If you want to use these later, freeze them before broiling and they will keep up to 2 months.

I am a full-time homemaker transplanted from Maryland to North Carolina in 1983. One of the things that I brought with me was the recipe for Crab-Melt-A-Ways. This dish originated in Maryland, and was made by my mother, who passed away May 27th, 2002. She loved to entertain and use seafood, which was plentiful, since we were close to the Chesapeake Bay.

I love this recipe. It is easy to prepare, it's delicious, and it can be used as an appetizer—or as a main dish by leaving the muffins whole. All the ingredients are kitchen staples, except for the crabmeat, so it's also convenient. After twenty years in North Carolina, our family and Carolina friends have come to enjoy the recipe as well. This year we have a grandson, and we look forward to introducing Crab Melt-A-Ways to his developing palate!

1 package English muffins
1 stick margarine, softened
A 7-ounce can of crabmeat, rinsed and drained
An 8-ounce package of cheddar cheese, shredded
2 tablespoons mayonnaise
½ teaspoon seasoning salt
½ teaspoon garlic powder

Slice muffins in half and cut each half into quarters. Arrange on a cookie sheet and set aside.

In a bowl, cream margarine then stir in the other ingredients. Spread on the muffin quarters. Place in freezer for 30 minutes.

Preheat the broiler. Remove the Crab Melt-A-Ways from freezer and broil until they puff up, are bubbly, and slightly golden brown. Serve hot.

YIELD: 48 appetizers

PIQUANT COCKTAIL MEATBALLS

SALLY OLIN

These are the very best cocktail meatballs, and are especially wonderful at the holidays. They were passed down to me from my maternal grandmother.

FOR THE MEATBALLS:

2 pounds of ground beef
1 cup of corn flake crumbs
2 eggs
2 tablespoons soy sauce
2 tablespoons instant minced onion
¼ teaspoon pepper
½ teaspoon garlic powder
⅓ cup ketchup
⅓ cup dried parsley flakes

Combine all of the ingredients and mix well. Form into small balls about the size of a walnut. Place in a pan, ideally 15 ½ x 10½ x 1".

FOR THE SAUCE:

1 can jellied cranberry sauce
12-ounce bottle of ketchup
2 tablespoons firmly packed brown sugar
1 tablespoon bottled lemon juice

Preheat oven to 350 degrees.
In a saucepan, combine the sauce ingredients. Cook over low to medium heat, stirring occasionally until smooth and melted. Pour over meatballs in pan. Bake uncovered for 30 minutes.

YIELD: 24 appetizer servings

HOT CRAB DIP II

PETER MEYER

This recipe was devised during research for the book, *Blue Crabs: Catch 'em, Cook 'em, Eat 'em.* We—wife, Cathy, and sons, Ben and Jason—spent many pleasurable hours capturing, cooking and consuming blue crabs. The final version of Hot Crab Dip, an epicurean delight, was reached by trial and error. Hot Crab Dip remains one of the Meyer family's favorite recipes.

8 ounces fresh crabmeat (5 to 6 crabs)
4 ounces light cream cheese, softened
¼ cup non-fat sour cream
1 teaspoon horseradish
1 tablespoon fat-free mayonnaise
1 teaspoon Worcestershire sauce
¼ teaspoon dried mustard
2 teaspoons milk
¾ teaspoon fresh lemon juice
1 to 2 ounces cheddar cheese
shredded paprika

Preheat oven to 350 degrees. Grease a small baking dish and set aside.

Sift crab meat through fingertips to remove all shell fragments and set aside.

In a bowl, combine the remaining ingredients and mix well, reserving half of the cheddar cheese and the paprika.

Fold in the crabmeat. Transfer the mixture to the baking dish. Sprinkle reserved cheese and paprika on top. Bake for 20 minutes or until bubbly on the outside. Serve on Ritz crackers, melba toast or whole wheat crackers.

YIELD: 8 appetizer servings

ANNE'S SHRIMP AND SAGA SANDWICHES

HEIDI FLICK

My mother introduced my family to pita bread, anchovies, brie, and béarnaise sauce in the '60s and '70s when all my friends were eating salmon patties, macaroni and cheese, meatloaf and fishsticks. She was a little ahead of her time because she had to fix dinner six nights a week and she got bored. This is a woman who spent two hours grocery shopping, perusing labels as if they were bestsellers, snatching up new products and muttering like a mad scientist about how it would combine with stuff she already had at home. Her inventions were 90 percent successful.

She came up with the shrimp sandwich one weekend, using shrimp we had brought home from the docks at Georgetown, South Carolina, on our latest vacation. It became a family classic. It works with frozen cocktail shrimp or even fried shrimp. These are definitely knife-and-fork sandwiches. Years later, when I was bartending at a restaurant, I made them as a late-night snack for the owner. She put them on the menu. We named them after Mom.

6 thick slices of French bread
Butter
8-ounce bag frozen cocktail shrimp, thawed or ½ pound cooked
    shrimp, peeled
4-ounce wedge of Saga blue cheese at room temperature
1 jar cocktail sauce

Preheat the broiler.

Spread the butter liberally over the French bread slices and toast them under the broiler until browned, then remove.

Drain cocktail shrimp and blot any additional liquid with paper towels; or chop larger shrimp into bite-sized pieces.

Slice the cheese thinly, then cover the toast slices with the cheese. The heat from toasting will melt the cheese just enough.

Pile shrimp on top of cheese, then spoon the cocktail sauce to taste over the open-faced sandwiches. Feeling fancy? Toss on some capers and chopped green onions.

YIELD: 6 servings

"LOWCOUNTRY COOKING"

a song from the hit musical "King Mackerel & The Blues Are Running"; lyrics and music by Bland Simpson and Jim Wann

This song includes recipes for she-crab soup and a fish muddle called pine bark stew. Numerous folks have said they've used the song to cook by…

Bland Simpson and Jim Wann's music and lyrics are part of *King Mackerel & The Blues Are Running: Songs and Stories of the Carolina Coast.*

Few dishes are as closely identified with South Carolina as she-crab soup, a seasonal delicacy made with fresh roe.

You melt the butter, stir in flour till it's smooth
You're making she-crab soup, get in the she-crab groove
So when you add the milk, don't you go full tilt
Do it nice, and steady and slow…
Then you ladle in them she-crab eggs
And all the meat your child can pick out of them she-crab legs
Don't you tarry, pour in warm sherry
You 'bout ready for the table, don't you know

CHORUS:
Lowcountry cooking, keep the skillet good and greased
Lowcountry cooking, hot and hot, if you please
And if you get a strike
Everybody's gonna like your Lowcountry cooking, way down
By the sea, yeah, Lowcountry cooking way down by the sea

Now say you want to make some pine bark stew
I'm a here to tell you exactly what to do
Cook a pound of bacon, lay it by,
Slice onions and potatoes in the grease
Let 'em fry, yeah
Very next thing you gonna do
Pour in boiling salted water, lay some bass across there too
Hurry with that curry, more layers of taters, onion, fish
Cook it half a day, serve over rice, now that's a dish, yeah

REPEAT CHORUS:
(Where's the pine bark come in? That's what you make your cook fire out of…)

VIDALIA ONION DIP

JESSICA GRAHAM

It was a beautiful fall day in the Carolinas when I first discovered the recipe that would change my social life forever…Vidalia Onion Dip. I had just arrived at the Junior League of Charlotte for a meeting. The breeze was blowing, the leaves were falling, the sun was shining, and I was stumbling towards the building, arms full of folders and all sorts of vital information. All of the sudden, I stopped. The most wonderful aroma had filled the air, and I spotted a perfectly coiffed woman walking toward the League building, carrying a baking dish.

"Stop!" I hollered, stumbling over. "I know you don't know me, but I need to know what you've got in that dish. It smells delicious."

She stopped, looking stunned, and then smiled a perfectly coiffed smile. "It's Vidalia Onion Dip." And she told me the recipe.

I get invited to more parties these days. I'm a lot more popular now that my party date—a dip—is on everyone's "must have" list. And I owe it all to the immaculate mystery woman with the baking dish, the woman who walked into the Junior League on a beautiful fall day that ended even better than it began.

- 2 cups shredded Swiss cheese
- 2 cups mayonnaise
- 2 cups chopped Vidalia onions

Mix together and bake in an ovenproof dish at 350 degrees until set.

YIELD: 5 to 6 cups of dip

THE TASTE OF A NEW LIFE

Amy Rogers

She was just 18 when she arrived at the refugee camp in Indonesia. Kim Loan had traveled from her hometown of Tamky, South Vietnam, with her little brother, who was 16. They were on their way to America—if they could find someone to sponsor them.

The trip cost a small fortune to the parents who had scrimped and saved and then stayed behind so their children could benefit from the opportunities that lay thousands of miles away.

Weeks went by, then a month, then two. Then two more. Ten months passed before Kim got the news she'd been hoping for. She and her brother had gotten a sponsor, Catholic Social Services. The names of the cities, towns and states where they might be sent were indistinguishable. She spoke no English and wouldn't have known the difference between North Carolina and North Dakota, if she had been given a choice of where to go, which she wasn't.

The agency brought her to Charlotte, North Carolina, in 1984. "Lucky me," she thought. She enrolled at Central Piedmont Community College and began to learn English. In class, she met a young man, Huy Vu, also from Vietnam. He had grown up near a U.S. military base in Bien Hoa. Kim and her brother were the only members of their family to emigrate to the U.S., but Huy was the first of many in his family who would follow.

Kim and Huy got jobs in a local textile factory, laboring long hours at the hard work that immigrants and local folk alike have done for generations. They married and joined a Vietnamese Catholic Church, where the Mass is celebrated in English. They became citizens and started a family of their own.

The children have Vietnamese names, but everyone calls them Lisa and Dustin, even the relatives back home, whom Kim has been able to visit just once in 19 years.

Kim and Huy don't work at the factory anymore. Like their parents, they saved everything they could, and in late 1999, they opened a small dry-cleaning business in Charlotte. It's next door to a sandwich shop and a nail salon, and across the street from a Starbucks coffee store, so they get a lot of traffic.

Kim will always cook the dishes that remind her of home, but now she reads the newspaper for recipes and goes to the public library for American cookbooks as well. On American holidays, her family eats American food. She makes spaghetti, turkey, mashed potatoes. Like every good cook she adds her own special touches—"my talents," she calls them—garlic and soy sauce on the turkey, or Asian spices from a market across town.

"I was homesick before I had my children," Kim says. "But now my life is here; I cannot live my life in Vietnam now. I know myself. I am changed."

KIM AND HUY VU'S VIETNAMESE COLD SHRIMP NOODLE ROLLS (GO'I CUÔN)

¼ pound rice vermicelli noodles
Package of rice paper wrappers*
Bowl of hot water for dipping
½ pound shrimp (steamed in shells, peeled and chilled)
⅓ pound prepared barbecued pork, sliced into thin strips*
1 small bunch fresh mint, cleaned and stems removed
4 lettuce leaves
1 bottle prepared fish sauce*

* available at Asian grocery or gourmet stores

Boil vermicelli according to directions; drain and chill.

To assemble the rolls: Dip a sheet of rice paper into hot water. When paper begins to soften, remove and lay flat on a plate. Place a portion of vermicelli, several shrimp and strips of pork on the rice paper. Top with mint and a lettuce leaf. Fold up the bottom of the rice paper slightly, then fold down the top the same amount. Then, grasp by one side edge and roll toward the other, making sure to tuck the ends in as you roll. You can re-moisten the seam with a dampened fingertip if needed to seal the roll. When finished, turn the rolls so the seam side is down.

Serve with prepared fish sauce for dipping.

YIELD: 4 servings

CARROT SOUP

GAYLE KELLY GARRISON

A number of years ago, our local newspaper in Walnut Creek, California, held a recipe contest. My neighbor won with a carrot soup recipe which was delicious. I have changed it to lower the fat. Most orange soups have curry as an ingredient and it is not one of our favorite spices; the orange zest and juice makes this a delicious soup. My adult daughter always asks me to make it when we visit her in Portland, Oregon.

- 1 quart of de-fatted chicken stock (refrigerate, then remove fat that rises to the top)
- 2 cups of sliced carrots
- 2 tablespoons dried onion flakes
- 2 tablespoons raw rice
- Zest of one-half orange
- Juice from one-half orange

In a large saucepan, place the chicken stock, carrots, onion flakes, rice and zest. Bring to a boil, then simmer until the carrots and rice are tender. Cool and puree in blender. Add the orange juice and heat, but do not boil.

YIELD: 4 servings

FAVORITE CONGEALED SALAD

MIGNON F. BALLARD

This is a recipe for a congealed salad that is light, refreshing and easy to make. It was a favorite in our household as I was growing up in Calhoun, Georgia, and I remember my mother serving it for Sunday dinner with a baked hen, rice and gravy, hot rolls, and green beans cooked a long time with streak o' lean. Now I'm making myself hungry!

Mignon Ballard, an author who lives in South Carolina, is well-known for her mystery books—but she also writes historical fiction.

A 15-ounce can grapefruit sections (snipped into smaller pieces)
1 small or medium can pineapple tidbits or crushed pineapple
Orange juice
½ small bottle maraschino cherries
½ cup broken pecans
*1 small (3-ounce) package lemon or orange gelatin dessert mix
    (I use Jell-O brand)

*I add about $\frac{1}{2}$ envelope of plain gelatin dissolved in a little juice or another $\frac{1}{2}$ package of flavored gelatin for better consistency.

Drain fruits and save juice. If you don't have two cups, make up the difference with orange juice. Heat one cup of juice until hot, remove from heat and dissolve the gelatin dessert in the juice. Add second cup of juice, then fruit and nuts. Pour into a mold or 9" square dish and refrigerate overnight.

YIELD: 8 or 9 servings

CHICKEN RICE SOUP WITH LEMON (AVGOLEMONO)

VASSILIOS KARAMITROS

I was born in Greece in 1960. I graduated from high school in 1978. During my service in the Air Force, I was thinking about what career to choose. What is the career of the present and what is the career of the future? I wondered. I chose to become a chef for several reasons.

1. The job will exist forever. People always will eat to survive.
2. There are many options for jobs: restaurants, hotels, hospitals, clubs, cruise ships.
3. I like good food so I can cook for myself and for my family — quality meals.
4. Savings. Wherever I work I will have at least one free meal. That means saving money.

1 whole chicken	6 eggs
Salt and pepper	½ cup lemon juice
2 cups parboiled rice	½ cup cornstarch

In a large pot, put the chicken to boil. Add salt and pepper to taste. When the chicken is cooked, remove it from the pot, strain off and reserve the broth. Remove the chicken from the bones, discarding the skin and bones, and chop into bite-sized pieces. Set aside.

Return the broth to the stove and bring to a boil. Add the rice and simmer until the rice is done and remove from heat.

Meanwhile, in a separate bowl, beat the eggs with ½ of the lemon juice and the cornstarch, then add ¼ cup of cold water. Blend well. Use a ladle to slowly add hot soup to the egg mixture, and stir constantly (this will keep it from separating). Keep adding soup and stirring until the mixture is hot. Then, pour the mixture back into the pot with the soup and rice; stir and return it to the heat. Bring the soup just to a boil, remove from heat, and add the cut-up chicken and remaining lemon juice. Correct the seasoning with additional salt and pepper if desired.

YIELD: About 8 servings

BOBBIE LOU'S VEGETABLE SOUP

BECKI NELL WILLIAMS

My Bobbie Lou made a mean soup from nearly nothing. I thought every child had a Bobbie Lou—a babysitter/grandmother, only not blood-related. How could a child grow up without one? She taught us how life was supposed to be—how to make lye soap as we watched from the other side of the basement, and how to make a toothbrush from a stick and brush with baking soda.

Everything she did was "for my own good," even when I challenged her by saying, "I ain't got no own good." She taught me to take whatever I had and always make the best of it. She would hunt around in the icebox and cabinets, pulling out all kinds of things, potatoes and beans or meat, and before long, a warm, full pot sat on the stove.

Like "stone soup," she put in what she had, seasoned it with love and trusted that those who ate it would receive it with love and be grateful. Then she'd say, "Honey, sit right down here and have you a bowl of soup. For your own good."

4 carrots, chopped
1 large onion, chopped
3 to 4 celery stalks, chopped
3 to 4 tablespoonfuls bacon drippings (may substitute vegetable oil)
1 good soup bone
32 ounces of water
32 ounces canned diced tomatoes and juice
(Optional—Home canned or frozen green beans, corn, baby lima
   beans or okra)
Salt, pepper and sugar to taste
Leftover cooked vegetables of all sorts
3 to 4 potatoes, peeled and diced

In a soup pot, sauté the carrots, onion and celery in the bacon drippings. Add the soup bone, water, tomatoes and juice. (If you are using the optional ingredients, add them now.) Taste and season with salt, pepper and just a little sugar to cut the acidity of the tomatoes. Simmer, covered, for about one hour.

Then add the leftover vegetables and the potatoes and simmer until potatoes are fork tender. Remove and discard the soup bone. Check seasonings again and serve.

YIELD: 8 to 12, depending on how many vegetables you add

NONNA'S CHICKEN SOUP

GILDA MORINA SYVERSON

One Saturday while shopping at Talley's Green Grocery, I saw a sign that read "Unadvertised Special, Fresh Chickens." The chickens were plucked clean and sitting on a bed of crushed ice behind the glass at the meat counter. I thought of when my grandmother, Nonna Egidia, was still alive and pictured her preparing chicken soup for my large Italian family. I had to buy one of those chickens.

Once home, I washed it thoroughly, flushed the cavity with water and placed the whole bird into a large pot, adding enough cold water to cover. As it boiled, I skimmed the scum from the top, peeled carrots, quartered onions, sliced stalks of celery, including the leaves. I put all the ingredients into the steaming water along with chunks of tomatoes, bay leaves, salt and pepper. Nonna's chicken soup simmered all day.

As I busied myself around the house, I thought of Nonna and how she'd brought home live chickens from the market in Syracuse, New York, where I grew up. She and her sister *Zia,* aunt in Italian, would each grab a chicken, lay the necks against their thighs, twist and snap.

They dipped the fowl in boiling water, then hurried the birds over to a table covered in newspaper. My grandmother and great aunt moved their hands swiftly, making short inhaling sounds through their teeth, while plucking feathers from the hot birds. The air smelled like skin singed from burnt hair. Afterwards, they carved the chickens open and scooped out the insides. Everything edible was saved—neck, gizzards, liver and heart. The chickens and all their parts were placed into large pots then filled with cold water.

Though I didn't start with live chickens, I used Nonna's recipe that Saturday at my home in North Carolina. Just before dinner, I scooped a spoonful of soup from the steaming pot and slurped it down. I swore I heard inhaling sounds around me as the smell of Nonna's homemade soup hung in every crevice of the house.

1 chicken (fricassee or soup chicken if available)
3 peeled tomatoes, fresh or canned
2 or 3 stalks of chopped celery including the leaves
1 chopped onion
2 chopped carrots or 3 to 4 whole carrots cut into four sections
2 or 3 bay leaves
Salt and pepper to taste
1 pound small pasta, such as orzo, pastina, or small elbow macaroni
Parmesan or Romano cheese (optional)

When buying chicken, ask for fricassee or soup chicken. (If not available, at the end add 2 bouillon cubes for extra flavor.) Flush out the inside and place in a stock pot or large saucepan. You can cut up the chicken if desired. Fill the pan with enough water to cover the chicken.

Bring to a boil and remove scum. Once clear, add tomatoes, chopped celery and onion, carrots, bay leaves, salt and pepper. Reduce heat, cover and simmer 2½ to 3 hours. Remove chicken and debone.

Boil the pasta according to package directions and drain. Place cooked chicken on large platter. Pour soup over pasta, and sprinkle cheese on the soup if desired and serve.

YIELD: 8 to 10 servings

Salsa—in Spanish, it means sauce. In the U.S., the spicy condiment made from tomatoes and chiles has found its way into countless kitchens. Here are two very different salsa soup recipes. One is served hot and the other, cold, but each is special for the memories it evokes.

BRENDA'S SALSA "SOUP"

MARSHALL CHAPMAN

The first time I tasted Brenda's salsa, I was sitting at a table in a wind-swept house on the beach at Gulf Shores, Alabama. It was July the 4th, 1988. It was me, Brenda, her husband Jan, and their son Tim, plus one or two others. Brenda said, "Let's make some salsa!" and I said O.K. That summer, I was heartsick over some damn Texas songwriter and had taken to following Brenda around like a puppy dog because she seemed to know everything worth knowing.

In the South, July the 4th usually signals the beginning of homegrown tomatoes being ripe enough to eat. That morning, Brenda and I had stopped at a roadside market and bought a brown paper sack full of ripe Bradley tomatoes. I'd never heard of a Bradley tomato. I'd always thought a tomato was just a tomato. "Bradley's are the best!" Brenda exclaimed as she held up a pinkish-looking orb that looked anemic to me. But I took her at her word.

Later at the beach house, she showed me how to rub the dull edge of a knife along the outside of the tomato, taking care not press down too hard lest you break the skin, causing the red juice with those little yellow seeds to come spurting out. With just the right pressure, the skin would separate from the tomato. Then all you'd have to do is grab an edge, and the whole thing would peel right off—just like human skin after a bad sunburn. So I tried it. When that first one came off all in one piece, I got almost as excited as I did twenty years earlier, when I first played Ray Charles' "What'd I Say" on the bass strings of a neighbor's guitar.

Nashville song-writer Marshall Chapman, a native of Spartanburg, S.C., contributed her songs to the touring musical, *Good Ol' Girls*.

After all the ingredients for the salsa were mixed together in the big bowl, I took a tortilla chip and dipped it in, then put it in my mouth. "Holy s---!" I exclaimed, "this is good!" Everyone agreed it was the best salsa they'd ever had. Then somebody crunched up the remaining tortilla chips by pressing down on the bag while the chips were still in it. The broken-up contents were then poured on top of the salsa. After that, it was every man for himself.

They say food always tastes better at the beach. But Brenda's salsa soup tastes good everywhere. That's because Brenda knows that if you take the time and do it with love, the beach will follow you wherever you go.

4 to 6 homegrown tomatoes (Bradley's if ripe and available)
6 to 8 spring onions (skinny scallions), finely chopped
2 to 3 tablespoons fresh cilantro, chopped
1 clove garlic, finely chopped
Juice of ½ lemon
1 chili pepper or jalapeño, steamed until tender, seeds and veins removed, then finely chopped
Sea salt to taste
1 bag "restaurant style" lightly salted tortilla chips

Remove skin and seeds from tomatoes, then dice. Then add the remaining ingredients, except for the tortilla chips, and mix together in a large bowl. Spoon the salsa into soup bowls. Crunch up the tortilla chips and sprinkle on top, serve at room temperature and eat with a soup spoon.

YIELD: 4 servings

SALSA SOUP

LORI LEROY

I love to serve delicious food like my grandmother would make when we visited her for the weekend. In my mind I see her dining room table with dishes spread across it, filled with good food. Oh, and the wonderful smell as it made its way through her house! Smells that come only from hours of preparation.

However, I am the queen of skipping steps when it comes to cooking. I'm always looking for shortcuts. One day I was making vegetable soup. Trying to avoid the task of chopping an onion, and realizing I did not have all the spices I needed, I dumped half a jar of salsa into the crockpot. As we tasted the savory soup that night, it was as if I'd waved a magic wand and was able to step back in time to my grandmother's table. The crockpot performed the long hours of kitchen labor, and the salsa provided zest—and my favorite, a shortcut to good flavor. It's been a hit with my family ever since. The soup is also becoming a favorite when our relatives visit. My mom and mother-in-law have asked for the recipe. Perhaps I'm beginning a new tradition.

HINT
Try adding peas, using frozen soup mixes, and leftover taco ingredients.

    2 pounds of ground round or beef
    46-ounce can tomato juice
    ½ jar mild salsa
    2 bay leaves (remove before serving)
    15-ounce can green beans
    15-pounce can corn
    15-ounce can carrots

Brown the meat and drain the fat. Combine all the ingredients in a crockpot and simmer for at least 3 to 4 hours.

YIELD: 8 to 10 servings

LIB'S JUNK SALAD—OR SOUP

DIANA PINCKNEY

HINT
You can also make soup from these same leftover vegetables. Now you can use the mushy ones, plus any little pieces of roast or meat hiding in the refrigerator, cut in small chunks. If anyone was silly enough not to finish the silver queen corn, slice it off the cob. No okra? Then use frozen. Chop a yellow or white onion, $1/2$ clove garlic, fresh carrots, put them in a big pot, add 2 cans of stewed tomatoes, juice from $1/2$ lemon, some Italian herbs, a cup of water, dried or frozen soup mix and beef bouillon. Let this cook slowly a few hours or all afternoon, then bring on the junk! Cook another $1/2$ hour. Enjoy in January.

My mother thought leftovers were sacred. In her hands they were also delicious. Salads on hot Columbia nights were all we wanted with a little cold chicken. Many of the ingredients came from the State Farmers Market on the outskirts of town, my father having given up his WWII victory garden. Most Saturdays found us at the market. My parents knew all the farmers. While my father talked weather with them, my mother poked among the eggplants, tomatoes, okra—everything from country hams to flowers and Christmas trees. I wandered from one stand to the next sampling the juicy tidbits, whatever was in season. It was blissful.

To this day I dislike enclosed malls with their stale smells, jangling sounds, but open markets—state, county or a single roadside stand—call out to me. More than once we've come close to a highway smashup because I suddenly spot peaches or cantaloupes and swerve off or I yell, "There's one!" startling my poor husband so badly he almost wrecks us. All is forgiven if he finds they're selling boiled peanuts from a steaming black kettle.

Now, back to the salad.

1 firm summer tomato, sliced
Several small cucumbers, sliced
Junk from your (as Lib would say) icebox
Any vinaigrette dressing

1 thinly sliced onion (Bermuda or Vidalia)
1 head of crisp lettuce, preferably Romaine, torn

Use the kind of tomato you slice and put between slices of white bread, spread with mayonnaise. Cukes hard and fresh, that you use for pickles, with no big seeds. Leftover green beans, butterbeans, carrots, avocado, any of the small squashes; again, no big seeds.

Use any leftover vegetable, as long as it hasn't been cooked to mush. If it is buttery from an earlier dinner, rinse under hot water, drain on paper towels. Marinate the leftovers first in any good vinaigrette dressing before tossing with the lettuce and other ingredients.

YIELD: 6 or more servings, depending on how much "junk" you add

SIMPLE SPRING SALAD

JENNY ROSENTHAL

What I like about this salad is that it's so fresh, simple and beautiful. I've made it dozens of times. When people ask me for the recipe, they're always surprised that it's so easy.

An 8 to 10-ounce bag of fresh baby spinach
1 to 1 ½ cups strawberries
Red onions or Vidalia onions (amount to your taste)
½ cup toasted, slivered almonds or more to taste
Your favorite salad dressing

Clean the baby spinach and place in a large bowl. Clean and slice the strawberries and add them to the bowl. Peel and slice the onions very thin; add to the bowl. Top with the slivered almonds and toss the salad. Top with your favorite dressing and toss again. (I use store-bought poppy seed dressing and it's as good as any.)

YIELD: 4 to 6 servings

CORN CHOWDER

ALLEN MAST

I'm always tinkering in the kitchen trying to create a new recipe or change an old one for the better. I am constantly reading recipes from books, magazines and newspapers. I found this recipe years ago, and doctored it to my liking. If I make it for a crowd and no one likes it, then there will just be more for me!

12 slices bacon
2 medium onions, chopped
4 medium potatoes, peeled and cubed
1 cup water
4 cups milk
Two 17-ounce cans creamed corn
1 teaspoon salt
Dash of pepper
1 clove garlic, minced

Fry bacon until crisp; reserve 2 tablespoons drippings. Set bacon aside to drain; sauté onions in drippings. Add potatoes and water, and pour into medium saucepan. Simmer for 20 minutes. Stir in milk, corn, salt, pepper and garlic. Cook over medium heat, stirring occasionally, until potatoes are tender. Crumble bacon into chowder and serve.

YIELD: 6 to 8 servings

LYNN KARMEL'S COLESLAW

ELIZABETH A. KARMEL

This coleslaw is as good as it is easy. My mother's "secret" was to peel the leaves of a very fresh cabbage and crisp them in ice water before grating on a box grater. My mother served this creamy version of coleslaw with corn sticks and fried fish, but I make it more often to accompany simple grilled meat or as a picnic side dish. If you use a whole cabbage, you will need to double the dressing.

- 1 fresh, green cabbage, cut in half
- ¾ cup real mayonnaise (I use Hellman's brand)
- 2 tablespoons apple cider vinegar
- 1 teaspoon sugar
- 1 teaspoon sea salt
- ¼ teaspoon white pepper

Fill a large bowl or one side of a clean sink with ice water. Peel the leaves of cabbage from the head and soak in the ice water for 15 minutes to crisp. Remove from water and drain on paper towels.

Meanwhile, make the dressing by combining the other ingredients. Dressing should be fairly thick. Set aside.

Grate the cabbage on the coarsest side of a box grater, or in a food processor. Mix cabbage and dressing and refrigerate at least 2 hours or overnight before serving.

YIELD: 6 servings

SUGAR-FREE ORIENTAL SLAW

KAREN PROCTOR

This recipe was prepared by one of my family members for a recent Thanksgiving gathering. It contained sugar and since I am diabetic, I decided to redo the recipe so that I could enjoy it without guilt. It is a good way to get in a lot of vegetables at one time and makes a great dish to take to events.

1 package fresh or frozen snow peas
1 small head of cabbage, finely chopped
2 packages of ramen-style chicken-flavored noodle soup
½ cup sunflower seeds
½ cup sliced almonds, toasted
¼ cup grated Parmesan cheese
1 bunch green onions, cleaned and chopped
¼ cup vegetable oil
¼ cup water
½ cup cider vinegar
9 to 11 packets of Equal brand sweetener

Steam snow peas, take off strings and slice crosswise, about ½" in length. Place in a large bowl and add cabbage. Set aside the seasoning packets from the ramen noodle packages. Break noodles into small pieces and add to the cabbage, then add sunflower seeds, almonds, cheese and green onions. Mix together.

In another bowl, mix together the oil, vinegar, water, Equal, and seasoning packets from the noodle soup. Pour over the vegetables and mix well.

YIELD: About 8 servings

MOM'S POTATO SALAD

TAMMY WILSON

The secret to good potato salad is celery seeds and sweet pickle juice, Mom said, though Dad would slosh vinegar all over his food to the point that it became an island in a sour, china pond. Mom would know he'd been busy when she saw naked gherkins lying limp in their jar, like beached fish. When it came to making potato salad, she had to beat him to the refrigerator.

Potato salad always accompanied us to a picnic or potluck. To make it, you had to boil at least two eggs that had been around long enough for the shells to peel off, and you had to peel the potatoes before boiling them. This was before the enlightened days of eating potato skins.

After the eggs and potatoes cooled, Mom diced everything, then added the Miracle Whip, sweet pickle juice and seasonings to taste. She never added onions or mustard.

"Mustard will give it a whangy taste and onions give your Dad heartburn," she said.

"You mean he's worried about heartburn after all that vinegar?" I asked. She shrugged her shoulders and rolled her eyes.

4 good-sized potatoes
2 eggs
⅓ cup of Miracle Whip brand
¼ cup sweet pickle relish or juice
Salt and pepper to taste
1 tablespoon celery seed
Dash of paprika for color on top

Boil the potatoes with the eggs. Poke the potatoes with a fork to be sure they are fully cooked. Peel everything and cut into cubes.

Mix together the Miracle Whip, pickle juice or relish, salt, pepper and celery seed. Top with the paprika. Cover, chill and serve.

YIELD: 4 servings

HINT
Some people use mayonnaise instead of Miracle Whip, though Mom insisted real mayo was too greasy.

MEDITERRANEAN TURKEY SALAD

KAREN M. SULLIVAN

Recipes from my mother's kitchen are as much about life as they are cooking. I learned about relationships, joy, citizenship and economics from cakes, casseroles, soups and stews.

I remember the first time I discovered a bottle of wine as I unpacked the week's groceries. I looked at the price tag, then at my mother. There were five children at our family's table. We needed more meat, not wine.

"It's for a dish I'm making Sunday," she said excitedly.

Her first subscription to *Bon Appétit* was definitely changing things. "I thought it might be what you plan to pass around to the boys when they ask for seconds," I muttered.

She was unshaken. "Buy your bread, but feed your soul with hyacinths," she said.

I recognized that as the voice of my late grandmother Harriet, a formidable cook. I knew the discussion was over.

On Sunday the table was set for a celebration. Mom presented a golden, succulent roasted chicken in an unforgettable wine sauce. I felt like I was dining in the South of France. We left the table wholly nourished if not completely full.

I never tried to recreate Mom's Chicken and Wine. Its perfume is still in the air and on my palate whenever I think about that night. What's important is the lesson that humble ingredients like chicken can achieve an almost mystic transformation when the cook finds inspiration. Here, I find it by buying pomegranate molasses, instead of hyacinths.

2 pounds turkey drumsticks, skin removed
Cooking oil
Salt and pepper to taste
1 tablespoon garlic powder
1 ½ cup walnuts
8 ounces fresh, soft goat cheese or cream cheese

¼ cup fresh dill, chopped

⅛ teaspoon or more cayenne pepper

Plastic wrap

10 ounces mixed field greens or other salad greens

1 cup fresh parsley leaves, loosely packed

½ cup plus 1 tablespoon pomegranate molasses, divided

3 teaspoons lemon juice, divided

½ teaspoon soy sauce

3 to 4 tablespoons extra virgin olive oil

3 green onions, finely sliced

1 avocado, peeled, pitted and sliced

1 can whole, pitted black olives

1 red bell pepper, seeded and julienned

Extra dill and parsley for garnish, if desired

HINTS

Turkey drumsticks are humble and inexpensive, yet wonderfully rich in flavor and low in fat. Pomegranate molasses is exotic, fruity and tart. I use the Sultan brand. Look for it in Middle Eastern markets and gourmet food stores. The turkey and the cheese log can be made in advance.

Preheat oven to 275 degrees. Oil the bottom of a baking dish. Rub the turkey with oil and place in the baking dish. Season with salt, pepper and garlic powder. Cover the pan with a lid or aluminum foil. Bake for 2 to 2½ hours, depending on the size of the drumsticks, turning once after 1 hour and 15 minutes. The meat is done when it releases easily from the bones when pierced with a fork. Allow to rest 30 minutes or until cool enough to handle.

While the meat cooks, toast the walnuts in the same oven for 10 to 12 minutes. Set aside to cool. Meanwhile, place the cheese in a small bowl. Add the dill, the cayenne and a pinch of salt. Mix well and adjust seasoning as needed. Using a rubber spatula, transfer the cheese mixture to the center of a sheet of plastic wrap. Shape the mixture into a log slightly taller than a quarter. Twist the ends and chill for at least 30 minutes.

Wash, dry and prepare the salad ingredients, and place in a large bowl. Add the parsley leaves. Once walnuts are cooled, chop to a medium fineness that resembles coarse bread crumbs. Unwrap the cheese log and roll it in the crushed nuts to coat evenly. Cut the log into coins about ⅜-inch thick. Then coat the cut sides of each coin. Cover with plastic and chill until 30 minutes before serving.

In a medium bowl combine 1 tablespoon pomegranate molasses, 1 teaspoon lemon juice and the soy sauce. Taste for desired sweetness. Remove and discard the turkey's bones and cartilage. Add the warm meat to the molasses mixture and mix well. Set aside.

Toss the salad greens with olive oil, coating well. Add salt to taste and toss. Transfer to a large serving platter or a wide, shallow serving bowl. Arrange the meat, cheese, green onions, avocado, olives and bell pepper on top. In a small bowl, combine the remaining ½ cup pomegranate molasses and 2 teaspoons lemon juice. Drizzle salad with half the dressing, offering the remainder at table. Garnish with dill and parsley.

YIELD: Serves 4

THE KITCHEN AT WILDACRES

Amy Rogers

Most people have never heard of Wildacres. Since the 1940s, it's been a gathering place for civic and interfaith groups, nestled in the North Carolina mountains near a town called Little Switzerland. Even some who visit year after year aren't aware of one of the most elemental ways the center upholds the spirit and heritage of its Jewish founders: by operating a kosher kitchen.

Wildacres isn't a resort like those made famous in the movies; rather, it's a retreat center where non-profit groups meet to learn everything from creative writing to leadership skills. Some of the groups are Jewish but many are not. But all share a common belief in founder I.D. Blumenthal's commitment to "the betterment of human relations."

Wildacres is a stunning place, with views of mountain ridges that emerge from the clouds, only to vanish with the next wind shift. The rustic lodge buildings hold a low profile on top of Pompey's Knob, and the serenity, quiet and isolation of the place are so breathtaking that retreat participants may never notice the hardworking men and women who plan, cook, and serve the meals at Wildacres.

While no one on the current staff is Jewish, they can serve three meals each day to 120 people at a time, all while observing the strict dietary laws called *Kashrut*.

Chefs Randy Snyder and John Wright have more than 40 years combined experience in the kitchen. Joining them is newcomer Wes Hall, a young and energetic prep chef who hopes to study culinary arts formally someday.

Crissy Pitman usually plans the meals, a week at a time, based on what the groups request. For those such as the N.C. Storytelling Guild, the routine is pretty straightforward, Pitman explained. But it gets more complicated when the Jewish groups begin to arrive. The dietary laws are complex, and plenty of otherwise observant Jews long ago gave up trying to follow the directives that prohibit pork and shellfish, forbid the combining of meat and dairy products at the same meal, and require that foods receive rabbinical approval. Kitchen workers at Wildacres are undaunted as they clean, sort, and prepare everything for their Jewish guests.

Row after row of drawers and cabinets are marked "Not for Kosher," "Meat," "Dairy"—and "Parve," indicating foods that are neither meat nor dairy and that can be served with either. Black-handled utensils are for meat, white for dairy, red for parve. The blue and green-striped dishes only appear to be random restaurant mix-and-match, but they are color-coded as well.

Produce comes from nearby growers when possible, and staple goods from restaurant supplier PYA/Monarch. Kosher Mart, more than 100 miles away in Charlotte, delivers the meat by trucking it up the steep, winding roads that allow the only access to Wildacres.

Unlike most restaurant kitchens that look out onto alleyways or parking lots, Wildacres opens out into the tops of trees, surrounded by wildflowers. It's a big change from the noise and commotion that seem to define the typical restaurant kitchen.

Despite the challenges of keeping kosher, there's a good-natured spiritedness about it all. "This meat looks like it was butchered with a weedwhacker," Hall proclaimed one afternoon when stir-fried beef was planned for the menu that night. Worse, he explained that the kosher salt used after slaughtering tends to overwhelm any other flavor the meat might have. Solution: sweet and sour sauce, with extra hot pepper flakes. (Horseradish works well, too.)

Snyder, who grew up in Mitchell County, is soft-spoken with a sense of humor that shows up in the occasional practical joke. He's got recipes—for everything from pickled corn to chocolate gravy—in a zippered binder. Wright, who spent 15 years cooking in restaurants around Atlanta, likes the change of pace "and the lower stress" at Wildacres.

Pastry chef Paula Bailey lived on Long Island for 35 years but came back to the mountains where she was born; Lynn Harrison remembers picking beans for 50 cents a bushel; Tamara Ellis likes her Wildacres job better than the factory where she used to work.

As in any kitchen, things can go wrong. The humidity and altitude affect baking, so Bailey doesn't even try to make biscuits. Once, Pitman had to step in for an ailing co-worker and bake 11 pound cakes. "Ten pounds of butter and 66 eggs," she recalled. Hall still shudders when remembering a nut-and-noodle dish he attempted called Praline Kugel. And everyone jokes about a recent visitor known to complain about her meals. At Wildacres, she complained that she couldn't find anything to complain about.

Lasagna with baby asparagus, salad with warm grilled pineapple, fresh tomato-basil soup and almond cake—it's a tremendous amount of work, requiring a level of mindfulness most cooks would rather reserve for the creativity that inspires them, not for the limitations they must follow.

Does the food itself define the experience, or is it something more? When asked what they got out of working at Wildacres, the kitchen crew turned thoughtful, with a kind of reverence. "It's something you have to feel," Harrison said.

Wright put it this way: "It's a way to get closer to God, through ritual and tradition."

Once the Jewish groups finish their sessions at Wildacres, the kitchen reverts to a regular restaurant facility, one where cheeseburgers are acceptable and there are no separate plates and utensils for meat and milk. The kosher plates will be put away and no one will have to read labels or check the color chart for which knife or ladle to use.

When winter comes, when the wind starts to blow across the mountain, staff will shut down the kitchen for the season, go to Florida, work odd jobs, or just sit by the fire at their homes in the countryside. Then, come spring, they'll drive the winding gravel road to the top of Pompey's Knob again, sort and wash cookware for the rabbi's blessing, separate the meat and the milk, and keep alive a tradition that goes back more than 5,000 years.

CRISSY PITMAN'S BROCCOLI SALAD

1 pound bacon (can substitute turkey bacon)
2 large heads broccoli, cut into florets
1 cup celery, diced small
1 medium onion, diced small
1 jar toasted sunflower seeds
2 to 3 cups red seedless grapes, sliced in half
3 cups mayonnaise
6 tablespoons white vinegar
1 cup sugar

Fry, drain and crumble bacon. Mix it in a large bowl with the next 5 ingredients.

In a separate bowl, combine the mayonnaise, vinegar and sugar. Pour over salad just before serving.

YIELD: 12 servings

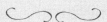

COLD CREAMY PEACH SOUP

RANDY SNYDER

I was raised in Mitchell County, North Carolina, with three brothers, and I live in the same county today. When I was young I started car-hopping at the local diner, and that's where I got interested in cooking. I worked there at least 27 years, and was a cook for the last 25. Managing the kitchen for the last eight years was quite an experience, but I enjoyed every aspect of it.

Working at Wildacres for the last three years has been a very rewarding experience for me. I enjoy meeting new people, exchanging ideas about cooking, and experimenting with recipes—like this one, for cold peach soup. It's very gratifying when people ask for my recipe or compliment me on my efforts to create an enjoyable meal.

Two 16-ounce cans of peaches, drained
½ cup dry white wine
½ cup ricotta cheese
½ cup plain yogurt
½ cup peach liqueur
2 tablespoons honey
Mint leaves for garnish (optional)

Puree peaches, wine and ricotta cheese in a blender, and pour into a chilled bowl. Add the remaining ingredients, except for the mint leaves, and mix well. Refrigerate for 1 hour.

To serve, divide among 6 chilled bowls and garnish with mint leaves.

YIELD: 6 servings

CREAM OF TOMATO SOUP

JOAN OSBORNE

HINT
Putting all ingredients in together cold should keep the milk from curdling, but don't be alarmed if it does curdle a bit. Once it comes to a boil and simmers for a little while, it usually comes back together.

I have made this recipe for many years. I got the idea from a cream of tomato soup my Aunt Royster made for her family. I don't know exactly how she made hers or where she got her recipe, but she probably just made it up. I think I remember that she used sugar in hers, but we like it with the tangy tomato taste. My son and husband eat theirs with crackers and mayonnaise stirred into the soup.

1 quart tomatoes, home-canned or store-canned
2 tablespoons butter or margarine
¾ cup milk
3 tablespoons flour
Salt and pepper to taste

Pour tomatoes into soup pot, and add butter.

In a separate bowl, mix together flour and milk until smooth, using an immersion blender. If you don't have an immersion blender, put milk and flour in a jar with a tight fitting lid and shake until flour is dissolved. Add to tomato mixture. Add salt and pepper to taste and bring to a boil slowly, stirring often. If you like your tomato soup without chunks of tomato, use the immersion blender in the soup pot. Once the soup comes to a boil, reduce heat to simmer and continue cooking for 15 minutes.

YIELD: About 4 servings

HUNGRY FOR HOME

2

Main Dishes:

BREAKFAST, LUNCH, BRUNCH, DINNER, AND SUPPER

HAPPILY EVER AFTER

Amy Rogers

Once upon a time, in a land called Germany, there lived a fair young maiden whose family grew grapes and made wine. For the first time in a long time, the country was no longer divided in two, and hope for the future was in bloom.

A handsome traveler from North Carolina came to the country, and at a gathering of friends he spied the dark-eyed beauty. But he couldn't tell her what was in his heart. Scott Wilson spoke little German and Ingrid Bialas barely spoke English, so they taught each other. Soon each was fluent in both, and in the language of love.

They traveled the countryside, drank wine and feasted together, but before they knew it, time had almost run out. "It was a minute before midnight," Scott remembered. The Fayetteville native had to decide if he would stay in Ingrid's country or return to his own.

The couple came to America, and the fate that befell the star-crossed pair when they set out on their journey seemed to be equal parts comedy and tragedy; in short, everything you'd expect from a fairy tale.

Scott and Ingrid never imagined their struggle to remain together in the U.S. would dominate their existence for years to come. To tell their story, Ingrid opened a bottle of Grafenberg, red wine from her family's vineyard. As she shared wine, bread, cheeses and ripe fruit, she and Scott described what they'd been through.

They understood that changes to immigration laws meant it would be difficult and expensive to enter the U.S. legally. Only a limited number of immigrants are allowed in each year. Nevertheless, Scott and Ingrid were determined to try. Scott found work as an architect. Ingrid, who holds graduate degrees from Heidelberg University, ran into trouble. "You need a visa to get a job, but you need a job to get a visa," she explained. She began making her way through the maze of rules, regulations, fees and procedures. She was diligent and found a job teaching middle school students.

Then the door slammed shut. Ingrid's supervisor got a call ordering the young teacher to leave campus—immediately. While Ingrid's visa application was being processed, the immigration limit had already been reached. She had been on the job for exactly one day.

She returned to her old job in Stuttgart. And Scott had a new job: bringing back the woman he loved. "I spent about three hours a day on work, and five on the phone making a nuisance of myself," he said. He called lawyers, lawmakers, anyone who could possibly help.

Scott and Ingrid got married. Then they got married again, to reassure both governments their union was real. They went back and forth across the ocean to renew Ingrid's visa more times than they could count. They submitted letters and records and documents to prove they were worthy of staying in the U.S. together.

At their wedding at the Wilson family farm in eastern North Carolina, in the house where Scott's parents were married, the minister asked the bride to repeat the words, "In joy and in sorrow, in sickness and in health . . ." Ingrid thought back to what they'd been through, everything that tested their resolve and challenged their commitment. She tried to say the words, but they caught in her throat—because she realized she and her husband had already begun to live up to the promises the words stood for, not in a fairy tale, but for real.

Then came the day of the interviews. Not just in two separate rooms, but in two separate countries. The questions would be specific, determined to reveal any contradictions. *What kind of wine does she like?* they would ask Scott, in the U.S. *What does she cook for your dinner?*

What does he eat for breakfast? they would ask Ingrid, in Germany. *"Which crops do his parents grow on their farm?"*

If officials pronounced the Bialas-Wilson marriage genuine, they would issue Ingrid a Green Card and she could stay in the U.S. as long as she wanted. Then she and Scott could embark on the rest of their lives, buy a little house, and make it a home with room for a child or two someday. But if not . . .

"We must learn to be patient," Scott told his wife. And so they did. Days went by, then weeks, and as the seasons began to change, the couple received an envelope in the mail. It contained something small and precious; their wish for a Green Card had been granted. Although it was something that for years they had hoped and prayed for, it really promised nothing—nothing but a chance for happily ever after.

INGRID BIALAS-WILSON'S GERMAN BACON TART

1 ½ cups flour
1 envelope packaged yeast
⅔ cup warm water, not hot
2 tablespoons oil
Salt
¾ stick of butter
2 egg yolks
8-ounce container of sour cream
8 slices uncooked bacon, chopped
½ cup onion, chopped
½ tablespoon caraway seeds

Put the flour in a bowl and set aside.

Dissolve the yeast in the water, then stir in the oil and a pinch of salt. Make a "well" in the flour and pour in the yeast mixture. Mix well until the dough is stiff enough to knead; add a little more flour if it is too sticky. Knead until smooth. Put the dough in a greased bowl, cover with a clean towel and set aside in a warm place to rise until doubled in size, about 1 hour.

Preheat the oven to 400 degrees. Grease a baking sheet and set aside.

Meanwhile, in a bowl, cream the butter. Add the egg yolks and sour cream. Then stir in the bacon, onions and caraway seeds. Knead the dough again briefly, roll it out into an oblong and spread it onto the baking sheet. Spread the topping evenly.

Bake until bacon is crispy, about 20 minutes.

YIELD: About 8 servings

WEEKEND APPLE PANCAKES

DENE HELLMAN

No kitchen was big enough for my husband and me to work in together. Since he was the more dazzling cook, I usually deferred to him. A Holocaust survivor, Werner came from a family that, before the Nazis shut them down, was in the food business in Berlin. That, plus having nearly starved to death during the war years, meant he could never take food for granted.

After moving to Charlotte in the 1980s, I took a job and he retired, which left him in undisputed control of the kitchen. Often, on a weekend morning, I'd dawdle my way downstairs and he'd be there making apple pancakes. His only recipe was in his head.

In time, Werner began lapsing into the haze of Alzheimer's. Still, sometimes I'd find him trying to make the apple pancakes. To ease his confusion, I had to put my instincts to work in order to bring him the right amount of ingredients. Enough flour; the right scoop of yogurt; the correct smidgen of baking powder. Eventually, I got it right. Satisfied, he would nod and stir, we'd share the stove together, and then cheerfully have our weekend breakfast.

1 egg
⅓ cup plain yogurt
½ teaspoon olive oil
½ teaspoon salt
Pinch of sugar
1 ⅓ cups milk
1 cup flour
½ teaspoon baking powder
2 Granny Smith apples, peeled, cored, sliced paper-thin
Cinnamon

Whisk together the egg and yogurt. Stir in the olive oil, salt and sugar. Add the milk, flour and baking powder, stirring to a slightly lumpy mixture. Fold in the sliced apples. Place a heatproof platter in the oven and heat the oven to 150 degrees.

Spray an 8 or 10" non-stick frying pan with cooking spray and heat it over a burner set between medium and high heat. When it is hot, pour in a ladle of pancake mixture. The pancake will be rather thin. Turn it when the edge is brown and the pancake has shown bubbles on the surface. Sprinkle with cinnamon. When the second side is brown, transfer the pancake to the platter in the oven. The pancakes are tender, so use care.

Repeat the process, adjusting the burner heat as necessary. Spray the pan between each pancake.

Serve with a drizzle of real maple syrup. A pat of butter is a good addition, too.

YIELD: 2 to 4 servings

MEDITERRANEAN MUESLI

CASSANDRA KING CONROY AND PAT CONROY

Cassandra King, author of *The Sunday Wife,* is also an accomplished reporter and teacher. She and her husband, novelist Pat Conroy, live in the South Carolina Lowcountry.

HINT

This is the consistency I like—in Egypt it was really soupy; in other places on the Mediterranean, thicker

Pat and I discovered this fabulous dish in Cairo and have been breakfasting on it ever since. Here's what's great about it: It's delicious, nutritious and really versatile, especially in summer when there are so many fruits and berries available.

1 cup plain yogurt
1 cup low-fat milk
1 cup raw oatmeal
¼ cup oat bran or wheat germ
¼ cup honey, or more to taste
½ cup dates, dried apricots and figs, chopped
½ cup walnuts, chopped

Mix together all the ingredients and store in the refrigerator. Serve as is or topped with fresh fruit, finely chopped melon or berries.

YIELD: 2 servings

CABBAGE, HAM AND CHEESE DISH

BARBARA APPLING

I have lived in North Carolina all my life. I am one of 14 children, and I learned to cook from my mom, who learned from her mom and just plain experience. We cook from memory only. I started at a very young age, since I was one of the five smaller ones still at home. I have never cooked anything by measuring. We learned that food is much better when you just throw in a little of this and a pinch of that. My grandmother once told me, if it smells good, nine times out of ten it is going to taste good!

- 2 ham hocks
- 2 heads of cabbage
- 4 slices of fatback
- 1 bag shredded cheese, any kind you like

Boil ham hocks until meat separates from bone. Set the meat aside.

Cut up the cabbage, put into a large pan and add just enough water to cover; steam until soft. Most of the water should be gone once cabbage is done.

Bake fatback at 350 degrees until golden brown. Add fatback grease to cabbage. Put the meat and cabbage into a deep casserole dish and sprinkle with cheese. Warm in the oven until cheese melts.

YIELD: About 6 to 8 servings

BUFFALO CHICKEN WINGS

SCOTT JAGOW

King Henri IV of France (1553-1610) is credited with the first speech that made reference to the importance of a chicken in every pot!

If you grow up in Buffalo, New York, chicken wings are a staple. Although they have become commonplace in restaurants around the country, wings were invented at the Anchor Bar in downtown Buffalo in the early 1960s when the bar's owner was searching for a late night snack.

This is our family recipe, written down for the first time here. A native of the Buffalo area, my father tinkered with it for years and taught it to me when I was mature enough to responsibly carry on the tradition. Vinegar was not part of the original recipe. We added it later when I tasted vinegar in the wing sauce at a Buffalo-themed restaurant in — of all places — Orlando, Florida. The vinegar adds the "sting" you feel on your lips once you eat a few.

Don't feel ashamed if you have to pull an ice cube out of your glass of water and rub it on your lips. Even an experienced wingman like myself resorts to that trick now and then. You'll also need plenty of napkins because the sauce will get all over your fingers, lips and face if you eat the wings right. Besides lots of water, a nice, cold beer (Genessee is made in upstate New York) will also help you get through the experience with a smile on your face.

I made these wings before each of the Buffalo Bills four straight Super Bowl appearances in the early 1990s, and obviously they had no effect on the team's success, since the Bills lost each of those games. But everyone who has tasted these wings — including Cowboys, Redskins and Panthers fans — has raved about them, so I guess that's some consolation.

Not really. I still make these at the beginning of every football season in the hope that the Bills will make it back to the Super Bowl and finally win one.

3 large packages of wings (9 in
  each package will yield the
  right amount)
Cooking oil
1 large bottle of hot sauce*
½ tablespoon Worcestershire
  sauce
1 tablespoon white vinegar
1 tablespoon tomato paste
1 handful seasoned salt, to taste
½ stick of butter
1 teaspoon cornstarch, optional
Dash of salt and pepper,
  optional

EQUIPMENT:

1 wok
Many napkins
Ice cold beer, preferably
  Genessee Cream Ale

*I use Texas Pete
brand, but you can
substitute your
favorite Texas- or
Louisiana-style hot
sauce.

Cut wings in half with a boning knife. Rinse and dry with paper towels.

Pour oil into wok; it should be about a quarter full. Heat on medium high.

Meanwhile, combine the remaining ingredients in medium pot and simmer on low heat. Stir occasionally. The tomato paste thickens the sauce so it will stick to the wings. Use less butter if you want the wings hotter; more butter to make them milder. Add the cornstarch if the sauce needs more thickening.

Once oil is hot, carefully add the wings; cook on medium to high heat until golden brown, about 10 minutes per batch. Cover wok to avoid splattering. Once wings are cooked, remove from wok, pat dry with paper towels on a large platter.

A few at a time, put the wings into the saucepot and stir until wings are covered with sauce. Serve immediately.

YIELD: About 50 wings

BRISKET JUBILEE

JENNY ROSENTHAL

Brisket is a cut of beef that is improved by long, slow cooking.

HINT
This freezes well.

This is the brisket recipe that always wowed everyone. I got the recipe from my mother, Ida Marie Berman, who got it out of the newspaper years ago. I've been making it as long as I've been married—23 years. When people would ask for the recipe, I would say, "No. You have to wait till I die. I'll just make one for you instead." I protected the recipe; it was a little something I could hold over them.

When I turned 50, I had a change of heart. I decided to give away the recipe on my birthday, May 20. I said, "Everybody can have it." And now, everybody does!

A 6-pound brisket
Fresh garlic
½ cup water
½ cup ketchup
½ teaspoon salt
¼ cup Worcestershire sauce

2 tablespoons vinegar
½ cup strong coffee
¼ cup sugar
Fresh ground pepper

Preheat oven to 275 degrees. Rub the roast with garlic, then put it in a roasting pan with ½ cup water. Bake 2 hours uncovered. If the pan has gotten dry, add a little more water (or wine), then cover with foil and bake 2 hours longer.

Meanwhile, combine the remaining ingredients in a jar and shake well. During the last hour of cooking, pour about half the sauce over the meat and let it finish cooking.

Remove the brisket from the oven, slice it, place the slices on a large dish or platter, and cover with the remaining sauce. Cover and refrigerate overnight so the fat will rise to the top. The next day, skim off the fat, reheat and serve.

YIELD: About 12, depending on the size of the brisket

SEAFOOD BLEDSONIA

JERRY BLEDSOE

The problem I encounter when I write about my cooking is that I tend to sound immodest, although Heaven knows that is not my intention, or my nature. Still, how does one talk about a dish he has created that is so divinely scrumptious as to be ambrosial without seeming to have an ego the size of Paul Prudhomme's belly?

I am not even going to write here about the dish for which I actually gained a modicum of fame—attention on national TV and a write-up in *Southern Living*. That would be my left-handed whelk chowder, which I cooked for literally thousands of people over the years at the Strange Seafood Festival in Beaufort, North Carolina, until that event became politically incorrect and was permanently banished.

Practically everybody who tried it told me that chowder was the best thing they tasted there, which may not be so impressive when you consider that some of the alternative dishes were a yukky yellow mole crab broth, steamed marsh snails, and glisteningly purple gonads from live urchins of the sea variety. Besides, it is practically impossible to get left-handed whelks anymore, and why, like the gourmet magazines, provide a recipe for which nobody can obtain the ingredients?

Instead, I offer something even better, the dish that people who have sampled it once beg me to cook for them again and again. (See what I mean about this immodesty thing?) I call it Seafood Bledsonia, because I created it after ordering a dish at an Italian restaurant owned by a fellow named Anthony. He called his Seafood Antonia. It was shrimp and fish in a watery white sauce over rice, and I was so unimpressed that I said, "I can make this a lot better." Somehow Seafood Jeronia didn't sound quite as impressive as Seafood Bledsonia, thus the name.

This is a dish that is rich by every meaning of the word, but quite simple. I am not a precise cook and I don't do measurements, so I will just tell you what you need and how to put it to together.

Jerry Bledsoe's first true crime book, *Bitter Blood*, reached #1 on the New York Times best-seller list.

55

MAIN DISHES

First, obviously, you need seafood, the more expensive the better. I use lobster, shrimp, sea scallops, grouper, or some other firm white fish, and lump blue crabmeat. Pan the seafood in a generous amount of butter at low heat until it loses its translucence but don't overcook.

You will need to have steamed up a pot of rice in advance. Spread the rice in the bottom of a casserole dish. Put the seafood over it. Slice some roasted red peppers and dot them about on the seafood for color and flavor. It will look so pretty at this stage that you will want to eat it immediately, but wait.

Now make a simple white sauce using clam juice and heavy cream (if you don't know how to do this, you really shouldn't be attempting this dish). When it begins to thicken, add as much sherry as you can take—don't be sparing. Pour this over the dish. Top with grated mozzarella, Swiss and Parmesan cheeses, and put it into a 400-degree oven until the cheese bubbles and gets little golden spots on top.

Once you've served it, just sit back and await the accolades, which, I'm sure, you will accept with all modesty.

YIELD: 6 or more servings, depending on the amount of seafood and rice

SARA'S SWEET SOUTHERN SUGAR-CANE PORK

SEAN A. SCAPELLATO

I'm a Southerner by transplant. When I married a Charleston girl, I had no idea there was a profound culture shift embedded in those wedding vows. Growing up a Pittsburgher in Atlanta was shocking enough. We were never "fixin' to do" anything. We didn't "cut on" lights, and "y'all" was reserved for a trip to Macon or Valdosta. I'd never once tasted catfish; I thought barbecue was grilled burgers and dogs. And Frogmore Stew…well, I won't say what I thought was in that. In any case, with my new wife, my taste buds experienced a broadening of sorts, and before long, I was talking about vinegar- and mustard-based barbecue, and my appetite for steamed oysters was as keen as anyone from Bowens Island or Murrells Inlet.

I'd married a woman who possessed prodigious skills in the kitchen, thoroughly schooled in Lowcountry cuisine. Her uncles are mayors of South Carolina towns like Yemassee, Varnville, and Hampton. Her cookbook from the Great Saltkehatchie Church in Ulmer is dog-eared and stained with the gold of her creations from it. Needless to say, she comes by it naturally, and judging from my waistline, I've adapted quite nicely myself. Simply say "meat-and-three," and I'm at the table looking for green beans, mashed potatoes, and mac-and-cheese.

My parents were so poor when they married that their first kitchen table was made of the shuffleboard from a Pittsburgh fire hall and some makeshift legs that screwed into the bottom of it. I inherited it at my wedding when neither Sara nor I had jobs, and a kitchen table was conspicuously absent from our list of wedding presents. Now, it sits as an island in our kitchen (it's really that small), and it reminds me of my Italian upbringing, but it also reminds me of my introduction to Southern cooking. As Sara began to perfect her culinary art, I became a test pilot for her dishes, quickly forming a list of favorites and a few dishes that I could "grow" into (I'm still working on fried okra and creamed corn). I can't go a winter without her chilis—red and white—and her vegetable soup simmering on the stove is a hedonistic mélange of meat and vegetables.

But then there was the pork. She's been making this since our first year of marriage. It is a nostalgic call back to our early days in Tennessee when we were eating off our expensive wedding china at our makeshift shuffleboard table and rickety stools. One of our first times entertaining as a couple included this dish, and it turned out so well that we couldn't get our guests to leave. I was a bit alarmed as Sara crouched over the stove, pouring syrup all over that meat, but as honey is to ham, so syrup is to pork, as far as she was concerned. Years ago, when a friend introduced us to the insouciant wine-drinking crowd of highly refined Clarksville, Tennessee, we discovered the fruity sweet of French Vouvray, and Sara—like any gifted cook—created the pork dish to accompany the wine in the consummate blend of food and drink.

I never know when she's going to surprise me with this dish, but I do know, when I see the pink of the tenderloin thawing in the fridge—along with some B&G Vouvray—I should probably skip lunch, take my afternoon nap, and dream of sweet glazed pork and the seconds I will undoubtedly have.

2 to 3 pounds pork tenderloin
Freshly cracked black pepper
Salt
Olive oil
3 tablespoons Dijon mustard
3 tablespoons cane syrup

Roll tenderloin in cracked pepper and salt. Heat olive oil on high in a skillet and sear the outside of the meat until brown. Reduce heat to medium-low. Add the mustard and syrup, stirring until blended with pan juices. Turn meat in pan to coat all sides. Cover and continue cooking for 15 to 20 minutes or until desired internal temperature (160 to 165 degrees).

YIELD: About 6 servings

HINT

Best served with mashed sweet potatoes and black-eyed peas. Wines include a sweet Vouvray or the Riesling of your choice. Oh, and don't forget the cornbread.

RATATOUILLE OR EGGPLANT CASSEROLE

KATHARINE W. OSBORNE

About 25 years ago, when my daughter Kathy returned home after spending a year in Paris, she accompanied me one morning to our local farmers market. The summer vegetables were at their peak, and as she spied a dark purple eggplant, she exclaimed, *"Aubergine,"* the French word for eggplant. She informed me that the female ushers at L'Opera in Paris were called *aubergines* since their uniforms were the color of eggplant.

She begged me to buy one, and I consented even though I did not know what to do with it. My mother had always made a delicious eggplant casserole, but I had no idea where to find the recipe for one.

Eventually, however, I did find what turned out to be the perfect recipe. It called for zucchini, green peppers, tomatoes and onions, as well as eggplant. Even the name, Ratatouille Provençal, was perfect. It is one of my summer favorites. This is my adaptation, as I never measure the ingredients. I just approximate.

HINT
Ratatouille is a versatile dish that can be served either hot or cold.

¼ cup olive oil
1 medium-to-large onion, thinly sliced
2 or 3 green peppers, thinly sliced
1 medium eggplant, peeled and sliced
2 or 3 sliced zucchini
3 or 4 sliced tomatoes
Salt and pepper

Place the oil in a deep skillet or casserole and randomly layer the vegetables, adding salt and pepper to each layer. Cover and simmer over very low heat for 35 to 45 minutes. Uncover and simmer for about 10 more minutes to reduce the liquid.

YIELD: About 6 to 8 servings

59

GARLICKY CRAB CLAWS

JOSEPHINE HUMPHREYS

Nowhere Else on Earth, the latest novel by Josephine Humphreys, who lives in the Low-country of South Carolina, is rooted in the history of the Lumbee Indians.

Tie half a catfish to a string weighted with a bolt or any small hunk of metal out of your father's toolbox. Throw the line into a lowcountry salt creek on the incoming tide. With the string looped around one finger, lie down on the dock, cheek against the hot pine, and wait. Oysters will tick, mullet jump, turtles surface snout first. On a lucky day the porpoise will come with a poof of breath and an arched blue back, and—if you are properly flat with your head down so he can't see you—he might come close, and might hurl himself fully out of his element onto the mudbank, throwing ahead a wash of flopping mullet to eat while you watch.

Doze now, dream things up, hurl your own self into memory or other people's lives, into love and danger and all that has not yet happened, or into the great mystery of your father at the creek's bend, throwing a cast net for shrimp, your mother and sisters catching toadfish and croakers from the bank. Something will come.

You will feel a pull—or not exactly a pull, more of a jitter, a tickle, a scratchy tug. Slowly raise the line until you can see, just under the water, a blue crab working the bait with his claws. A good one is big and rusty, barnacled over. With your free hand, gently let the long-handled net down behind the crab, and then scoop fast. Repeat until the bushel basket holds twelve crabs and your head a dozen seeds for stories you'll write in years to come when this place, these loved souls, and your young heart have changed beyond recognition.

In the catching and cooking of blue crabs there is, built in, a certain amount of horror. Maybe some will escape the basket on the way home and scuttle into hidden parts of the car. Or when your father upends the basket over a pot of boiling water, some will miss the pot and clatter to the kitchen floor. Loving minor risk and drama as you do, these are the parts you'll like best. If the boiling alive is too much for you, you can try another method, although it too is violent. Clean the crabs first, by pulling off the backs, legs, claws, and the dead man (lungs, which can't be eaten). Steam the bodies and pick the sweet white meat from its intricate shelly compartments. Save the claws for this best of all crab dishes:

Crack each of 24 uncooked fresh crab claws (the whole arm) in a couple of places with a mallet or a nutcracker or the bottom of an old-timey green Coke bottle, careful not to smash the meat. Heat a stick of butter or ½ cup of olive oil in a big cast iron skillet. Mince four or more cloves of garlic and sauté with a teaspoon of grated ginger on low heat until soft and just barely golden. Add ¼ cup finely chopped parsley and the cracked claws. Salt and pepper to taste. Cook until the claws turn red and then another minute. Serve hot with good bread and plenty of paper napkins.

SERVES FOUR

SOUTH AFRICAN BEEF CURRY

ELLEN WILLIAMS

Curry powder can contain up to 20 different herbs and spices

My husband is originally from South Africa. He was only two years old when the family arrived at Ellis Island and headed south to settle. He really is just as Southern as I am.

One of my favorite dishes my mother-in-law cooks is beef curry. I quickly learned that this was not the mild yellow curry I am used to; this spice is red and very hot like something you taste in Indian food. My in-laws would have it custom mixed to their taste on their trips back to South Africa.

I have tried over the years to duplicate this taste with my mother-in-law's basic recipe. I have had to make some adjustments to my taste and to the availability of ingredients. The best way to cool your mouth between bites is with condiments such as tomatoes, fruit and chutney. My favorite is bananas. Enjoy!

4 to 8 tablespoons oil
2 pounds stew beef
Flour

* Check specialty food stores for red curry powder.

3 to 4 teaspoons red curry powder*
1 teaspoon ground ginger
½ pound onion, chopped
2 cans beef broth
1 stick cinnamon
½ clove garlic, peeled
2 whole cloves

Heat about half the oil in a heavy pan over medium heat. Coat beef in flour and brown in the oil. Remove beef but leave oil in pan. Add curry powder and ginger to the pan; stir until brown, then scrape the seasoned oil into the reserved beef. Heat the remaining oil and cook the onion until dark brown. Add to the beef.

Place all ingredients in a crock pot and cook a minimum of 4 hours on medium-low. Serve over rice.

YIELD: 4 to 6 servings

GROUNDNUT STEW WITH CORN PORRIDGE (AZI DETSI WITH AKOUME)

DON BOEKELHEIDE

When The Peace Corps decided to send me to Togo, I had to look in the atlas to find this a narrow strip of land sandwiched between Ghana to the west and Benin to the east. At the end of the fourth week of training, a veteran Peace Corps volunteer named Lance asked if I'd like to visit his village. I squeezed onto the back of his little Yamaha motorcycle, and we rattled down a dusty road through the African bush, dodging goats, chickens, people and trucks.

After a long, sweaty, bumpy ride, we veered onto a narrow dirt path through a sea of corn, passing huge kapok and baobab trees, and red termite mounds. The path led to a cluster of clay houses. A small crowd surrounded the motorcycle, greeting Lance like a lost brother. In the shade of a palm-thatched hut, tepid bottles of local beer appeared. We drank to everyone's health and good fortune, taking care to pour a little taste on the earthen floor, for the ancestors.

Lance introduced me, in French, as his *"petit frère,"* his "little brother." Then he proudly announced, "This is my family, Kofi is my Togolese dad." Kofi was a short, barefoot man clad in a faded khaki shirt and torn pants, with a battered brown fedora on his head. He shook my hand shyly, his grasp strong and his palm leathery as a baseball glove.

I fielded questions in my best textbook French. Kofi smiled when I told him I was from California—he had heard of Hollywood. And he was a great fan of President Jimmy Carter. "Is it possible that he is really a farmer who grows groundnuts, the chief of the greatest nation on Earth?" Kofi wanted to know.

"Mais oui!" I said. "He's a peanut farmer!"

Kofi shook his head sadly, clicking his tongue in that West African way. "Too bad you have a new president, the actor. Soon, he will have Carter shot, *n'est pas?"*

Palm oil gives West African dishes a distinctive flavor. It is available in the U.S. at some specialty food stores.

As Lance was explaining that things didn't work that way in America, Kofi's first wife bustled in. Lance spoke to me softly.

"*Ecoute, mon frère* . . . Listen, brother, eat everything they bring and just keep smiling,"

"*Oui oui!*" I replied, "but I'm a vegetarian."

We were interrupted by a young girl, wrapped in a bright blue and white cloth, and carrying an upside-down enamel bowl on a metal plate. She gracefully set it on the rickety knee-high wooden bench in front of me. Her sister followed, placing a little covered stewpot next to it.

"You are the guest of honor, little brother!" Kofi said. "My wife makes the best groundnut stew! Eat!"

With a flourish, the girls uncovered the food. Under the bowl was a glistening yellowish mound of something that looked like day-old grits. The pot was filled with a hot, thick, brownish liquid with a reddish oil slick on top, embedded with unidentified chunks. My glasses fogged up and my eyes began to tear. There was something else too—feet, chicken feet, sticking up out of the steaming concoction.

Lance smacked his lips loudly. "*Evivi!*" he said, grinning ear to ear (that's Ewe, a local dialect, for "Very sweet! Very delicious!").

I sat staring, my mouth gaping open.

"Don't hesitate, little brother!" Kofi insisted. "You are our guest of honor. You eat first!"

What was I supposed to do? Everyone in the room, now crowded with a full extended family of Ewes, watched attentively. Lance leaned close. He spoke in a whisper.

"Look, 'little brother,' my family just killed a chicken for you, and that chicken is a major part of this family's wealth. I don't care what kind of vegetarian you are. If you respect my family—hell, if you respect that chicken—you're going to eat it. And enjoy it. And the chicken's feet, see, that's the most delicious part. That's why you get 'em: you are the honored guest. Any questions?"

"But what do I do with them?"

"You suck the toes, to get the jelly, and spit out the rest."

I sat up straight, picked up one clawed foot, and popped it into my mouth; then sucked out the goo, which wrestled mightily with the hot peppers. My eyes watering, I spit out the bones, gulped down the goop, smacked my lips, smiled, and took a long pull on my lukewarm beer.

With chuckles of contentment and approval all around, everybody dug in.

Next thing I knew, I was so busy eating and laughing and talking I forgot all about those chicken feet. The "groundnut stew" was simply delicious, robust and spicy, yet a tiny bit sweet from the red palm oil. Those mysterious floating chunks were fresh West African vegetables. We ate with our right hands, though I noticed spoons placed discreetly where Lance and I could reach them if needed.

We lingered through the long African afternoon, and didn't get back to the training site until dusk. Sitting by myself, watching night swiftly swallow up the twilight, as it does in Togo, I realized something had forever changed.

That memorable meal marked the moment my heart opened to Africa, the moment the boundaries of my world began to fall. I had crossed the bridge to Africa. My life would never be the same again.

FOR THE GROUNDNUT STEW:

1 large sweet onion

1 clove garlic

¼ cup palm oil (or peanut, corn or canola oil)

1 small can, 3 to 6 ounces, tomato paste

1 pound fresh tomatoes, chopped

2 cups water, plus ½ to 1 cup additional

1 cup smooth peanut butter (I use organic unsweetened)

A 1" piece of fresh ginger root, chopped, or ½ teaspoon ginger powder

A fresh hot pepper to taste, chopped and seeded (optional; I use habañeros)

4 bouillon cubes

1 tablespoon soy sauce, Maggi sauce or "liquid aminos"

1 teaspoon salt, to taste

OTHER INGREDIENTS:

1 pound soaked textured vegetable protein (TVP), or soy "chicken"

2 cups chopped vegetables, including:

Eggplant, peeled and cubed

Okra, sliced

Greens, such as collards or chard (spinach or cabbage will do in a pinch)

HINT

This is the version we make at our house. If you want to use chicken in place of vegetarian protein, add the meat from 1 whole chicken or 8 chicken breasts, boiled and cut up. Reserve cooking water in place of bouillon and water. Groundnut stew is plenty good on its own; you don't have to sacrifice your chicken to make it—unless, of course, you have a special guest, or want to use the feet for garnish.

In a large pot, gently sauté the onion and garlic in the oil until transparent and beginning to brown. Add tomato paste and sauté for about 5 minutes. If you are using vegetarian protein or chicken, cut into chunks and add to the pot. Sauté for a few minutes. Then add the tomatoes and vegetables, as the spirit moves you, and sauté and brown a few minutes more.

Add ½ to 1 cup water to the peanut butter, stirring to form a paste. Then add the peanut butter paste, ginger and hot pepper to the pot. Be careful! If your family doesn't care for hot pepper, you may want to omit it.

Combine the remaining 2 cups of water with the bouillon cubes and soy sauce (or Maggi sauce or aminos). Add to the pot and simmer about 20 to 30 minutes, stirring occasionally, until the sauce thickens and the vegetables are tender. If necessary, add broth or water as needed to maintain a thick, stewy consistency. Just before serving, add salt to taste.

FOR THE CORN PORRIDGE:

2 cups cornmeal, finely ground

6 cups water

Salt

Mix cornmeal into 1 cup cold water in large kettle or saucepan. Put over medium heat, gradually add remaining water, stirring constantly. The technique is similar to adding liquid to a thickening sauce—let it begin to boil and thicken, add a bit of water to thin, let that thicken, add more water, and so on. Stir in salt (I use about 2 to 4 teaspoons since the cornmeal is so bland).

When all of the water has been added, keep stirring until the cornmeal forms a thick batter that "lifts" slightly off the bottom and sides of the pot. Turn heat to lowest setting, cover pot, and let it steam for about 20 to 30 minutes, stirring occasionally, until the mush no longer has a bitter taste.

Spoon into a round-bottomed bowl, pressing down so it takes the shape of the bottom and allow to cool. To serve, turn over onto a plate so the smooth "dome" side is up.

To serve: There are at least two ways to eat this dish, with a spoon or fork, or with your hand (right hand only, please). If you serve it the conventional way, pour the stew over portions of the porridge. To eat this traditionally, keep the two separate, and dip small bits of akoume into the azi detsi.

YIELD: 4 servings

MEAT BALLS WITH PRUNES

JOAN MEDLICOTT

Joan Medlicott, who lives in the mountains of North Carolina, is the author of *The Ladies of Covington* series of novels.

This recipe traveled with my grandmother from Lithuania, and is the only food she made that I loved so much that I stood beside her and memorized the details while she cooked. I enjoy the sweet rich flavor infused by the prunes. To me it is comfort food, and I love it with rice smothered in its thick gravy. It can, however, taste great with gravy over potatoes or noodles.

When my grandmother left her native land at age 17 to marry a man she had never seen, her mother placed a series of family recipes in her satchel. On the ship to America the satchel, with all her possessions, was stolen. Her clothing, her precious family pictures, and the recipes vanished, as if they had been cast into the sea; everything, that is, but one piece of paper, this recipe, smudged and ragged at the edges when found on deck by a crew member.

Meat balls with prunes were served every year on December 15th, my grandmother's birthday, and on my birthday in September, and on my mother's birthday in November and on other family members' birthdays and anniversaries. Thus, it took its place as a tradition in our family.

Because I wanted to keep the recipe alive, I shared it with readers in my third Ladies of Covington novel. I am honored to have it included here.

1 can tomato paste
1 or 2 onions, chopped
Olive oil
1 ½ pounds of ground beef, round or sirloin
1 egg for every 1 ½ pounds of beef
Seasoned bread crumbs
A box of pitted prunes
Salt, pepper and other seasonings, as desired

Mix tomato paste with at least 1 quart of water. I use a blender: fill with water, add the tomato paste and whir a second or two. But you can also use a bowl. Just mix well. Pour into any deep pot you'd use to make stew.

Sauté onions in olive oil, then drain and add to the tomatoes.

Put meat in a bowl. Crack the egg into it and work with a fork or your hands. (Add a few bread crumbs if needed, but make sure to reserve enough for coating the meat balls once formed.) Form round balls of meat in your hand, and insert a prune into each ball. Be sure prune is surrounded with meat and not visible. Use a light coating of bread crumbs to hold together well.

Heat a skillet, add olive oil. When hot, brown meat balls quickly on all sides. Remove and drain. Add meat balls to pot. Add the rest of the prunes to the pot. Add water if needed to cover meat balls; season to taste. Cover. I use tin foil under the cover to make a tight seal. Bring to boil, then reduce to medium heat (bubbling slightly) for approximately ½ hour. Lower heat and simmer, covered for about an hour.

Then uncover and bring back to boil for ½ hour or less. You'll need to watch it, for the gravy will become nice and thick without adding flour or anything at all. Do not let all the liquid boil out, or it will burn the bottom of pot.

Enjoy with rice, noodles or potatoes.

YIELD: 8 to 10 meat balls, depending on size

KAREN'S BARBECUED SHORT RIBS

KAREN A. GEIGER

I don't remember when I first started making these, but they are great on a cold day and make the house smell great. I use boneless ribs if I can get them, but even if they're bone-in, the meat just falls off the bone. Serve with mashed potatoes because you will love the sauce.

¼ cup shortening
5 pounds beef short ribs
¾ cup water
1 medium onion, chopped
½ cup diced celery
¼ cup cider vinegar
2 teaspoons salt
1 ¼ cups ketchup
1 cup honey barbecue sauce
¼ cup light brown sugar
1 ½ tablespoons Worcestershire sauce
2 teaspoons hot prepared mustard

In a large Dutch oven over medium-high, heat the shortening till hot, then add the ribs and brown well on both sides.

Meanwhile, in a medium bowl, combine the water and remaining ingredients and pour over ribs. Heat to boiling. Reduce heat to low, cover loosely and simmer 2½ hours, or until ribs are fork tender, stirring occasionally. Add more water if necessary to prevent sticking.

YIELD: About 8 servings

ATHENIAN CHICKEN

VASSILIOS KARAMITROS

After I graduated from the culinary school in 1984, I worked in hotels and restaurants for six years before I moved to the U.S.A. from Greece. I wanted to learn a lot about cooking so I tried to work in different types of restaurants. Today I know how to cook Greek, Italian, French and American food.

- 1 stick margarine or butter
- 2 bunches green onions, chopped
- 1 pound fresh mushrooms, sliced
- 1 tablespoon garlic, chopped
- A 16-ounce can artichoke hearts, drained
- 2 pounds chicken tenders
- Flour for dredging chicken, plus ½ cup more for the sauce
- 2 cups chicken broth
- ¼ cup fresh lemon juice
- Salt and pepper to taste
- ½ to 1 cup Parmesan cheese
- 1 pound spaghetti (can be cooked and drained ahead of time, or while chicken is baking)

Preheat oven to 350 degrees. Grease a large baking sheet and set aside.

On the stove over low to medium heat, melt the margarine or butter in a large frying pan or Dutch oven. Add the green onions and mushrooms. Sauté until cooked, then add the chopped garlic and artichoke hearts. Reduce heat to low and simmer.

While the vegetables are simmering, lightly dredge the chicken tenders with flour and place on baking sheet. Bake until golden brown, about 20 to 30 minutes, then remove from oven.

HINT

Combine the flour with a small amount of broth to make a smooth paste before adding the rest of the broth. This will prevent lumps in the sauce.

While chicken is baking, combine the remaining ½ cup flour with a small amount of chicken broth to make a smooth paste; then add the rest of the broth. Stir into the simmering vegetables, then add the lemon juice. Stir until thick, then add salt and pepper to taste. Add the cooked chicken to combine and stir to keep from sticking.

Run hot water over the spaghetti if cooked ahead, and drain; add the Parmesan and chicken and serve. Enjoy!

YIELD: 4 to 6 servings

THAI-INSPIRED FISH CAKES

ALYSSA WOOD

The first time I met Claire she was working on a large clay piece that looked like a huge stomach, an animated one. She was scrawny and six feet tall, and she wore a long straight braid that hung down her back and a small bar through her nose. We started a kind of all-consuming friendship. We did absolutely everything together—runs to the hardware store for supplies, making art, teaching, grocery shopping, eating. Food became a part of our friendship. We treated each other to chocolates, milkshakes and root-beer floats, and huge meals at breakfast joints and Thai restaurants. Sometimes, we would cook Thai meals together, I as her apprentice.

We were in grad school, getting our MFAs at Carolina, trying to make a body of work, and not kill each other while sharing a small studio, large ceramic heads on my half of the room, fantastical sculptures of fossils and golems on hers. The cooking and eating and sculpting tumbled together into one creative and sometimes smelly mess.

Our friendship has changed since I moved away. We no longer see each other every day, or even every month, but I find that the friendship has followed me so that when I cook Thai food or make art or stop by the lumberyard, Claire is here.

Fish sauce, popular in the cuisines of Southeast Asia, is a salty, fermented condiment. In Vietnam it's called nuoc nam; in Thailand it's called nam pla. In the U.S., you can find fish sauce in Asian grocery stores, as well as specialty food stores.

3 cans of salmon
1 bunch of scallions, thinly sliced
2 cloves of garlic, pressed or minced
¼ cup cilantro, minced
2 limes, plus more for garnish if desired
Peanut oil for frying

FOR THE SAUCE:

¼ cup fish sauce
¼ cup light soy sauce
2 chili peppers, with seeds (should be spicy!)

HINT
Fry the fish cakes in
batches and put them
in a warm oven while
you finish frying the
rest.

Combine the salmon, scallions, garlic and a scant ¼ cup cilantro in bowl, reserving a bit of the cilantro for garnish. Mix well. Halve the limes and add their juice to mixture. Set aside.

In a small bowl, combine the sauce ingredients and set aside.

Pour oil into a heavy frying pan, about ½" deep. Heat over medium until oil is hot but not smoking. Meanwhile, form small patties, about 4" in diameter. Fry in the hot oil about 5 minutes until patties begin to brown, then turn to cook the other side until brown. Drain on paper towels.

Drizzle sauce over just before serving. You can garnish with reserved cilantro or wedges of lime if you wish. Serve with thin wedges of seeded cucumber and jasmine rice.

YIELD: 4 servings

CARROLL'S BARE HANDS
BAKED COUNTRY HAM

DAN HUNTLEY

This recipe came from Carroll Robinson of York, South Carolina, the best natural-born, story-telling cook I've ever known. The father of three South Carolina schoolteachers—I married his eldest, Susan (I better name the others if I don't want to get smacked, Cindy and Leigh).

My start in cooking all began with Carroll. A welder, a plumber, a roofer, a shade-tree mechanic, a 76-year-old steel worker, he can fabricate any iron cooking rig I can dream up. He's always treated me like a son he never had. I first met him when I was 15 and hitchhiking home from Charlotte to York. He asked me if my parents knew I was out on the highway. I told him no and he didn't tell on me, which impressed me to no end.

From the first time I tasted his food—30 years ago—I was a goner. Thank God he had pretty daughters. He was cooking a catfish stew in a huge, iron wash pot in his backyard. Steam was fogging up his glasses and he was stirring the stew with a cypress boat paddle. He said, "Here, Danny, stir this pot while I drink me a Bud."

He has always gone for the gusto, both in his cooking and in his life. When I worked on a shrimp boat in Key West, Florida, I told him I had five pounds of fresh conch meat and asked him if he knew how to cook a chowder. At the time I don't even think he knew that conch was a seafood but I'll be darned if he didn't learn. He taught me how to grind the meat to tenderize it, stew it in a milk-based roux with bacon fat, baby red-skinned potatoes, fresh corn and a sprinkling of chopped green scallions. It's so rich and down home good, it'll make you climb on the roof and holler.

Carroll doesn't give out recipes, he gives advice: "Now Danny, you have to get you a big cooter (snapping turtle) for your stew and when you get that sucker cleaned, you call me now, hear?" The best cooking trick

Carroll ever taught me was never be a slave to a recipe. "You got a tongue, get you a spoon and taste it. Forget about that recipe writer, you're not cooking for them. You make it taste good to you and who is sitting at your table."

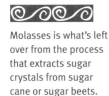

Molasses is what's left over from the process that extracts sugar crystals from sugar cane or sugar beets.

A 12- to 15-pound cured country ham. The best are always bought hanging in a white cotton sack. Don't buy no kind of ham sealed in plastic.
½ cup brown sugar
½ cup apple cider vinegar
A jar of brown mustard
1 cup blackstrap molasses
1 handful of cloves
1 jigger of the best bourbon you can find, two jiggers if you dare

A true Carolina country ham is salty and you have to soak it in water overnight. You need a roasting pan large enough to completely cover the ham. Next morning, trim excess fat but leave enough to keep your meat seasoned. Be healthy but don't be a dang fool about it.

Preheat the oven to 325 degrees. Drain water, wash excess salt from ham and place it back in roasting pan and fill with water again until half of ham is covered. Add brown sugar and vinegar to the liquid. Put it in the oven and bake, covered, until tender, about 20 minutes per pound. Test with a meat fork; meat should be able to flake off in fibers.

Now coat the top of ham with the mustard; any kind'll do, but I like Zatarain's brown Creole mustard. Pretend like you're frosting a cake. Pour molasses over top of ham and sprinkle with the cloves. Pour bourbon over the ham. Now if you have an audience and you want to get fancy, you can ignite the bourbon and then pour it over to the meat. Supposedly, you're burning off the alcohol while keeping the smoky flavor of the bourbon and it actually does help caramelize the molasses. But I think that's mostly for show and a waste of good alcohol. If it's just me, I take a little nip to make sure it's still potent and keep my matches in my pocket.

Place ham back in oven and brown at 325 degrees for about 20 minutes. Remove from oven, cover with lid or foil, keeping meat from being exposed to air. Now here's the secret to this dish: Leave ham alone until water is cool enough to reach into the ham water with your bare hands and lift out the ham, 45 minutes to an hour. Don't ask me why, that's just the way the man taught me how to do it. And all you need to know is, it works. It's the best country ham I've ever put in my mouth. And let me tell you, this farm boy has put away some pig meat.

YIELD: 12 to 15 servings, enough to serve the whole family, with enough left over for redeye gravy and biscuits the next morning

TAH-CHEEN (PERSIAN CHICKEN)

NOUSHIN HEIDARI

Exotic, yellow-orange saffron is the world's most expensive spice. It comes from crocuses. But don't try to grow your own — you would need more than 10,000 flowers to make one ounce of saffron.

I was born and raised in Iran and came to the U.S. back in 1983 to continue my education. I returned home, got married in 1990 and moved back to the U.S. and have lived in Columbia, South Carolina, ever since.

I got to know Mary Ann Rogers through Lucy Johnson, who came to my rescue when I was desperately in need of help. What was supposed to have been a routine task turned out to be an ordeal I'll never forget.

After shopping at Columbiana Mall, I was putting my youngest daughter, Mina, in her stroller. She managed to tip the stroller over and landed face-down on the ground in the parking lot. Lucy just happened to park next to my car and witnessed the whole event. She came to my rescue, and I could not thank her enough for her kindness.

I invited Lucy and her friend, Mary Ann, over for dinner at my home.

"What followed was a wonderful evening of Persian food," Mary Ann said later. "My delight in the meal, the conversation, and the cultural openness was exceeded only by the realization that adventures are before us every day—even as close as a parking lot."

1 pound cooked chicken, deboned and minced
3 to 4 cups basmati rice
Salt
1 ½ cups plain yogurt
2 teaspoons lemon juice
Pinch of saffron
1 egg
Oil

In a large saucepan, put the rice and enough water to cover by at least 2". Add salt generously, about 4 teaspoons or so (it will be rinsed off). Bring to a boil, and cook uncovered only until rice is half-done. Check the cooking time on the package, or watch for the grains to swell while they remain chewy inside. Drain rice, add cool water and drain again.

In a bowl combine the yogurt, lemon juice, a little more salt, saffron, and mix well. Then mix in the egg.

Put ½" of oil in the bottom of a large non-stick pan or pot. Add yogurt mixture, about ⅔ of the rice and stir to combine; spread into an even layer. Put the chicken on top of the rice and yogurt layer; spread into an even layer. Cover with the rest of the rice, put on medium heat and cook uncovered until moisture evaporates. Then carefully cover with 2 paper towels, put lid on, and continue cooking. The cooking time should be at least 1 hour. It's ready when you shake the pan and it will feel "loose" inside, and when underneath it has a golden-brown crust. Serve with Kookoo Potato (See Chapter 3).

YIELD: 4 to 6 servings

CHICKEN FOR WAYLON JENNINGS

WILL D. CAMPBELL

Preacher Will Campbell, a graduate of Wake Forest University, was a finalist for the National Book Award for his memoir *Brother to a Dragonfly*.

When one writes rare books for a living, paydays can be irregular events. Some years back my wife came over to the cabin where I write those rare books and told me that one of us had to get out and get a real job.

Waylon Jennings was a friend and neighbor and I told him I needed a job for a spell. He said, "Be on the bus at one o'clock Thursday morning and plan to be gone for about a month." Waylon never liked to be bothered with trivia, but after three days of riding and watching concerts and playing gin rummy while the buses rolled on to the next gig, I still didn't know what my job was. So I asked him.

"Damned if I know," he said and looked at his wife, Jessi.

"What can you do?" Jessi asked. After considerable deliberation it was agreed that about the only absolutely essential thing I had been seen doing was opening and closing the microwave oven more than anyone else. So it was decided. I would be the tour cook.

How was I going to feed all those mouths? Well, you have to be creative. Sometimes it was as simple as deciding whether lunch was going to be at Hardee's or McDonald's. Sometimes supper would be a buffet provided by the venue. Breakfast on your own. And a few times I actually made a dish of some sort.

I pretty much made it up as I went along. For one concoction, I drew on what I remembered from an Amish chicken dish I had eaten in Indiana. Of course, I had to do a lot of doubling up for a crowd, but I'll give you the measuring for four servings. Sometimes Jessi joined me in the galley and made peach cobbler. Jessi is a charismatic Christian and she begged me to talk to Waylon about the state of his soul. Even as a boy preacher years ago I had trouble being an ecclesiastical Peeping Tom. But late one night I said, "Waylon, what do you believe?"

"Yeah," he replied. Way down in his throat.

Conversations need not be rushed on a stagecoach. Eventually I mumbled, "Yeah? What's that supposed to mean?"

Several more minutes of silence. Then, "Uh huh." At first I thought Waylon was telling me to stick to cooking. Upon reflection I decided and told Jessi that was the most profound affirmation of faith I had ever heard.

I've thought a lot about that trip since we buried Ol' Waylon way out on an Arizona desert. I miss him but have no fear of how he's doing. If you ever find yourself rolling down one of America's highways some night on a country and western tour bus, maybe going from Greensboro to Tampa, you might try this recipe. Or try it in your own kitchen.

Food for the body. Food for the soul.

1 stick of butter
4 chicken breasts (with or without skin or bones; any will work)
1 or 2 onions, peeled and sliced
2 to 3 cloves of garlic, peeled and sliced
2 tablespoons flour
1 cup hot water
2 to 3 bouillon cubes
Salt and pepper to taste
Fresh chopped basil or parsley (dried will work)
2 or 3 new potatoes, peeled and quartered

In a large, heavy skillet, melt the butter. Add the chicken and brown on both sides over medium heat. Remove the chicken and set aside; add the onions and garlic to the pan and cook until soft. Then put the chicken back in the pan and continue cooking.

In a small bowl, mix the flour with just enough hot water to make a paste, then add the bouillon cubes and the rest of the water; stir until the cubes dissolve. Add salt and pepper to taste.

Add the potatoes to the skillet. You can add the basil or parsley now, or upon serving, or both. Pour in the hot liquid mixture, cover and simmer for half an hour or so until the chicken is cooked through and the potatoes are tender. Serve with additional basil or parsley if desired.

YIELD: 4 servings

HEIDI'S KITCHEN

Amy Rogers

Heidi's kitchen is a loud and colorful place. Mismatched towels and mugs cheerfully share their space with dishes and ceramic pitchers in a riot of colors. On the yellow walls, Heidi has stenciled red, green, and blue knives, forks, and spoons; plus coffee cups and pots.

Heidi has no signature dish, no special skill she acquired at cooking schools in France or New Orleans. She never serves fussy little foods or those tiny little appetizers that please the eye but leave the stomach grumbling for more. Instead, Heidi heaps her table with pork roasts and potatoes, cobblers and frittatas. She makes her own liqueurs and bottles her own vanilla extract. Plain olives won't do, so she stuffs rosemary and lemon peels into their jars, then pours the brine into salads that are both simple and satisfying.

Last year, Heidi underwent treatment for breast cancer and through it all, everyone tried hard to behave normally, to laugh and joke with her as always, and we avoided talking about what was happening to her, unless she brought it up first, which was almost never. She is undisputedly the best cook among us, and so none of us could deny the seriousness of her illness when the day finally came that Heidi lost her appetite.

Food has always been such a central reason for our gatherings—for birthday buffet dinners, for Sunday pancake breakfasts—that when we couldn't do those things anymore, we didn't know what to do instead.

And so, wanting to do something—even if it turned out to be the wrong thing—we began calling her husband, Will, at his office. "Should we bring over some bagels tomorrow? Or a pound cake?" we would ask. "Or how about a roast chicken?"

"No, not just yet," he would answer gently. "Maybe in a few days." So we sent flowers and cards instead, and waited for the call from Will, when enough time had passed, telling us Heidi had weathered the worst of it.

It's often said that illness affects not only the person who is ill, but her entire family as well. If that's the case, all of us in Heidi's family of friends felt our own appetites diminish. We stopped jumping into the car on Saturdays to search for apples in the mountains, or canning jars, or places to buy maple syrup in those little tins shaped like log cabins.

One wintry Sunday, my husband and I went to visit Heidi. It had been only two or three days since her last treatment and Will had warned us she was feeling iffy.

"Please, just let us come by for a minute. We won't stay long," I had promised, and Will had finally relented.

When we stepped onto the porch, we heard the dogs barking and the stereo playing flamenco music inside the house. Will opened the door. It was hard to read the expression on his face. "She's in the kitchen," he said.

On the table was a platter full of olives in garlic brine, roasted red peppers, pickled onions, crackers, and in the center, a big wedge of blue cheese. A pot of coffee was waiting for us.

The room was in a state of disarray we hadn't seen in months, cabinets open, dishes in the sink, a light dusting of flour all along the kitchen counter. The dogs were begging for scraps of turkey or crusts of bread while the cats pretended not to care.

And while the oven pre-heated, Heidi was rolling out pie crust, fitting strips of dough into a pan heaped high with apples and cinnamon and brown sugar and allspice.

I began the rehearsed speech, said we could only stay a little while, and bent down to hug her.

She leaned toward me.

"You CAN stay and eat with us, can't you?" she asked.

HEIDI'S SMOKED TURKEY AND BRIE SANDWICHES

HINT
Don't use fresh cranberries for this recipe. They are too tart.

4 croissants
½ pound smoked turkey, sliced
Sweetened dried cranberries, ¼ to ½ cup (optional)
A 4- to 6-ounce wedge of Brie cheese
Fresh ground black pepper

Preheat the broiler. Lightly grease a baking sheet and set aside.

Split the croissants in half lengthwise. Divide the turkey equally among 4 of the halves. Top with the cranberries.

Divide the Brie among the other 4 halves and top with ground pepper. Place all 8 halves on the prepared baking sheet, then broil just until the Brie begins to bubble. Remove from oven and carefully assemble the sandwiches by placing one half with Brie on top of one half with turkey. Serve immediately.

YIELD: 4 servings

GRAMMA BUTNER'S STUFFED PEPPERS

SHERRY AUSTIN

This recipe comes from my Great-Gramma Anna Butner, who lived in an apartment above the Chinese laundry in downtown Winston-Salem, back in the 1930s.

This is different from all those stuffed pepper recipes you see with tomato sauce and rice. Mama Willie and Aunt Teeny (Great-Gramma Butner's granddaughters, who just about worshipped her because they were orphans and she took them in) made their stuffed peppers this way. To put any kind of tomatoes or rice or cheese or spices other than salt and pepper in this recipe is a crude violation. The kind of very young green peppers that they used are hard to come by in the stores. You just about have to get them from somebody's garden. Also, you'll notice the recipe calls for leftover cathead biscuits. Catheads are buttermilk biscuits that were patted down before they were baked so they come out of the oven flat and shaped roughly like a cat's head. Any kind of buttermilk biscuits, even store-bought will do, though.

    6 to 8 very small green bell peppers
    1 pound stew beef
    2 cathead or other buttermilk biscuits, crumbled
    1 medium onion, chopped up fine
    Black pepper, a good bit of it
    1 half pound bacon, untrimmed

Preheat oven to 350 degrees.

Cut the tops off the peppers but leave them whole, remove the seeds, then briefly blanch the peppers (plunge into boiling water for about a minute, then remove and drain).

85

In a skillet, cook the beef, salted to taste, until it falls apart. Mix up the cooked beef, including a cup or so of the beef liquid, with the crumbled biscuits and chopped onions. Season with black pepper. Mixture should be wet or else it will get too dry when it bakes.

Stuff each pepper with the mixture, packing it in tight. Over each pepper drape an entire piece of bacon, fat and all. Lay the peppers in an iron skillet, greased with bacon fat.

Bake until the bacon is crispy and the peppers are starting to shrivel up, about 35 to 45 minutes. Let set for 10 to 15 minutes before eating, if you can hold out that long, which is doubtful.

YIELD: 4 to 6 servings

SRI LANKAN CHICKEN

S.J. SEBELLIN-ROSS

A long time ago, I belonged to the management team at a company with a large staff of employees. The good news was that we would hold potluck lunches. The bad news was that the managers would eat cake and casseroles with other managers, while the employees would enjoy tabouli and falafel with other employees.

I was far more interested in the intriguing dishes the employees brought. So there I was among a rainbow of faces, tasting this and that as they encouraged me to try different dishes, teased me about my reaction to the spices, and laughed as I spluttered and coughed.

I fell in love with a chicken dish from Sri Lanka and asked the chef for the recipe. But she was shy about sharing it, telling me it was only a simple family dish. I told her I, too, wanted to make this for my family. She finally relented, and using the palm of her hand to indicate ingredient sizes, taught me this recipe. I'm so glad she decided to share her family's dish. I think about her every time I serve it.

¼ cup soy sauce
4 small or 3 large tomatoes, quartered
1 tablespoon curry powder
1 tablespoon chili powder
4 cloves crushed garlic
Generous pinch of salt
4 boneless, skinless chicken breasts cut into large chunks
Cooked rice

Put the soy sauce and half of the tomatoes in a large skillet on medium-high heat. Stir in nearly the full allotment of the four spices. Stir in the chicken, ensuring all sides are coated with the spicy mixture. Ideally, your tomatoes will be juicy enough to keep the dish moist, but not so juicy that the chicken is swimming in liquid. If there is too much liquid (more than ⅛" deep), use a turkey baster to remove and discard the excess. If there is not enough liquid, add a tablespoon or two of soy sauce.

Simmer uncovered and stir periodically for 20 minutes, then add the remaining tomatoes and spices. Cook for another 3 minutes. When chicken is cooked through, serve over cooked rice with a crusty bread, salad and red wine.

YIELD: 4 servings

VARIATION:

Omit the chicken and rice; cut the tomatoes into small pieces, mix the other ingredients in a skillet, and heat on medium-high for five minutes. Coat chicken breasts with this mixture and grill. It can also be used as a dip for nachos.

MAMA ALLIE'S "TALKING DOGS" FRIED CROAKERS

CONNIE WILLIAMS

Mama Allie, her grown son, Uncle Horace, and his family all lived together. Uncle Horace said every night at around midnight, dogs would meet and go on a scrounging journey, sniffing out the overflowing trash cans that gave them the largest, meatiest bones and bread sopped in greasy brown gravy, dripping of syrupy sweet potatoes. But their favorite cans were the ones that carried the delicious smell of fish, especially if there had been a fish fry. The smell made the dogs lick their long tongues all around their mouths.

Mama Allie's family had always fried fish for supper on Friday night. Her mother fried fish; her mother's mother fried fish; and her mother's mother's mother fried fish on Friday night, as far back as she could remember. So her trash can was a favorite because that family tradition continued.

Well, these dogs would gather in the neighborhood and decide where to search. A pack of ten to twelve dogs with their leader, the dog with the most brains, would attack and turn over Mama Allie's trash can and scatter the garbage all over the alley in back of the house.

You see, Uncle Horace worked hard on his job at the railroad all day and needed his sleep at night. And each time the dogs turned over the garbage, it was his job to get up very, very early the next morning to clean up the trash before going off to work.

One day after Uncle Horace became tired of having to get up early to clean up the mess the dogs made the night before, he decided he would hide the trash can. Then the dogs wouldn't be able to find it and Uncle Horace could get his sleep.

So on Friday night after supper, Uncle Horace closed the lid very tightly on the can, put it in the barn, locked the barn door and went to bed. In the meantime, the dogs gathered as usual to go looking for food. After

Croakers are members of the drum family, which includes kingfish, redfish and spots. Drum—and croakers—are named for the unusual sounds they make.

MAIN DISHES

they checked all of the cans at the local stores they rounded the corner to where Mama Allie and Uncle Horace lived. But to their surprise, when they arrived they could smell the delicious fish that made their mouths water, but there was no garbage can.

They huddled and the group decided that the dog with the most brains would ask the question. So he began, "Roo, roo, roo-roo-roo-roo-roo. Roo, roo, roo-roo-roo-roo?" There was no response. So he asked again, "Who, who, who moved that garbage can?" When no one answered, he began to howl louder, because he knew that the other dogs wanted to know what had happened to that garbage can with the fish in it. So he demanded, "Roo, roo, roo-roo-roo-roo-roo? (Who, who, who moved that garbage can)?"

Uncle Horace, awakened by the commotion, decided to give the dogs a good scare. He loaded his old shotgun and shot into the air with a loud *boom*! And the dog with the most brains led the trembling pack away as he told them, without looking back, "I know now. I know now."

4 cups peanut oil
4 medium-sized croakers (heads removed; cleaned and split open)
Salt and black pepper to taste
1 egg, beaten
Yellow cornmeal

Heat the peanut oil in a deep fryer until hot but not smoking. Wash and drain the water from the fish.

Add salt and pepper to the beaten egg. Dip the fish into the beaten egg, then roll in cornmeal and fry until golden brown in the hot peanut oil. Serve hot.

YIELD: 4 servings

HINT
Mama Allie used Crisco to fry her fish. I use peanut oil for a crispier taste. I believe she would be pleased.

CHICKEN MACIEL

VIRGINIA MOORE

I have a recipe I have not shared with anyone except my daughter. When I lived in Kansas City, the chef at the Kansas City Club was a man named Joe Maciel. Our church, Central Methodist Church, annually held a special dinner as a fund-raiser. The chef had a recipe that he reluctantly gave to one of our church members for use at the dinner. My daughter must have this dish for her birthday dinner each year, or the day is ruined. We named our version of the recipe Chicken Maciel in honor of the chef.

HINT
This can also be prepared ahead and heated in a casserole in a 350-degree oven.

2 pounds of stewed chicken breasts, skin and bones removed
¾ stick of butter
1 teaspoon curry powder
½ teaspoon paprika
1 pint of cream
1 heaping teaspoon cornstarch
2 ounces sherry
1 cup cooked rice
Swiss cheese

Preheat the broiler. Grease a casserole dish and set aside.

Dice the chicken. In a pan, heat the butter, curry and paprika, then add the chicken and sauté until chicken is well coated with the butter mixture.

In a large saucepan, heat the cream to just below boiling. Meanwhile, dissolve the cornstarch in the sherry. Stir the sherry mixture into the hot cream and stir until thick. (Reduce heat if needed to prevent scorching.) Stir until thick.

Fold in chicken and rice, and pour into the prepared casserole dish. Sprinkle with grated Swiss cheese. Brown under broiler.

YIELD: 6 servings

LITERARY GUMBO

LEE ZACHARIAS

The dish we know as "gumbo" gets its name from the African word for okra.

I learned how to make gumbo shortly after visiting New Orleans for the first time in the late '70s. I had been to an AWP (Associated Writing Programs) conference and picked up *The New Orleans Cookbook* in a bookshop in Pirate's Alley. Because I like to cook, I soon changed the Collins' recipe into something of my own.

Whenever I've moved, I've gone ahead to the new house to make the gumbo for the crew of friends who did the hauling. Generations of writers who passed through the Writing Program at UNCG ate this gumbo while they worked on their MFAs. My fiction workshop once hauled it to Ocracoke for a final workshop at the beach. I've served it to dozens of visiting writers. John Frederick Nims, Arturo Vivante, Gracy Paley, Hilary Masters, Ann Stanford, Jim Whitehead, George Garrett, James Alan McPherson, Gordon Weaver, Frederick Bush, Richard Ford, Reg Gibbons, Tobias Wolff, Bob Shacochis, Lewis Nordan, and George Singleton are just a few of the guests who've eaten this gumbo at my table. When Dale Ray Phillips lived in town he used to drop by all the time to have an extra bowl put on.

All of my colleagues have dined on this, but when Jim Clark asked for the recipe and students started telling me they'd had Jim Clark's famous gumbo, I realized it was time to fight back. The gumbo, kids, is mine.

½ cup flour
½ cup canola oil
2 medium yellow onions, chopped
4 green onions including the green tops, sliced
3 garlic cloves, minced
1 pound of smoked sausage, chopped
A 28-ounce can of diced tomatoes with their juice
3 quarts of water
2 pounds of cleaned shrimp, fresh or frozen

1 pound of crab meat, fresh or frozen

2 pounds of sliced okra, fresh or frozen

A *lot* of chopped parsley, fresh or dried

5 bay leaves

Thyme, no more than 2 teaspoons dried

Creole seasoning

Juice of 1 lemon

Up to ½ teaspoon allspice

6 to 8 cloves

To make the gumbo you must chop everything before you start the roux, which is made by stirring the flour into the oil in a big soup pot over medium-low heat. Keep stirring. The roux needs to cook for 20 minutes or so, until it turns a medium brown.

To the roux add the yellow onions, green onions and garlic. Continue cooking and stirring over low heat for approximately 10 minutes. To this mixture add the sausage; stir then add the tomatoes and their juice. Add the rest of the ingredients. Use lots of Creole seasoning, a mixture of salt, pepper, and cayenne pepper, and shake the shaker vigorously over the pot at least 3 times or more, depending on how much spice you like. Bring to a boil, then lower the heat and simmer uncovered for about an hour, stirring occasionally to keep the roux from burning. Serve over cooked white rice in soup bowls.

YIELD: About 10 servings

NORTH CAROLINA-STYLE PULLED PORK

ELIZABETH A. KARMEL

I grew up in Greensboro and for a while my family lived across the street from the Stamey family (owners of the legendary Stamey's Barbecue). So, naturally my first taste of North Carolina barbecue was at Stamey's restaurant. All year, I looked forward to Christmas parties where the hostesses would inevitably serve the moist, smokey and slightly piquant meat in silver chafing dishes; or my annual summer drive to Camp Seafarer that was punctuated by a stop at Wilbur's in Goldsboro. As I aged out of camp, I went to college out-of-state and ended up moving to Chicago where barbecue is defined by ribs—something that at the time, I thought to be quite odd and incorrect! I stood by my claim that the only true "barbecue" was that of my native state (In my heart, I still secretly believe this but have fallen in love with of all forms of 'cue).

Soon I realized that nary a person in my adopted town agreed with my "point of 'cue." So, if I wanted to eat pulled pork more than the once-a-year visit home, I was going to have to barbecue it myself! That was more than a decade ago and since then, I've made pulled pork more times than I can remember and have converted a hefty group of out-of-staters to my way of thinking.

GRILLING METHOD: INDIRECT/MEDIUM HEAT

Wood chips or chunks (optional)
A Boston butt, pork shoulder or end-cut boneless pork roast,
    7 to 9 pounds
Kosher salt to taste
Freshly ground pepper to taste
North Carolina vinegar sauce (see Chapter 7)
North Carolina coleslaw (see Chapter 7)
White hamburger buns

Soak hickory or other flavor wood chips in water for 30 minutes. Meanwhile, season pork with salt and freshly ground pepper. If using a gas grill, place soaked chips in a smoker box and place in grill during the preheat stage. If using a charcoal grill, wait until coals are covered with a white-gray ash to place chips directly on briquettes.

Place seasoned meat in the center of the cooking grate and cook slowly over low heat for 3 to 4 hours or until an instant-read meat thermometer registers 180 to 190 degrees F. If using a charcoal grill, be sure to add coals each hour to keep the heat constant. The meat should be very tender and falling apart. If you are cooking a cut of meat with a bone in it, one surefire way to tell if it is done is if the bone can be easily pulled out—clean as a whistle—without any of the meat sticking to the bone. Remove meat from grill and let rest 15 minutes.

While pork is still warm, pull the meat from the skin, bones and fat, reserving crispy parts of the pork and fat, known to barbecue aficionados as "burnt ends." Chop the meat finely or shred with two forks. Mix with enough sauce to moisten, adding the "burnt ends." Mix well and set aside.

At this point, the meat can be either refrigerated or frozen and re-heated. The best way to re-heat is over a covered double boiler but few have patience with that process as it takes about an hour per quart of frozen barbecue. If you lack patience, thaw the sauced pork in the refrigerator and microwave covered on medium heat until warmed through.

Serve warm on white buns and top with coleslaw that has been dressed with North Carolina vinegar sauce (never mayonnaise-dressed slaw). Serve additional sauce on the side, if desired.

YIELD: About 10 to 12 servings

PIERRE'S ROASTED BONELESS LEG OF LAMB WITH FETA CHEESE AND OIL-CURED OLIVES

TRICIA CHILDRESS AND PIERRE BADER

You have never had a scrambled egg until Pierre Bader cooks one for you. The egg white and yolk are not blended into a monochromatic taste. Rather by folding the eggs together, he allows the tastes of egg white and yolk to be intertwined, yet distinct.

As you can tell, cooking is very important in our home. Since the restaurant is only closed Sunday, that's the day Pierre and I can create dinner together. Our Sunday night menus are usually the result of whatever is fresh at the farmers' market. We like simple dishes in which the food speaks for itself. Young eggplants are sliced and then slathered with olive oil and slapped on the grill and then served with anchovies. Newly dug fingerling potatoes are roasted and simply seasoned with sea salt and pepper. In September heritage mountain apples become the stars. In June, we pick cherries in southern Virginia.

Lamb is Pierre's signature dish. He created this unforced and appealing lamb recipe for a family get-together one Sunday night. The feta cheese virtually melts into the lamb. The herbs for this dish come from our kitchen garden.

1 boneless sirloin end (top half) leg of lamb, about 3 pounds
4 cloves of garlic, thinly sliced
3 tablespoons olive oil
1 tablespoon Dijon mustard
Salt and pepper
2 sprigs fresh rosemary
1 large onion, thinly sliced
6 ounces feta cheese, crumbled
6 ounces of oil-cured black olives, pitted and halved

1 medium vine-ripened tomato, chopped

1 tablespoon fresh rosemary, finely chopped

1 teaspoon fresh thyme

Preheat oven to 450 degrees.

If the lamb is tied with a string, untie it. Spread the lamb open and with a knife make incisions into the lamb. Insert slivered garlic into these incisions. Rub the lamb with 1 tablespoon of olive oil, front and back. Repeat with a mustard rub. Season with salt and pepper. Before re-rolling lamb, add sprigs of rosemary to the inside. Roll, and using three lengths of kitchen twine spaced evenly, re-tie lamb roast.

Roast the meat in the oven for 10 minutes. Reduce heat to 350 degrees and continue to roast until an instant read thermometer inserted in the center registers 140 degrees for medium rare, about 1 ½ hours.

Meanwhile, sauté the onion in the remaining olive oil until the onion is softened and light brown in color. In a mixing bowl, combine onions, crumbled feta, olives, tomato, and herbs. Toss until mixed.

To serve: Slice the lamb and arrange in the center of the plate. Spoon feta-onion mixture on top and serve.

YIELD: 6 servings

MOM'S SPAGHETTI SAUCE

ANN H. HOWELL

Not every tomato is red, or even green. Some varieties are yellow, purple, gold, pink, rose—and striped!

Years ago, my new mother-in-law, Bette Burgin Howell Pryor of Waynesville, North Carolina, explained her recipe for spaghetti sauce while I observed her making it. Over the years it's been adjusted to the needs of our changing lives and tastes. More tomato, thicker, and with soy rather than beef after my husband's triple bypass surgery. I've gotten it down to a concoction one of my youngest son's fellow football players touts as "off the chains."

But where's the chocolate? I *love* chocolate. I'm convinced in a previous life I was an Aztec, or one of their ancestors, Olmec Indian, or Mayan. Montezuma, the Aztec ruler, valued *xocolatl* so highly that the Spaniards found only large quantities of cacao beans when they raided his treasury for gold and silver. The Mayans worshipped the cacao tree—cacao is a Mayan word meaning "God Food." Vianne Rocher from the book and movie *Chocolat* swirls us into the depths of chocolate's Mayan roots.

Why not incorporate chocolate's lusty, dark, mysterious flavor into the sauce and see if anyone guesses? I'll share the secret with you now. Are you brave enough to try?

A 16-ounce package of soy crumbles, or 1 pound of ground beef
1 medium onion, chopped
1 tablespoon minced garlic, or garlic to taste
Olive oil
A 15-ounce can tomato sauce
A 15-ounce can crushed tomatoes or 8-ounce can tomato paste
A 15-ounce can diced tomatoes
2 teaspoons sugar
1 tablespoon A-1 brand Steak Sauce (Bette's touch)
Red wine vinegar, about 1 teaspoon
1 heaping tablespoon dried oregano, or fresh chopped
2 teaspoons dried basil, or fresh chopped

Bay leaf or two
Generous sprinkle of black pepper
½ teaspoon cinnamon (suggested by my son's Italian friend)
1 teaspoon Hershey's cocoa
Spaghetti

In a large, heavy pot, "brown" the soy crumbles with onion and garlic in a little olive oil. If using ground beef, sauté until brown and drain well. Add the remaining ingredients. "Rinse" each of the tomato cans with about ¼ can of water; add the water to the sauce. You can add more or less tomato products and water according to taste and thickness. Feel free to experiment with the amount of any of the ingredients according to personal taste.

Simmer over low heat, covered, at least 30 minutes but the longer the better. Prepare spaghetti according to package directions, drain, then serve with the sauce. (After my husband's bypass surgery, the hospital dietician suggested spaghetti made from Jerusalem artichokes. It looks and tastes like regular spaghetti.)

YIELD: At least 12 servings

HINT
There's enough sodium in the tomato products that you can omit salt from this recipe. Also, sugar helps cut the acidity of the tomatoes.

STEW BEEF

NADINE CARRIKER HYATT

I grew up in Mint Hill, North Carolina, and my education began in 1934. When I was a girl at home we had good food. Mother was a good cook but when we had company, most of the time Daddy cooked the meats. He was very particular when he was cooking, doing a little something extra to make the results better. Some people think it isn't necessary to do all he did, but it's worth it. I've taken Daddy's recipe and added two ingredients that my family likes. We think it adds a little extra flavor. This recipe is special to me because both of my parents are now deceased, but I still have memories of that delicious stew beef.

1 ½ to 2 pounds stew beef
⅓ cup flour
3 cups water
3 or 4 medium potatoes cut in chunks
2 medium onions, chopped
2 or 3 carrots, cut into chunks
Salt and pepper to taste
¼ cup ketchup
1 teaspoon Worcestershire sauce

Brown beef in a hot fry pan. Remove from pan to a pot for cooking. Brown about ⅓ cup of flour in frying pan and add 3 cups of water, cooking until thickened. Pour over meat and cook over medium-low heat until tender. (If pressure pot is used, cook at 10 pounds pressure for 20 minutes.) Add chopped vegetables, salt and pepper, ketchup and Worcestershire sauce. Cook until vegetables are tender.

YIELD: 4 servings

ST. DAVID'S CHICKEN SPAGHETTI

ELIZABETH C. BURGESS

When the women of St. David's Episcopal Church in Laurinburg, North Carolina, were asked to come up with a fundraiser, my friend Carol Whitehead hit upon the idea of a "Chicken Spaghetti Candlelight Supper." Recipes were passed out to the women of the church, a date was set, and the event turned out to be a big success because nobody had ever heard of chicken spaghetti. Carol claims it is an old Episcopal recipe.

She and I were fellow Episcopalians and teachers, and Carol and her family were stars in Paul Green's play, *The Lost Colony,* held each summer in Manteo, North Carolina. The day after the Saturday night "Chicken Spaghetti Candlelight Supper," Carol, ever the actress, announced that she had no idea so many Episcopalian women could not read a simple recipe—because she kept getting so many calls about it. The one thing that threw us was the instruction to "Combine all ingredients."

What we all wanted to know was "The spaghetti, too?"

The answer was "Yes!"

1 hen, 4 to 5 pounds

1 cup fat from broth that hen was boiled in, or 1 stick of butter or margarine

1 tablespoon garlic, minced

3 cups onions, chopped

3 or 4 stems celery, chopped

1 bell pepper, chopped

1 cup flour

5 or 6 cups chicken soup or broth

A 28-ounce jar prepared spaghetti sauce

1 tablespoon Worcestershire sauce

1 pound box of spaghetti

"Some hae meat and canna eat. And some wad eat that want it; But we hae meat and we can eat, And sae the Lord be thankit."
—The Selkirk Grace (1793)

HINT
This freezes well.

Season to taste and boil hen very early, or a day before you plan to serve. Boil about 20 minutes per pound. Cool. Remove chicken from bone and skin, chop coarsely, and refrigerate. Refrigerate strained broth and let the fat come to the top.

Place fat in a large skillet or roaster, and sauté the garlic and vegetables about 10 minutes. Combine 1 cup broth and 1 cup of flour in a Mason jar and shake well. Add to the vegetables and simmer until thick. Add the jar of spaghetti sauce and the Worcestershire sauce. (I use Prego and Lea & Perrins brands.) Simmer, covered, while you cook the spaghetti.

Meanwhile, break the spaghetti, cook in a separate pot according to package directions; drain and add to the sauce mixture.

Remove chicken from refrigerator, add the chicken and remaining broth to the sauce mixture. Simmer, covered on low heat about an hour, then serve.

YIELD: About 12 servings

"LADY FOOD"

LEE SMITH

Progress is not my thing. I don't have a microwave, for instance. I drive a car until it has 200,000 miles on it; and I write books in longhand, on a legal pad. But even I have to admit that American food has dramatically improved in recent years. You can find good bread almost everywhere. You can buy good lettuce, though you still have to grow your own tomatoes. Fancy restaurant food has moved from ubiquitous steak and baked potatoes to include, well . . . everything. Food is healthier and more innovative than ever before.

Still, I often find my Luddite streak kicking in when I am presented with a menu as long as a novella, offering rhapsodic descriptions of something like "fresh grilled newly dug tiny potatoes served on a bed of roasted corn-bacon relish and collards frisée." I don't like the way they put the sauce *under* the food either, instead of on top of it; and frankly, I'd love to have a cocktail with one of those little paper umbrellas in it.

My first idea of an elegant meal came from my mother, whose bridge club met every Thursday at noon for lunch and bridge, rotating houses, for years and years until its members began to die or move to Florida. I loved the cut flowers, the silver, the pink cloths on the tables. The food my mama gave the bridge club was wonderful, though it was very clear to me even then that the way these ladies were was a way I'd never be. They feasted upon molded pink salad which melted on the tongue (back then I thought all salads were Jell-O salads); a canned asparagus/Velveeta cheese soufflé; and something called Chicken Crunch that involved mushroom soup, chicken, Chinese noodles, pecans and Lord knows what else. All of Mama's bridge lunch recipes required gelatin or mushroom soup and pecans. This was Lady Food.

When my mother died a few years ago, I inherited her recipe box. I sat down and read it like a novel—for in fact, our recipes tell everything about us: where we live, what we value, how we spend our time. My

Best-selling novelist Lee Smith, who now lives in Hillsborough, N.C., began writing in her hometown of Grundy, Virginia.

103

MAIN DISHES

mother made all her own bread, for instance. Her recipe for Salvation Cake had a Bible verse listed beside each ingredient (the almonds came from Genesis 43:11), and the only instruction given for baking was the cryptic Proverbs 23:14. Fat content was *not* a consideration. Biscuits called for lard, and Chocolate Velvet Cake required one cup of mayonnaise. A hearty beef-and-cheese casserole was named "Husband's Delight."

Then I realized that I, too, have written out my life in recipes. As a young bride, I had eleven dessert recipes featuring Cool Whip as the main ingredient. Then came the hibachi and fondue period, then the quiche and crêpes phase, and now it's these salsa years. Just this past Christmas, I made cranberry salsa for everybody.

My mother would not have touched salsa—let alone sushi!—with a ten-foot pole. She would not have recognized a portobello mushroom. I think I'll make some biscuits right now, in her memory, if I can just find some lard. One thing she used to say is, "No matter what is wrong with you, a sausage biscuit will make you feel a whole lot better."

MY MOTHER'S CRABMEAT CASSEROLE

1 pound lump crabmeat
1 egg, beaten
1 finely cut green pepper
1 jar pimientos, chopped with juice
Plenty of mayonnaise
Salt and pepper to taste

Preheat oven to 350 degrees. Grease an ovenproof dish and set aside; a flat casserole pan works best. Combine all the ingredients, spoon into the dish and bake for 15 minutes.

YIELD: About 4 servings

CHICKEN CRUNCH

½ cup chicken broth

2 cans mushroom soup

3 cups cooked, cut up chicken

A 7-ounce can of tuna

¼ cup minced onion

1 cup diced celery

1 can mushrooms

A 5-ounce can of water chestnuts, sliced

A 3-ounce can of Chinese noodles

¼ cup almonds

Preheat oven to 350 degrees. Blend broth and soup in 2-quart casserole. Mix in the other ingredients, except almonds. Bake 40 minutes and sprinkle almonds on top during the last few minutes.

YIELD: About 8 servings

"BAKED STEAK" AND BEEF STROGANOFF

Amy Rogers

Beef Stroganoff, named for a Russian count, was very popular in the 1960s. This variation uses tomatoes in place of beef stock, in combination with the traditional sour cream.

Monday was KFC and Tuesday was pizza; Wednesday was hot dogs from the arcade and Thursday was Burger King. On the weekend our Dad would take my sister, my brother and me to a family-owned Italian restaurant nearby, or we'd get take-out Chinese and eat in front of the TV. The next week the cycle would begin again.

For several years this was our family's routine. It was also how and when I learned to cook, not at the knee of a doting grandmother, not in my mother's own house, but in my father's small apartment kitchen. At 15, I became the female head of the household when my mother entered the hospital for four years of on-and-off illness and convalescence.

When we moved from my mother's little house on Long Island to my father's apartment in Miami, not only did we leave behind our playmates and the home we knew, but we abandoned every vestige of our food habits—of food familiarity and identity—as well. Gone were the Sunday pot roasts and slow-simmered spaghetti sauces my mother made for us. Gone were her meatloaf sandwiches, her Beef Stroganoff, her homemade holiday dinners. They were replaced with the weekly rounds of taking out and ordering in, highlighted by the occasional meal at a relative's house.

For a while anyway, it seemed to be a kid's culinary dream come true. But I knew it couldn't last indefinitely, if only because of the expense. I was drafted as the family cook.

I read the directions on frozen pizza boxes and got the expected results. Kraft macaroni-and-cheese was a big hit. Mrs. Paul filled our freezer and I soon became adept at preparing the kind of food you'd find in any below-average school cafeteria.

My sister and brother, then 11 and 9, suffered withdrawal from their fast-food fixes. They looked ready to rebel as they sat down to meals at home that were as bad as those they endured each day at school. I branched out into Rice-A-Roni and soon Hamburger Helper was on the table more nights than not.

Once I turned 16, I got my driver's license. I decided to impress everyone with a real steak dinner and drove to the grocery store. Once there I was faced with a dizzying array of cuts: sirloin, t-bone, flank steak, round steak, top round, ground round; plus roasts, chops, livers and more. I bought an inexpensive package of skirt steak, something I'd seen—sliced thin and arranged on a platter—on our table countless times, and brought it home.

Now, if you buy a 79-cent bag of rice there are directions on the bag. The same is true for any box of pasta. Even coffee and tea come with instructions. But not meat, which as the centerpiece of the meal is the most expensive and easily ruined component. *Well,* I thought, *nearly every grown woman does this, nearly every day. How hard could it be?*

So with my best friend, Diane, I set about making my first-ever fancy dinner from scratch. The oven had to be hot, that we knew for sure. But how hot? Diane, much more a daredevil than I, suggested going all the way. We compromised and turned it to 500, which first required some maneuvering to light the pilot. We remembered from home ec class that ovens need to preheat, so we let that happen while we prepared our feast. Giggling, we sprinkled the inch-thick steak with smoked salt, a concoction that was my father's favorite. Suddenly I pictured my mother in the kitchen of our old house; she always left the oven door open a crack, so we did that, too. I even found the proper broiling pan, and my confidence rose.

We slid the glistening meat into the oven. We waited. Then we heard it—the sizzle of fat. After another minute or so, the aroma began to find its way into our hopeful nostrils. We peeked inside.

Almost nothing appeared to be happening. The steak was still mostly pink, but a dull tan color had begun to creep up the sides. Where was the brownish-black coating of fat that would crunch satisfyingly in our mouths? Then it hit us—we had to turn the steak over to cook the other side. Surely that's when it would happen.

We did, and it didn't. So we cooked it a little longer and after 20 minutes or so, we declared it done. It smelled all right, but it looked all wrong. It was uniformly tan, the color of a Birkenstock sandal, and every bit as appetizing. We tried to eat it but couldn't. The extra time in the oven while we waited for browning to occur had made the bargain cut of meat too tough to chew. We had to throw it out.

By now you realize that we didn't broil the steak, we baked it. My mother's oven was electric, and I had watched her put steaks on the top rack of the oven, with the dial set to broil so the element would cook from above. But in my father's gas oven, of course, the flame was at the bottom. Broiling could only take place by putting the meat underneath the flame, in the lower compartment I mistakenly assumed was a storage drawer.

What we ate instead that night has long since been forgotten. Diane and I laughed when it happened and we've laughed about it lots of times since, because the teenaged antics of two girlfriends learning their way around a kitchen were bound to produce some comic mishaps.

Eventually my family struck a balance between taking out and making our dinners, and I felt a little less anxious as my skills improved. By the time I was 21, I was working as a caterer's assistant.

But what none of us could bring ourselves to say back then, and only discuss rarely even now, is that without my mother in the kitchen, nothing was the way it should have been. The familiarity of food and its routine, even an imperfect one, is so much a part of life that when it changes, nothing seems quite right. Even if that first steak had turned out perfectly, with crisply browned fat and the desired pink color, its taste would have left us all hungering for something we did not know how to ask for.

ELAINE ROGERS' BEEF STROGANOFF

HINT
You can add fresh mushrooms to this dish; just cook them along with onions.

3 tablespoons olive oil

1 ½ pounds cubed steak

2 onions, sliced

1 can tomato sauce

½ to 1 cup water

1 teaspoon salt

1 tablespoon Worcestershire sauce, to taste

An 8-ounce container of sour cream

Egg noodles

In a heavy sauté pan, heat the oil, then add the steak and onions and cook until both are browned. Add the tomato and Worcestershire sauces, ½ cup water and salt. Cover and reduce heat to simmer, and cook for 45 minutes. Check about half-way through the cooking time; if the pan is getting dry, add a little more water.

Toward the end of the cooking time, boil and drain the noodles according to package directions. Keep warm. Just before serving, stir the sour cream into the meat until the sauce is well blended.

Put the noodles on a deep platter, then spoon the Stroganoff on top. Serve immediately.

YIELD: 4 servings

MAMA NELL'S FRIED CHICKEN WITH WHITE CHICKEN GRAVY

ANNELLE FRYE WILLIAMS

Don't discard those drippings! Use them to make white chicken gravy.

I never could help myself. As a child, whenever we would visit our grandmothers I went right for the fried chicken. I didn't care about the big pieces. I was looking for the crispy little wings lying off to the side, kind of like nobody cared about them, within easy reach of my short arms.

Nobody ever acted like they knew they were gone, except Mama Nell who had laid them just right on the plate so I could grab one and get out of the way before anybody noticed. She'd watch me and give me a wink.

First, I'd pull all the skin and meat from the bigger side and cram it all in my mouth. It was just too good for words or breath and sure enough, I would nearly choke holding the meat in my mouth, not being able to chew until it cooled a little. After that first bite, I was more in control, and I picked that double bone clean before starting on the crispy coating of the little piece that most people throw away.

I have been frying chicken for nearly 40 years pursuing that taste and texture—the meat so moist and the skin a crispy brown that could sell as a delicacy, if anyone could figure out how to do it. I know it starts with a big iron skillet that has cooked more chicken than I'll ever see, and it ends with the most important ingredient of all—time. You can't get in a hurry. You just have to fry the stuff, browning on both sides, covering for a while to let it get down at the bone, then uncovering and crisping it up. That takes time and more precisely, someone who loves you enough to stand there and do it.

1 fryer chicken	2 teaspoons pepper
1 cup plain flour	1 cup shortening, more if needed
2 teaspoons salt	

Preheat oven to 350 degrees.

Cut fryer into pieces: 2 legs, 2 thighs, 2 wings, 4 breast pieces, the back and the neck. Put chicken pieces in bowl of salted water and clean them, removing any pieces of feather and excess fat. Remove chicken from water, drain and pat dry.

Mix flour, salt and pepper in a brown paper bag. Heat shortening to medium-hot in a large iron skillet. You'll need enough shortening to come about half-way up the chicken pieces after you place them in the pan.

Put chicken into paper bag with flour a few pieces at a time and shake to coat. Remove chicken from bag, shake off extra flour and slide each piece into the hot shortening, skin side down. Keep shortening at medium-high temperature; it should always be sizzling. Temperature is important. Don't let it drop too much, and don't let it get so high that it smokes and burns. You just have to watch it.

Don't aggravate the chicken. Put it in the pan, brown on one side about 10 minutes, then turn and brown the other side about 4 minutes. You may have to cook in batches because you don't want to overcrowd the pan.

After browning, cover the pan and put in the oven for about 10 minutes, turning once while in the oven. You can use a pizza pan or foil if you don't have a lid. This will make sure the chicken is done all the way to the bone. Remove lid, bring the skillet back to the stovetop to medium-high heat and crisp the chicken pieces a minute or two on each side.

Remove chicken from pan and drain. Try not to burn your fingers and mouth eating it before it cools enough to handle!

FOR THE GRAVY:

2 tablespoons oil from the skillet

2 tablespoons seasoned flour left over from flouring the chicken

2 cups of milk

Salt and pepper to taste

Remove excess oil from skillet, leaving about 2 tablespoons. Mix the flour with a little bit of the milk to make it smooth, then add the rest of the milk. Pour milk-and-flour mixture through sieve into hot pan with drippings, and stir until it thickens and all the little crispy pieces are deglazed from the bottom of the pan. Add salt and pepper to taste, and more milk if gravy is too thick.

YIELD: 4 to 6 servings

CHICKEN BRUNSWICK STEW

JANET BRIGHT

I love living in the southern mountains of western North Carolina. Like my mother, I'm more of a collector of recipes, as there aren't enough hours in the day to cook much. I was inspired to create this recipe by a canned Brunswick stew, and made my own version of it, which my family thinks is yummy.

1 whole chicken
A 15¼ ounce can whole corn, undrained
A 14¾ ounce can cream-style corn
A 10-ounce package frozen tiny lima beans
4 large carrots, sliced in rounds
3 large potatoes, diced
Two 28-ounce cans whole tomatoes, cut up
1 large onion, diced
4 chicken bouillon cubes
½ teaspoon black pepper
½ teaspoon parsley
½ teaspoon basil
½ teaspoon thyme

In a big pot, cover chicken with water and simmer until tender, skimming foam and fat off top. Remove chicken from broth, debone and cut into small pieces. To broth, add chicken, whole corn, cream-style corn, lima beans, carrots, potatoes, tomatoes and onion. Add bouillon cubes, pepper, parsley, basil and thyme. Cover and simmer, stirring occasionally, until vegetables are done and chicken has "shredded." Add additional water or chicken broth if necessary, but stew should be slightly thick.

YIELD: About 8 servings

BAKED FISH DRAUGHON

PATSY B. KINSEY

The late Pat Draughon was a dear friend of our family. He and his wife, "Miss Joyce," lived on what Pat called a pond, but was really a huge lake near Dunn in Harnett County, North Carolina. Pat started out as a school teacher and found out quickly that he could make more money providing catering services and garbage removal to the military. He made a lot of money.

He instilled in my boys his passion for quail hunting and deep sea fishing. His other two passions were his family and East Carolina University, his alma mater.

One time when we were visiting, he baked fish for our dinner. Afterwards, I complimented him on the dish and asked if he would share the recipe with me. He gave it to me and, after looking it over, I asked what kind of fish to use. He replied, "Honey, if you use enough tomatoes and onions, it don't matter."

Onions, sliced
Tomatoes, sliced
Salt and pepper, to taste
1 to 1½ pounds fresh fish, cleaned and filleted
1 can cream of shrimp soup
1 cup white wine or sherry
½ cup Parmesan cheese, grated
¼ cup cracker crumbs

Preheat oven to 350 degrees.

In broiler pan or baking dish, put a layer of sliced onions, then top with a layer of sliced tomatoes. Sprinkle with salt and pepper. Top with the fish; if it has skin, place skin-side down.

In a bowl, mix cream of shrimp soup and white wine or sherry. Baste fish with the mixture. Sprinkle with half the Parmesan cheese, then the cracker crumbs, then the rest of the cheese. Pour the rest of the sauce over the fish and bake, covered, about 20 to 30 minutes until done and the fish loses its translucency.

YIELD: About 4, depending on how many onions and tomatoes you have

LOWCOUNTRY SEAFOOD BOIL
(ALSO KNOWN AS FROGMORE STEW)

NANCY PATE

The easiest way to catch Atlantic blue crab is to set out a baited crab trap at low tide and come back at the next low tide and haul in your catch. But if you're a kid, it's more fun to go crabbing with some cotton twine, a couple of raw chicken necks, a few sinkers, a scoop net and a bucket.

That was the standard equipment we used on Edisto Island back when I was growing up. Sometimes we borrowed a dock, lying face-down on the sun-warmed, weathered boards, waiting for our weighted lines dangling in the water to twitch. More often, we set off on expeditions in the station wagon to Crab Creek, where an old bridge arched over the marsh and we squished across the mud flats, scattering fiddler crabs that made the little ones squeal. The hot, humid air smelled of salt and fish and Coppertone, with a little eau-de-marsh—think of the inside of a tennis shoe—for good measure. We all wore Keds then, because flip-flops tended to get lost in the mud and afforded little protection if a crab scuttled toward your toes.

Crab stew or a Lowcountry boil was the reward for our labors. We kill and clean our crabs before we cook them. It's not a task for the squeamish, so ask someone else exactly how to do it. But once that crab is cooked, just hand me that nutcracker, please.

2 gallons of water
3 tablespoons salt
4 tablespoons prepared seafood seasoning or shrimp boil, such as Old Bay brand
2½ pounds spicy smoked sausage, cut in 2" pieces

4 to 5 pounds small new potatoes
12 to 20 fresh crabs
10 to 16 ears of fresh shucked corn, broken into 3" chunks
5 pounds raw, unpeeled shrimp

In a large stockpot, combine the water, salt and seasonings, and bring to a boil. Add sausage and potatoes and boil uncovered for 5 to 7 minutes. Add the crabs and the corn and boil 5 to 7 minutes. Add the shrimp and boil 3 minutes. Drain and serve immediately on paper plates at a newspaper-covered picnic table.

YIELD: Feeds about 10

3

On the Side:
FRUITS, VEGETABLES
AND SIDE DISHES

FOR THE LOVE OF THE GRAIN

Amy Rogers

It's not just the mosquitoes that will get you. You've got to watch out for the snakes, too. It's summer in South Carolina, hot and swampy, and the air is thick as sweat.

Here is Campbell Coxe, sunburned and sandy-haired, working his rice fields down along the Pee Dee River in Darlington County. Two hundred acres or so, on land where he once grew cotton.

Each and every day during the summer, he walks the fields, checking water levels, inspecting the crop, watching for problems.

The fields must be flat for planting in the spring. Coxe grows a variety of rice called Della, notable for its distinctive aroma. Rice is semi-aquatic, not like wheat or corn. When the grassy-green shoots are six inches tall, Coxe floods the fields with water to a depth of three to five inches, making sure not to submerge the young plants. Without tides to push water in and pull it out, Coxe and fellow farm workers must pump it from the river. As the rice grows taller, to waist-high, the water level will be increased. It's called "stretch water." About a half-inch evaporates every day and needs to be replenished. Some years there are drenching rain storms. Other years, blistering droughts.

Coxe planted rice for the first time back in the mid-1990s. Although his yields are improving, raising rice can be a struggle. "This is not the 'Old South,' with hoop skirts and mint juleps," he's fond of saying. "There is nobody left alive to tell you how." Still, he is determined. So is Meredith, his wife.

They've got about 25,000 acres in all at Plumfield Plantation. "We want to derive a living from this land," says Coxe, "whether from row crops, recreation, forest products or gravel." To educate himself, he read industry journals and traveled to the Gulf states to see how most U.S. rice is grown.

The grain has been cultivated for more than 7,000 years, but it can be temperamental. It likes to be warm and wet. Insects or diseases can attack and ruin an entire season's crop.

Once the plants have matured, Coxe lets the water off. In a week or two, the rice will be ready to harvest, but until then, the plants run the risk of becoming "head-heavy" and breaking. The harvested rice is air-dried in bins, then sent to an Arkansas mill to be cleaned and polished. The result is a deeply aromatic grain unlike anything else on a typical grocery store shelf.

Other landowners are planting rice, but Coxe explains that for most it's a hobby. Even a successful rice planter can't compete with commercial growers in Louisiana, Texas and Arkansas. Coxe warns, "Before you grow anything, you'd better find a market." It's something he's worked hard at, getting his cloth bags of Carolina Plantation Rice into stores where customers will pay a little more for quality food grown locally.

He has no illusions of reinvigorating the South Carolina rice economy. "This crop will not come back like it was," he says. He's right. It was only in the hands of slaves, before the Civil War, that large-scale Carolina rice production was profitable.

"One man can't manage but so many acres," explains Coxe when asked about expanding. He's working with several contract growers. He hopes to develop a line of rice flour products. He's planning to build a milling facility on his land so he won't have to send his rice out of state; once the mill is running, he can process rice for other planters, too. Producing and buying local and heirloom foods is better for everyone, he believes, and says, "It keeps us all growing."

When cool weather comes, the fields will remain a source of sustenance, now for the migrating wild ducks and geese who find food and shelter in the rice straw left after the harvest. When laws permit, hunters will arrive; many will leave with food for their families. "It's not for everyone," Coxe admits. True enough; the work is strenuous, the outcome uncertain. But the appeal remains genuine, and the result authentic—especially for the rare men and women who feel the pull of history, and the urge to wade in the water.

MEREDITH COXE'S PECAN-PARSLEY RICE

1 cup Carolina Plantation Rice
2 cups of water
1 teaspoon salt
¾ pecans, chopped
¼ cup fresh parsley, chopped

Put rice, water, and salt in saucepan. Bring to a boil. Cover and reduce heat to low. Simmer without lifting lid for 18 minutes. Fluff with a fork. Add pecans and parsley and stir. Cover and let sit for 10 minutes.

YIELD: 4 servings

SPICY GARLIC CHEESE GRITS

DAN HUNTLEY

This recipe comes from Harvard Bardwell, a culinary genius and "seriously eccentric Cajun chef" from Baton Rouge. He's renowned for his gumbo, crawfish and crab—and something he calls Red Whammabamma Sauce (see Chapter 7).

- 1 cup of grits, uncooked (preferably stone-ground or quick, but not instant)
- 4 cups water
- 1 teaspoon salt
- ½ cup (1 stick) butter
- 1 tablespoon minced garlic
- 6 ounces cheddar cheese
- 6 ounces Monterey Jack cheese
- 2 tablespoons Worcestershire sauce
- A pinch of paprika

Preheat oven to 350 degrees. Grease a 2-quart baking dish and set aside. Cook grits in salted water according to package directions. Once grits are cooked, add butter, garlic, cheeses and Worcestershire. Stir until butter and cheeses are melted. Place in the prepared baking dish and sprinkle with paprika. Bake for 15 to 20 minutes or until hot.

YIELD: 4 servings

COMPANY SWEET POTATO CASSEROLE

SHEILA FREEZE

My brother was born with food allergies and asthma. As an adult, sugar became an added enemy and had to be avoided. During the holidays, when the family was indulging in lots of sugar, wheat, and milk-based products, Phil chewed on carrot sticks. The dinner table was especially frustrating for him, especially when he was eating his baked sweet potato sprinkled with fake brown sugar and watching us enjoy the same potato smothered in real brown sugar, real butter and thick sweet syrup.

I wanted to be fair to him, and at the same time not take a treat away from the rest of the family, so I scoured my cookbooks, tested recipes, and eventually came up with my own to satisfy everybody's taste buds.

You can use real brown sugar, but the potatoes taste great with the fake stuff. Any kind of margarine or butter will work, and try different fruits to suit your family's taste buds. My own recipe changes a little from year to year, but the ingredients remain essentially the same. Most of all, everybody loves it.

HINT
These can be prepared a day ahead and baked for one hour at 325 degrees. They freeze exceptionally well and can be easily reheated in the microwave.

5 large sweet potatoes
1 stick low-fat margarine
1 Granny Smith apple, peeled and chopped
¼ cup imitation brown sugar
½ large can frozen orange juice concentrate
2 teaspoons cinnamon
Salt to taste

Cut sweet potatoes in quarters, place in large pot. Cover with salted water, bring to a boil and simmer approximately 20 minutes. When a fork easily pierces the skin and the center, drain the potatoes and let cool.

Preheat oven to 350 degrees. Grease a large baking dish and set aside.

When cool, peel skin off potatoes, then place the potatoes in large bowl or back in cooking pot, add 5 tablespoons of the margarine, and beat with electric mixer until light and fluffy. Add finely chopped apple and other ingredients and mix just until blended. Place in the prepared baking dish, dot with remaining margarine, sprinkle with extra cinnamon if desired and bake for 30 minutes.

YIELD: 6 to 8 servings

VIDALIA ONION PIE

ELIZABETH C. BURGESS

This recipe was given to me by my mother's good friend of many years, Florrie Trollinger. She was a second mother to me and the one person that I would go to when I needed serious advice.

My mother and Florrie met in the 1950s when they lived in the foothills of the Blue Ridge Mountains. Our family lived in the mill village of Hudson, and Florrie lived in nearby Lenoir. In 1955, Florrie was widowed and later moved to Laurinburg, North Carolina, to marry a distant cousin. She and my mother lost contact.

Two years later, our family also moved to Laurinburg when my dad accepted a position in a cotton mill there. On Christmas Eve, the doorbell rang and there stood Florrie on our doorstep.

"Florrie!" my mother exclaimed. "What are you doing here?"

"I came over to ask you the same thing," said Florrie. "I live around the corner."

Florrie and my mother renewed their friendship, and now I had my second mother back. This recipe always makes me think of her.

2 cups saltine crackers, crushed
¼ cup plus 2 tablespoons margarine or butter
2 large Vidalia onions sliced into rings
½ cup of chicken broth
3 eggs, whipped
Salt and pepper to taste
2 cups shredded cheddar cheese

Preheat oven to 350 degrees. Melt ¼ cup butter, mix with crackers, and press into bottom of pie plate or casserole dish.

In a skillet, melt the remaining 2 tablespoons of butter and sauté the onions until soft. Pour over crackers.

In a separate bowl, combine the chicken broth, eggs, salt and pepper. Pour over onions.

Bake the pie for 45 to 50 minutes or until eggs are set. During the last 5 to 8 minutes of baking, sprinkle cheddar cheese on top.

YIELD: 6 to 8 servings

COOKED COLESLAW
(BARBECUED COLESLAW)

ELIZABETH A. KARMEL

HINT
You can also make this in a preheated 350-degree oven. Follow the same directions and place the cabbage directly on the oven rack or a cookie sheet. Bake until tender and the leaves pull off like an artichoke.

My family recipe for coleslaw is very simple. It's what I think of as classic fish-fry coleslaw. Nothing but cabbage and a vinegar-mayo dressing with sugar, white pepper and salt as the seasonings. I remember having this slaw for picnics or on the few occasions that my mother would serve fish at home. My sisters and I usually filled up on my grandmother's hot-from-the-oven corn sticks, passing the coleslaw and the fish! Now that I'm all grown up, I appreciate the nostalgia of the coleslaw, but I much prefer my cabbage barbecued.

METHOD: INDIRECT/MEDIUM HEAT

1 medium-sized whole cabbage
1 tablespoon of your favorite barbecue spice rub
½ stick of butter, cut into pats, plus more for basting
¼ cup barbecue sauce, either homemade or pre-mixed (optional)

Remove the core of the cabbage with a sharp paring knife, leaving a hole about 3" deep. Gently loosen cabbage leaves. Sprinkle the interior of the cabbage with spice rub, and spread pats of butter in cavity and between the leaves. Wrap the cabbage in heavy-duty aluminum foil so that all but the top is covered.

Place the cabbage in the center of the cooking grate for about 1 ½ to 2 hours, or until very tender and the leaves pull off the core easily. Baste occasionally with the barbecue sauce and butter in the cabbage core. Cut into wedges and serve.

YIELD: 4 to 6 servings

EMMYLOU HARRIS: MUSIC FROM THE KITCHEN

Amy Rogers

The distinctively sweet yet powerful voice of singer-songwriter Emmylou Harris is no secret to music lovers across the country—and across musical genres. More than simply Southern, her voice and her music transcend the places that have inspired her work.

Even her most devoted fans probably don't know that Harris has a connection to the Carolinas. The Alabama native attended the University of North Carolina at Greensboro before blossoming into the unique musician who, after more than three decades of performing, continues through her songs to tell stories that captivate listeners everywhere.

Singer-songwriter Emmylou Harris has performed and recorded with countless musicians, including Roy Orbison, Linda Ronstadt, Neil Young and Bruce Springsteen.

EMMYLOU HARRIS' BROCCOLI NUT CASSEROLE

Two 10-ounce packages frozen, chopped broccoli
1 can cream of mushroom soup
1 cup mayonnaise
¾ cup pecans, chopped

2 eggs, well-beaten
1 medium onion, chopped
1 cup grated sharp cheese
2 cups buttered bread crumbs

Preheat oven to 350 degrees. Grease a 1½ to 2-quart casserole dish and set aside.

Cook broccoli according to package directions; drain. Add the soup, mayonnaise and pecans and mix well. Add the eggs and onions. Pour into the prepared casserole dish and sprinkle with the grated cheese, then top with the buttered bread crumbs.

Bake for about 30 to 40 minutes.

YIELD: About 8 servings

GRAN RICE

NANCY GAILLARD

When you marry into a family that has its roots deep in Mobile, Alabama, there are many things that you learn to appreciate. These include Alabama football, the only real holiday (Mardi Gras), and the art of Southern cooking.

I became aware of this when I met my future mother-in-law, Helen Amante Gaillard, affectionately called Gran by nearly everyone. Gran is a fantastic cook and I quickly realized that if I were to become part of the family, I needed to learn how to cook my soon-to-be husband's favorite dishes. To start with, I picked something simple. There is some discussion about the name of the recipe, but he and his children just called it "Gran Rice."

I asked Gran for the recipe. When she looked at me and smiled, I knew what was coming—there was no recipe. And what was worse, I found this to be true of all the favorite family dishes. She and I discussed how these were concocted, with "a little pinch of this and a little touch of that." It was quite clear that this marriage would not survive unless I could figure out the equivalents.

So Gran, the quintessential Southern lady, worked with me to write the recipes down. "Gran Rice," having been transported to North Carolina, is still a favorite dish at all family occasions. We even experiment with it now and then, adding new seasonings, a pinch of this and a touch of that at a time.

1 cup rice (raw)	Sprinkle of marjoram
2 cans beef broth	Sprinkle of thyme
1 stick of margarine or butter	1 small onion, sliced

Preheat oven to 350 degrees.

In a casserole dish, pour beef broth over rice and butter. Sprinkle in spices to taste. Place the onion slices on top of mix. Cover and bake for 1 hour.

YIELD: 4 to 6 servings

BLAZING BEER BEANS

LEAH E. BURRIS

"I have always loved beer," my boyfriend of three years, Brian, told me. "And today, I still love it!"

I grew up in the small, Southern, God-fearing town of Concord, North Carolina. I lived with my parents who attended the local Methodist Church, held every position within it, and did not keep beer in the house.

On the other hand, Brian grew up in a Catholic family in Tallahassee, Florida, where alcoholic beverages were not only kept in the house, but were free-flowing with every meal. "It's what we do," he said, "we're Catholic!"

Five years ago, Brian moved to Charlotte, North Carolina. He was one of many young, non-North Carolinians comprising the population of the city. He quickly realized that his ideas about food and alcohol fit in nicely with the mix of backgrounds, origins, and young adults that made Charlotte great. He also came to know me—and I have come to appreciate beer.

Brian took his love of beer and my love for the Southern flavors and created the wonderful dish we call "Blazing Beer Beans." It is, like Charlotte, a mix of the best of both worlds without harmful side effects or hangovers.

A 12-ounce bottle or can of beer
1 can black beans, drained and rinsed
1 can kidney beans, drained and rinsed
3 jalapeño peppers, seeds removed and finely chopped
6 cloves garlic, chopped
1 small yellow onion, chopped
½ teaspoon ground sea salt
¾ teaspoon fresh ground black pepper
¼ cup fresh grated Parmesan or Romano cheese

In a saucepan, combine beer, black beans, and kidney beans. Allow to sit for 10 minutes prior to cooking. Then, while heating the mixture, add jalapeño, garlic, onion, salt, and pepper. Increase heat just to a boil, then reduce to a slow simmer. Simmer beans, uncovered, for 1 to 1 ½ hours, stirring every 10 to 15 minutes. This should reduce the amount of liquid by at about least ⅔. Add cheese in the last 10 minutes of simmering and stir. Serve hot over rice, or plain.

YIELD: 6 servings

MARY SCHENCK'S MACARONI AND CHEESE

LINDA STROUPE

Our large and extended family loves reunions. Playing second fiddle only to seeing our cousins, aunts, and uncles is a large spread of our favorite foods. Everyone looks for my mother's macaroni and cheese. She always brings a large casserole of this favorite comfort food. I don't believe she ever takes home leftovers, and people are disappointed if there's not enough to go around.

The recipe won a contest in May 1992, sponsored by the *Gaston Gazette*. Contestants were asked to send in recipes passed down from their moms. Mother's macaroni and cheese thus became famous in our part of the world. Today, I make it for my own family, including my four children who are now grown with kitchens of their own. My greatest pleasure is spoiling them with home cooking whenever they come back for a visit. Their grandmother's macaroni and cheese still holds a place as one of their favorites.

2 cups macaroni, uncooked
1 tablespoon flour
1 egg
2 cups milk
½ teaspoon salt
Dash of white pepper
1 stick margarine, melted
8 ounces grated sharp cheddar cheese
Paprika

Preheat oven to 375 degrees. Grease an 11 x 7" baking dish and set aside.

Cook macaroni according to package directions. Drain. If you have time, cover the macaroni with cold water and set aside until the macaroni swells up.

In a small bowl beat the flour with the egg. Add milk, salt and pepper.

Beat until there are no lumps.

Make a layer of half the macaroni. Pour half the melted butter over the macaroni and sprinkle with half the cheese. Repeat the layer. Then pour the milk mixture over the layers. Sprinkle with paprika.

Bake about 30 to 45 minutes until set (not juicy) and slightly browned.

YIELD: 6 to 8 servings

PEANUT BUTTER STUFFING

CISSIE DARR ROTH

This recipe comes from my mother, who was a gourmet cook. It is a wonderful, different and tasty stuffing for family gatherings of several generations. Little children who do not care for highly seasoned stuffings will really go for it. It is usually dry and needs lots of gravy. Leftover stuffing is great on sandwiches (with sliced cranberry sauce) or cooked like potato cakes.

HINT
Any dressing can become dry. Plan to serve with gravy.

A 16-ounce jar of peanut butter, preferably crunchy
1 teaspoon onion powder
1 stick butter at room temperature
Approximately 8 ounces dry bread crumbs
Salt to taste

Thoroughly mix together the first 3 ingredients. Add bread crumbs and mix with your hands until the mixture sticks together enough to be handled easily. Add salt and more onion powder to taste. This is how the stuffing will taste when cooked.

Stuff a 12- to 15-pound turkey about ¾ full, and roast according to size. Or, you can bake in a greased oblong baking dish at 325 degrees for 30 to 40 minutes.

YIELD: About 8 servings

GRILLED TOMATOES

S.J. SEBELLIN-ROSS

My mother knew nothing about cooking or nutrition until I was eight or nine. Then, she discovered the world of good food and became a self-taught gourmet cook. Unfortunately, for my eight-year-old palate, that was the end of white bread and processed luncheon meat. But, fortunately for my adult palate, that was the introduction to a world of interesting flavors.

I enjoyed all of my mother's culinary experiments, the failures sometimes more than the successes, and not just because they resulted in her ordering pizza. But of all the dishes I enjoyed, I liked the simple, classic dishes best, like this recipe for grilled tomatoes.

When I first moved into my own home, I asked my mother to show me how to make it. Because of her gourmet background, I naturally thought this was a complicated recipe with all sorts of hidden ingredients. I was surprised when she said it was so simple she could just tell me. So, sitting at the kitchen table, she did.

Many years later, I still remember—and have since learned how to make—the gourmet dishes my mother created. But it is the simple dishes, such as this one, that have become the heartfelt staples of our daily meals.

2 beefsteak tomatoes	Dash of black pepper
½ cup freshly grated Romano cheese	Dash of paprika
1 tablespoon shredded fresh basil	

Preheat the broiler.

Slice the tomatoes into ¼"-thick slices and place on a non-stick cookie sheet. Combine the Romano cheese with the basil and generously cover each slice with this mixture. Dust the slices with the pepper and the paprika, and broil until the cheese is bubbling and brown. This dish goes especially well with steak and asparagus.

YIELD: 6 servings

"FRIED" GREEN TOMATOES

JOANNA VIRKLER

I think I've finally figured out fried green tomatoes. The secret is: No frying—instead, baking. Yes, that's it. No heavy grease to steal away that wonderfully tart freshness of a firm green tomato straight from the garden.

I really fell in love with the idea of fried green tomatoes when I saw the movie version of Fanny Flagg's book, *Fried Green Tomatoes at the Whistle Stop Café*. Scenes of huge batches of tomatoes being cooked and eaten during steamy, hot Southern summers were as irresistible as the menu of female characters.

Recently my husband and I stopped off at a little roadside restaurant on the way up to the North Carolina mountains. The restaurant had placed framed photos of the movie's stars, Kathy Bates, Jessica Tandy and Mary Stuart Masterson, on its walls, and served fried green tomatoes as its specialty of the house in homage. No doubt about it, those tomatoes were good.

Looking through cookbooks when I got home, I realized recipes for fried green tomatoes are indeed a rare delicacy, hard to find even in *Joy of Cooking*. Nevertheless, here is my *baked* version—I think it beats fried tomatoes hands down—and is incredibly easy.

½ cup toasted fine bread crumbs
½ cup grated Parmesan cheese
2 tablespoons cornmeal
Salt and pepper
8 medium-sized fresh green tomatoes
Seasonings: try thyme, oregano and/or cayenne
Non-stick spray, olive oil or butter

Preheat oven to 325 degrees. Grease a cookie sheet with olive oil or nonstick spray and set aside.

Mix the bread crumbs, Parmesan cheese and cornmeal. Add salt,

HINTS
The crumb mixture may be stored in the refrigerator for use later; it works fine on fish, too. And forget using red or yellow tomatoes—they will turn to mush.

pepper and any other seasonings you care to add—though salt and pepper are just fine by themselves.

Slice the tomatoes thick or thin according to your preference. I like my tomatoes thick.

Dip the tomatoes in the crumb mixture, coating on both sides. Place on the cookie sheet. Depending on which you use, spray with non-stick spray, drizzle with olive oil, or dot with butter.*

Bake for about 20 to 30 minutes total, but keep checking after the first 15 minutes. The breading should be lightly browned, the tomatoes still firm. If you like, you can flip the tomatoes once, but it's more important to watch that they don't overcook.

YIELD: About 8 servings

* Though you may want to experiment with butter or olive oil on the breaded green tomatoes, I think they stay crisper with just a "spritzing" of the non-stick spray.

MASHED POTATO PATTIES

WENDY H. GILL

I love mashed potatoes . . . always have. As a child, I adored their gooey texture and used them like mortar to glue a couple of peas and a bite of pork chop together onto my fork for one glorious mouthful.

But I always practiced restraint on mashed potato night, hoping my family wouldn't scrape the bottom of the serving bowl. If there were extras, on the following night we were sure to eat mashed potato patties.

My penny-wise mother mixed and molded the ingredients into round, flat patties and placed them in a preheated cast iron skillet to sizzle. When butter, onions and potatoes met in the pan, they sent a heavenly aroma into the air. The patties fried up golden and crispy on the outside, with pale yellow, creamy potato integrity inside.

They were served as a side dish for a simple supper. Although other family members considered the patty a second-class citizen, on my plate, its return engagement received top billing. Mom often spooned on leftover gravy, but I preferred mine topped with just a pat of butter that melted instantly into an amber puddle.

These days, making potato patties transports me back to an age of home and the art of economizing. An age when all of us sat together at our metal kitchen table each and every night for a nourishing meal. An age when even a lowly leftover spud seemed sacred.

2 to 3 cups mashed potatoes, chilled	Salt and pepper to taste
1 egg, slightly beaten	1 tablespoon butter or
Finely minced onion (optional)	margarine

Into the potatoes, thoroughly mix the egg, onion, salt and pepper. Form into 3 or 4 hamburger-sized patties.

Heat the butter or margarine in a skillet or frying pan, then cook the patties over medium-high heat until brown, turning once.

YIELD: About 4

SARITA'S REDUCED FAT MACARONI AND CHEESE

SARITA OSBORNE

I have loved macaroni and cheese since I was young, and have loved to cook since I can remember. I liked the boxed macaroni and cheese, but being a cheese lover, I didn't think it was cheesy enough. So we started adding slices of American cheese to the boxed kind.

This was pretty good, but I like many different kinds of cheeses, so we started shredding up whatever we had on hand and adding it to the macaroni. Soon I was trying to cook my own and make my own sauce. I hardly ever make it the same way twice, but it always seems to turn out tasting good. My mom is trying to eat healthier, and so I came up with this recipe, which satisfies my taste for the cheesiest macaroni and cheese.

1 tablespoon margarine
1 teaspoon mustard powder
2 tablespoons flour
1 ¼ cups milk
Fresh ground pepper to taste
1 slice 2% sharp cheddar
1 slice 2% Swiss
4 ounces 2% mild cheddar, finely shredded

3 tablespoons Southwestern Ranch dressing, fat free
¼ cup salsa
4 cups cooked macaroni shells
1 ounce of ⅓-less-fat cream cheese

Mix together all ingredients except the macaroni and cream cheese, cook until thickened over medium-low heat. Turn to low and add cream cheese, stir until melted, remove from heat and add cooked shells. Stir well to mix with cheese and serve.

YIELD: 4 main-dish or 8 side-dish servings

SUMMER SQUASH CASSEROLE SUPREME

SYLVIA LITTLE-SWEAT

The squash casserole was a staple at my playhouse diner outside under the oil drum on my grandfather's farm in Union County, North Carolina. Mother never complained that I would make a daily run to the garden to pick the fatter squash that lay under the wilting vines. I would slice the squash, mix the rounds with water, add grass or chinaberries from the adjacent trees, and bake in the summer sun before selling it to patrons who would flock to my diner for huge servings of this most delicious item on my menu.

However, my shepherd, Major, would always turn his nose up whenever I put a plate for him to try and preferred instead to flop down in a cooler spot under the chinaberry tree while I stirred more servings.

When I outgrew playhouse diners and left the farm, I still was prompted to create my own recipes for real guests. My original version of the staple squash casserole has become a favorite at family reunions, Sunday school socials, and dinner parties at my home. Grass and chinaberries have been replaced by more palatable ingredients, but the imaginative fun of play-cooking continues to this day, a half-century later.

3 pounds of fresh, tender yellow summer squash, sliced
2 large white onions, sliced
1 can of undiluted Campbell's brand cream of chicken soup
1 cup of sour cream
1 cup shredded colby cheese
1 cup shredded extra sharp cheddar cheese
1 cup finely shredded fresh carrots (uncooked)
Freshly ground black pepper and salt to taste
6-ounce can of French's French-fried onion rings

Preheat oven to 350 degrees. Grease a 13 x 9 x 2" casserole dish and set aside.

Steam squash and onions for five minutes in a vegetable steamer. Set aside. In a saucepan combine the soup, sour cream, cheeses, carrots, salt and pepper. Cook over medium heat until bubbly, then remove from heat.

Place the steamed squash/onion mixture in the casserole dish. Pour the heated soup/cheese mixture over it and make sure it reaches to the bottom. Bake for 30 minutes, then remove and top with the fried onion rings. Return to the oven for five minutes, or long enough for the onion rings to brown.

Serve with almost any entree: turkey, ham, chicken, pork chops, even grilled salmon or other seafood.

YIELD: 8 to 10 servings

TOMATO PIE

ASHLEY WARLICK

Like any good writer, I have stolen my favorite family recipe from some-body else's family, changed a few details to improve on reality, and called it my own. I make it religiously every summer when tomatoes are good, and every New Year's Day when tomatoes are not, and every time people ask me for the recipe. Every time. The Ritz crackers are key, trashy as they might seem, as is the high-guilt mayonnaise.

At the age of 23, novel-ist Ashley Warlick be-came the youngest winner of the Houghton-Mifflin Prize. She grew up in North Carolina but now lives in South Carolina.

1 unbaked pie shell, preferably homemade
3 to 4 large, ripe-as-you-can-get tomatoes
1 small sweet onion
About 1 cup real mayonnaise
3 cups sharp cheddar cheese, grated
Salt and pepper
1 bunch fresh basil, about a dozen whole leaves, stemmed
½ sleeve Ritz crackers, crushed
½ stick butter

Flute your pie shell and preheat the oven to 350 degrees.

Slice the tomatoes. Halve and thinly slice the onion. Mix together the mayonnaise and half the cheese and blend with a wooden spoon.

Line the bottom of the pie shell with tomato slices. Salt and pepper to taste, and top with half the onion. Spread the mayonnaise mixture over all, then top with basil leaves. Repeat tomato and onion layers, topping with remaining cheese. Bake for one hour. Melt butter and mix with cracker crumbs, sprinkle over top and bake another 15 minutes. Great with a green salad, and/or anything off the grill.

YIELD: 6 to 8 servings

ON THE SIDE

KILLED LETTUCE AND ONIONS

SHERI MORETZ

This is a good dish to go along with pinto beans and cornbread. Corn or vegetable oil can be substituted for bacon drippings, but your lettuce will not "kill" as well. I love going to Granny and Papaw Moretz's house in the early summer because I know the lettuce is coming in from the garden. Whenever Granny knows I'm coming, she makes a big ol' bowl of lettuce and onions. It's my favorite dish, and no matter how many folks are at the table, it seems that I eat the most. I can make a real meal of it.

Leaf lettuce
Onions, chopped or sliced, depending on their size
Salt
Apple cider vinegar
Water
Bacon drippings from 3 strips of bacon

Gather and wash enough leaf lettuce to fill a large glass or ceramic bowl. Drain and tear into smaller pieces. Chop onions and put over the top of the lettuce. (I like lots of onion, so put however much you want). Salt to taste. In a small pot, mix vinegar and water, using a little more vinegar than water, especially if you enjoy the tang of vinegar, and the bacon drippings. You should have enough to almost "cover" the wilted lettuce when it "kills" down. Bring these to a boil. Pour over lettuce and onions making sure to distribute as evenly as possible; toss slightly. Cover this with a plate or bowl lid to allow the lettuce to wilt.

YIELD: Varies; from 1 large head of lettuce, about 3 to 4 servings

AUSTRALIAN CRISPY PARMESAN POTATOES

CYDNE HORROCKS WATTERSON

When I really want to impress my dinner guests, I make crispy Parmesan potatoes from Australia. Just mentioning Australia gets everyone's attention, and not only are these potatoes delicious, they have the sophisticated flair long overdue the ordinary Idaho spud.

This recipe is from the kitchen of Claudette Taylor, wife of Ian Taylor, renowned plastic surgeon, and talented cook. Claudette didn't allow us in the kitchen; Australian kitchens simply weren't big enough. My husband and I, along with dinner guests from around the world who had come to study with Ian, watched from the other room for gifts the master chef would deliver for our palates.

"Peel the potatoes early in the day and leave them in water until an hour or so ahead of time," Claudette taught me. "Use large potatoes and flatten one side so that they sit rounded as a ladybug on the plate. Remember to salt generously and forget the fancy grated Parmesan cheese—Kraft Parmesan cheese in the can works beautifully."

Follow her instructions as I did, and these potatoes will quickly become an entertaining favorite.

10 medium potatoes
½ cup oil
Salt
Grated Parmesan cheese (Kraft brand in the can works best)

Preheat oven to 350 degrees.

Peel potatoes early in the day and immerse in water until you are ready to cook them. Trim to a smooth, rounded shape. Cut a thin slice from the base of each potato so they sit flat. Using a sharp knife, carefully make cuts about ¼" apart across the top of the potato; cut from the top of the potato almost through to the base.

HINT
These are not suitable for freezing or microwaving.

Place potatoes flat side down in a large baking dish. Brush well with oil and salt generously. Bake for 40 minutes. Brush occasionally with oil during cooking time.

Sprinkle liberally with the Parmesan cheese; bake another 20 minutes until potatoes are crisp on the outside and tender inside. Do not turn potatoes during baking.

YIELD: 10 servings

SAUTÉED SWEET POTATOES

LYNN VEACH SADLER

After we tired of the latest "ovenfull" of baked sweet potatoes, my mother sliced the remaining ones and fried them. I didn't like their over-cooked taste and came up with this version when I was about eight years old. I still love these and occasionally substitute other toppings, such as cayenne, chopped nuts, or coconut. These, prepared with sugar and cinnamon, are especially good as a side dish for a brunch or company breakfast.

2 tablespoons butter or olive oil
4 medium-sized sweet potatoes, peeled and sliced about ¼" thick
Sugar
Cinnamon

Heat the butter or olive oil. Sauté the potato slices until golden brown. Remove them to a platter, draining them on paper towels as necessary. Immediately sprinkle each slice with sugar and cinnamon.

YIELD: 4 servings

HOME-COOKED CANDIED YAMS

JACKIE DENISE CURETON

At the age of twelve, I began preparing meals for my entire family. I am now 38 and the mother of two, and I still enjoy cooking and experimenting with different seasonings and foods. This can be served as a side dish with dinner, or as a dessert. It's even better topped with your favorite ice cream.

6 or 7 sweet potatoes (canned; or fresh and cooked until done, then peeled)
1 tablespoon vanilla extract
2½ cups of sugar (I use Dixie brand)
2 tablespoons evaporated milk (I use Carnation brand)
½ stick of margarine, softened

Slice potatoes thickly and place in a large saucepan.

In a bowl, combine the remaining ingredients and stir until blended. Add the mixture to the potatoes, and heat while stirring to make sure it doesn't burn. Reduce to a slow simmer and cook 45 minutes to 1 hour until the juice on the yams thickens.

YIELD: 4 to 6 servings

KOOKOO POTATO

MARY ANN ROGERS

Kookoo Potato is Persian, and I first enjoyed it at a dinner that Noushin Hedari prepared for my friend Lucy Johnson and me. *Kookoo Potato* accompanies *Tah-cheen*, (see Chapter 2) an unusual chicken dish. Noushin kindly shared both recipes.

3 or 4 medium-sized yellow potatoes
2 eggs, lightly beaten
Dash each of salt and pepper
¼ teaspoon garlic powder
¼ teaspoon baking powder
Oil for frying

Peel potatoes and grate them with a medium-sized grater. Put them in a strainer and press to remove excess moisture. Then, place potatoes in a bowl.

In a separate bowl, combine the eggs, salt, pepper, garlic powder and baking powder. Add to the potatoes and mix well with a fork.

Pour enough oil in a heavy frying pan to coat the bottom, heat it over medium heat and be careful not to let it burn. With a big spoon, take a spoonful of mixture and drop it into the pan. Repeat, keeping space between each. Cook over medium heat, and lift the edge to check browning. When the underside is golden-brown, use a spatula to flip to the other.

When browned on both sides, remove to cool and drain on paper towels. Enjoy!

YIELD: 4 servings

RAY'S NOODLE PUDDING

LYNDA CALABRESE

I never really thought of noodle pudding as my mother's signature dish even though she always brings it to friends' and family gatherings. New to the Internet, and a Web TV subscriber, my mother, Ray, keeps her noodle pudding recipe in her "Favorites" file, ready to be sent to new wives of her grandsons, and to granddaughters who hunger for the cinnamon scent in their college apartments.

Back in third grade, clearing the first course of a dinner with my cousin, we couldn't help ourselves. With each trip to the brown Formica counter we would pick another raisin or glazed walnut from the crispy top till it looked like mice had ravaged the Pyrex dish.

My father died in April, 2002, after an ugly fight with Parkinson's Disease. Before his funeral, as we made trips to the airport to pick everyone up, my mother made noodle pudding. She had just lost her Bernie of 62 years and she was cooking.

Six rectangles browned in her sad oven as all the kids descended on Boca Raton. "Why?" I almost screamed at her.

"Because everyone likes it and we need the smell of sweetness," she said. "He'd be happy. It always meant company was coming."

10 eggs
1 cup of sugar
½ cup light brown sugar
1 teaspoon vanilla
½ teaspoon salt
A few shakes of cinnamon (not too much)
1 pound of wide egg noodles
1 stick unsalted butter
1 cup of raisins
1 cup of walnuts, slightly chopped

Preheat oven to 350 degrees. Grease a 3-quart baking dish or spray with non-stick spray and set aside.

Put the eggs, both sugars, vanilla, salt and cinnamon into the blender and combine until just blended. Set aside.

Cook the noodles according to package directions, drain, and place in a large bowl. Add the butter to the noodles. Then add the egg mixture and combine, then stir in the raisins and walnuts.

Pour into the prepared pan, and bake in the center of the oven for about an hour. After about 20 minutes, press down with a large spatula on the top of pudding so that the liquid comes to the top. This helps keep the noodles from drying out while baking. You can do this several times. Don't let it get too brown, just golden. Enjoy!

YIELD: From 10 to 16 servings, depending on size

BLACK BEANS

MARISA ROSENFELD

As kids we didn't need a calendar to know if it was a weekday or the weekend; we knew by what was on the table. On weekdays, our midday meal always included black beans and rice. Even more, we knew that weekday mealtime was fast approaching by the smell of onions and garlic being sautéed for the beans.

I can't quite recall life before black beans, their aroma through the house, through any house that I knew. Black beans are such a basic food in my childhood home of Rio de Janeiro, you could count on them from school cafeteria up to company cafeteria. You could serve them with anything.

Since I have no idea how I reacted to my first spoonful of black beans, I took the opportunity, when my daughter was a baby old enough for solid food, to try it on her. She sat tall in the high chair, bib in place, curious eyes staring at this dark food coming her way. After her first gulp she smiled at me, showing all her eight teeth, her mouth mustached in black, excitedly asking for more.

1 pound dry black beans (check and remove any pebbles)
Salt to taste, about ½ teaspoon
2 bay leaves
1 small onion, chopped
2 teaspoons of minced garlic
6 tablespoons of vegetable oil

Soak beans overnight in water enough to cover them.

The next day, drain the soak water, put the beans in a pan and add water to cover, plus an additional two inches. Add salt to taste.

Bring contents of the pan to a boil. Reduce heat to medium-low and cover tightly. Every 15 to 20 minutes, stir slowly and check for consistency. When the beans seem almost cooked, add the bay leaves.

In a separate pan, sauté the onions and garlic in the oil till clear; then add to the beans. Continue cooking, and when the beans reach a creamy consistency, they are ready. This will be 2 to 3 hours, depending on the beans.

Serve with collard greens and rice if desired.

YIELD: 6 to 8 servings

SAUTÉED COLLARD GREENS BRAZILIAN STYLE

MARISA ROSENFELD

I knew my Brazilian collard greens had made an impression when Martelle, a tall, full-sized black woman and great soul-food cook, asked me to bring them to the next covered dish luncheon at the research company where we worked. That was quite a compliment to my collards! For the next six years I knew what I would be cooking for company lunches.

Collard greens made my adaptation to Southern living much easier when I moved to Charlotte in 1987; finding the greens in supermarkets brought me joy and comfort. After all, I had grown up picking them from our garden as a child and eating them regularly. Mom would tell my brother or me to go get a few leaves for the next meal and we would go running and give them to Maria, our live-in maid. She was from the state of Minas Gerais, where this recipe comes from. Nobody cut the greens as thin as she did. It was so impressive that we kids loved to watch her.

When I bought my first home in Charlotte, I planted collards in my garden and let them grow the way we do in Rio, taking only the leaves and letting the plant continue to grow. Soon I had six-foot-tall plants and everybody would ask what they were.

"Collard greens," I'd say, to their surprise.

I always got the same reply: "They look like bushes." Besides enjoying one of the favorite tastes of childhood, I could show everyone an alternate way of growing them.

After many years in the South, I still like to invite people over and serve them collard greens with rice and black beans. All my guests go for seconds.

Bunch of collard greens (1 ½ pounds,
    about 15 medium-sized leaves)
4 to 5 tablespoons of vegetable oil
1 medium onion, finely chopped
2 teaspoons of minced garlic (optional)
Salt to taste

Remove stems from the leaves so the leaves can be folded lengthwise.
Wash the leaves and dry them. Fold each leaf, stack them and roll the
bundle lengthwise very tightly, forming a cylinder. Hold tightly, place on
a wood cutting board and cut with a sharp knife, as thinly as possible.

In a large pan, heat the oil, then add the onions and garlic and sauté
until they are almost clear. Turn the heat to high, throw in the collards
and add salt to taste. Stir quickly with a wooden spoon until the collards
become bright green, no more than five minutes. They are ready to eat.

Serve with black beans and rice if desired.

YIELD: 4 servings

JAMES TAYLOR'S "BAKED" BEANS

Amy Rogers

Singer-songwriter James Taylor was just a child when his family came south from Massachusetts to Chapel Hill, North Carolina. Although he's long since moved back north to coastal New England, he generously agreed to share one of his recipes with us, especially for this book.

Even if the Tarheel State can't claim him as a resident any longer, we like to think he'll always return to Carolina, in his mind.

4 pounds dry beans (pinto, red, pink or black-eyed)	A 12-ounce slab sliced bacon, frozen
A 12-ounce jar of prepared mustard	2 tablespoons sugar
6 large onions	2 tablespoons salt
7 large cloves garlic	Dash of pepper
	Hot sauce

Soak the beans overnight in enough water to cover them, after you cull out the "losers."

The next day, drain off the soak water, cover with fresh water and bring to a boil in a LARGE stock pot (at least 12 quarts). Back off to a simmer, and add the mustard.

Chop the onions and steam them in a large steamer for an hour, and save the steamer juice. Add the onions to the beans, then cook the reserved steamer juice until reduced to 1 cup. Add it to the beans.

Put the garlic cloves through a press and add them to the pot. Cut the FROZEN bacon against the grain into ⅛" slivers and fry until brown; drain the bacon and add it to the pot. Then add the sugar, salt, pepper and hot sauce to taste. Cook the beans on low heat all day, stirring frequently to avoid burning the bottom.

YIELD: 12 to 16 *servings*

SHERRY TOMATOES

GINA JONES DELISLE

Growing up in the South, we always grew tomatoes in the summer. Of course when you grow tomatoes, there is always that point when you ask yourself, "What am I going to do with all these things?"

I believe my mother made up this recipe on the fly. She has always been a great cook and is very good at coming up with recipes to suit the ingredients on hand. The sherry is a perfect complement to the sweet tomatoes. I recommend this recipe for company since it's so easy and very elegant.

4 ripe tomatoes, cored and cut in half
8 tablespoons dry sherry (can substitute vermouth)
8 teaspoons dill weed
8 tablespoons Velveeta brand cheese, cut into small cubes
8 tablespoons mayonnaise

Preheat oven to 350 degrees. Grease an ovenproof casserole dish and set aside.

Pierce tomato halves with a fork. Place cut side up in the casserole dish. Drizzle the tomato halves with sherry and top with dill weed. In a bowl, mix the cheese and mayonnaise, then divide equally to top the tomatoes.

Bake 30 to 40 minutes or until golden brown and bubbly.

YIELD: 8 tomato halves

GROWING AWAY FROM HOME

Amy Rogers

Uncle Fernando tends the family garden behind the house in the old part of the city. He grows vegetables and a little coffee, too, for the family. Sometimes he grows raspberries, because they are his young niece's favorite.

His sister, Lola, is an expert cook who prepares the traditional Ecuadorian dishes: the pork with fried hominy and plantains; *arroz de leche,* a rice pudding made with cinnamon and cloves; and "Monday Soup," eaten the first of the week to guarantee God's bounty for the rest.

Lola and Enrique Guzman's three daughters, Consuelo, Andrea and Janeth, are good cooks, too. "I started practicing peeling onions and potatoes when I was about eight. By 14 or 15 I could cook on my own and would get together with friends to cook," recalls Janeth, who is now 19. "Consuelo was my inspiration."

It's a close-knit family, one of countless throughout the world. As years go by, children grow up, and one day a child says to her parents *I want to go to the U.S.A.* In the Guzman family, it was Andrea who said it first. She wanted to learn English to get a better job. So she came to the states to work as an *au pair.*

Then it was Janeth's turn. She came to North Carolina to join Andrea. "My parents weren't happy. They were missing my sister too much," she says. "Then I got a chance to study, and now they are O.K."

With her long dark hair, striking features and coloring, she could be Arabic or Greek, and her fellow students have told her so. But she is Ecuadorian and proud to explain that her city, Ibarra, is called "City of the Lakes," for its beauty in the highlands of her home country. She describes the freshness of the food that comes from farms all around the city, then talks about the differences in the cuisines of the people descended from the Spanish explorers and indigenous Indians. She lists the flavors of her favorite dishes: avocado, lemon, cilantro, *achiote*. She admits to being homesick.

Her English is good, even if some speakers talk too fast for her to fully comprehend just yet. She took placement tests and did well, but there are many more exams to come in the culinary arts program where she's now enrolled.

Janeth hopes to visit her parents at year's end. She's getting accustomed to North American meals—cereal and milk, hot dogs and fast food, and Mondays without soup. Today for lunch, she's having grilled chicken served on pita bread.

She dreams of opening a restaurant someday, "Somewhere I can sell food from my country." Where that might be, she can't say. In the U.S., culinary adventurers and Latin American immigrants would likely enjoy the native Ecuadorian dishes. Unique restaurants are sometimes wildly successful. But Janeth Guzman isn't sure she can forever leave behind her country of jungles and mountains, her friends and family, or the uncle who grows raspberries, just for her.

*HINT
Achiote seeds to flavor the oil can be found in Latin American grocery stores. You can substitute olive oil, but the tortillas won't have the distinctive Ecuadorian flavor.

JANETH GUZMAN'S LLAPINGACHOS (TORTILLAS DE PAPA)

4 large potatoes
1 large white onion, chopped; plus another large slice of onion
1 tablespoon salt
*4 tablespoons oil de achiote, plus more for frying
2 egg yolks
¼ pound white cheese, such as white cheddar or Monterey Jack, finely
   shredded

155

Peel potatoes, place in a large saucepan with enough water to cover, add the large slice of onion and bring to a boil. Simmer until potatoes are tender, then add salt. Stir, remove from heat, and drain. Mash the potatoes thoroughly and set aside.

In a heavy frying pan, heat 4 tablespoons oil and add the chopped onions; cook until brown. Remove onions with a slotted spoon, reserving the oil. Stir the cooked onions and the egg yolks into the mashed potatoes and mix well.

Take a small handful of the potato mixture and form a flattened ball. With your finger, poke a hole into the center, making a cavity. Fill with cheese, then pinch the hole closed. Repeat with the remaining mixture.

Add extra oil to the pan if needed, heat the oil, and fry the formed potatoes, turning once, until they are browned (the cheese will have melted inside).

For a traditional Ecuadorian meal, serve with fried pork, sliced avocados, lettuce and tomatoes.

YIELD: 4 to 6 servings

4

*Breads, Biscuits,
Muffins and More*

BLUE-RIBBON BISCUITS: MADE BY HAND

Amy Rogers

You can smell the biscuits through the screen door the moment you set foot on the porch. Inside, Virginia Jackson's blue ribbon hangs above the mantle, right next to her family photographs and praying hands plaque.

The afternoon trains are passing through Kenly, and their whistles blow from just across the street where the tracks cut through town. Virginia is reminiscing.

She grew up with tobacco and cotton, spending summers in the fields with her family. Thinking back on the days she worked alongside her father, Delie, she says, "The most cotton I ever picked was 150 pounds in one day. But even though he was in his seventies then, I still couldn't beat him. I made $100 for five or six weeks' work."

Given a choice, Virginia always preferred baking to picking cotton. She learned as a child.

"When my mother would get sick, she'd tell me how to make the biscuits—how much flour to put in, then lard, then milk," she says. "My brother used to tease me about them being hard."

Her mother, Lulah Richardson Hinnant, used what Virginia calls a "bread tray" to mix biscuits. The oval-shaped, shallow wooden bowl always hung from a nail on the wall in their kitchen. One day the tray fell and cracked right down the center, but Delie put it back together with a piece of leather strap.

Virginia still uses that bread tray every time she makes biscuits.

It was hard when Virginia's husband, James, died suddenly at age 45. She was left to raise their four boys by herself. But today she's happy just having Larry, Johnny, Randy and Rodney living nearby.

"Time is precious," she says.

None of Virginia's sons ever showed a knack for baking, but everyone near Kenly knows about Virginia's famous biscuits. She's baked thousands of them – four at a time in her own kitchen, and in batches of 800 at the Hardee's over in Smithfield.

Once, Virginia worked at a restaurant called Patrick's. The owner was concerned about cholesterol in the biscuits. Virginia told him, "Mr. Moore, I'm going to make them like you want, but they won't hold up." She lightened up the recipe, then said, "Now let me make some like I make at home.

"I sold him."

Good cooks often work without recipes, but the N.C. State Fair requires that you submit your recipe with your entry. Virginia didn't know about that rule when she decided, "I'll just bake some biscuits and carry them down there." They turned her away and she had to wait another year to enter and win.

Virginia can't remember all the contests she's won, but she never forgets the key to making perfect biscuits.

"Keep your mind on what you're doing; don't just throw them together," she advises. And forget using a mixer or even a spoon; Virginia mixes every batch with her hands.

It seems so simple: three ingredients. So there must be a secret, something that makes one biscuit – or cake or pie or bread – different and special. If that something else doesn't come from the store or out of a book, where does it come from? Can it be measured like so much flour and shortening?

In Virginia Jackson's strong, brown hands lies at least part of the secret. When your hands have worked the fields, tamed a garden and cared for children, almost anything is possible. Virginia's touch is unique. A talent like hers can be learned, but it comes only by doing, with care and with practice. And learning takes time, an investment too few are willing to make. But there's something else, still, something that comes from the heart.

Virginia remembers the time a neighbor tried to describe just what it was he liked so much about one of her biscuits. He thought about it a while, then decided it wasn't the color, the texture, or even the taste.

"Virginia," he pronounced, "that biscuit's got 'tender loving care.'"

VIRGINIA JACKSON'S BUTTERMILK BISCUITS

2 cups self-rising flour
1 tablespoon lard or shortening
¾ cup buttermilk

Preheat oven to 500 degrees. Grease a baking sheet and set aside.

Measure flour into a bowl. Make a well (or "hole") in the flour. Add the shortening and buttermilk and mix together. When the dough has lost some of its stickiness, "pinch" off a piece the size you want each biscuit to be. DO NOT ROLL OUT DOUGH. Pat each biscuit into shape and place on prepared baking sheet.

Bake until browned, 7 to 8 minutes for smaller biscuits, 9 to 10 minutes for larger biscuits.

YIELD: 6 large or 8 small biscuits

HINTS
Use your hands to mix the dough. You'll learn by feel when it's right. Lard helps hold the biscuits together, but shortening will work. Virginia believes the less time the biscuit is in the oven, the better. Make sure your oven is hot enough.

About ⅔ of the way through cooking, use a spatula to lift one of the biscuits to check the browning underneath. If the biscuits are getting too brown, switch on the broiler for the rest of the cooking time, but WATCH CAREFULLY to avoid burning.

Biscuits—the word itself almost makes your mouth water. In the Carolinas and throughout the South, everyone has a favorite kind. With or without lard, yeast or sugar; formed with a biscuit cutter, by hand or dropped from a wooden spoon; and devoured with jam, jelly or gravy—we love our biscuits. Here are several more recipes, and the stories of what makes them special.

FLOYE LONG'S ANGEL BISCUITS

DEBRA LONG HAMPTON

Flaky piecrusts, perfectly fried chicken, moist Christmas fruitcakes with finely chopped fruits and nuts, tender dumplings in soul-soothing chicken stew—those were only a few of the fruits of a grandmother's labor. Floye Elizabeth Hough Long honed her talent for many years in the kitchen of her bungalow-style house on Monroe Road right behind Charlotte's old domed coliseum. My Dad and aunts and uncles have said many times that they never knew who or how many would be at the table each meal when they were growing up. Anyone was welcomed and I'm sure if there didn't seem to be enough to go around, my grandmother would say, "Land sakes, I can fry another hen," or "Bert, go down to the cellar and get another jar of beans!"

The recipe that I consider a true heirloom adorned every meal and was something you not only expected but wished for with great anticipation. Angel biscuits—lightly browned, cloudlike circles with thin and delicate, crispy edges—did, in fact, seem truly heavenly. Early in my career, I worked down the street from her house, and I would often go there for lunch. "There's a biscuit on your plate that I've already *buttuhed,*" she would say in her thick Southern brogue as I arrived. And there on the plate I'd find one of those clouds with butter oozing out all around. I can still smell that heavenly steam, still feel the crusty edge of the bottom of the biscuit in my mouth. The memory of this recipe is a part of her that lives on in me and each member of my family. These are "the angel's biscuits."

- 1 package active dry yeast
- 2 or 3 tablespoons warm water
- 5 cups all purpose flour
- 3 tablespoons sugar
- 1 tablespoon baking powder
- 1 teaspoon salt
- 1 teaspoon baking soda
- 1 cup shortening
- 2 cups buttermilk

Preheat oven to 400 degrees. Grease several baking sheets and set aside.

Dissolve yeast in warm water and set aside. Sift flour, sugar, baking powder, salt and soda together. Cut in shortening, stir in yeast mixture and buttermilk.

Roll out on a floured surface, cut with biscuit cutter, and place on baking sheets. Brush the tops of the biscuits with melted butter and cover loosely while the biscuits rise in a warm place until ready to bake.

Bake for 10 to 20 minutes, until golden brown.

YIELD: 4 to 6 dozen

MAMA FRYE'S BISCUITS

PATTI FRYE MEREDITH

We were North Carolinians living across the state line in southwest Virginia. But to my mother, we might as well have been living in the Swiss Alps. She never made the adjustment from Sandhills girl to Mountain woman and insisted on frequent trips back to Carthage where circumstances had my grandmothers, both widows, living together in a tiny, white board house.

Many a Friday, we'd take off after Daddy got home from work. My sister, Annelle, and I would sleep on the way, but we'd sit up when the car slowed down and the lights of Main Street poured in through the windows. About a mile down the road, we'd pull up behind Mama Frye's house and a light would go on—a yellow bulb with a string pull.

Hellos and hugs were quick as we headed into the kitchen and Daddy didn't stop until he got to the stove. He'd reach in and pull out baked sweet potatoes resting on a pie tin. "You know, we used to call this Southern Ice Cream." He said that every time.

My sister would be sneaking fried chicken and Mama would be talking about how they shouldn't have gone to all the trouble, but she'd be talking with her mouth full of biscuit—the big, fluffy kind Mama Frye made.

Sitting at the table with the red checkered plastic cloth, I'd eat, taking my time because I knew when I was ready for more, I could have it. Having something you dearly love in abundance for you to use or squander as you see fit is a wondrous thing—that's what those meals were, but more accurately, that was the love of my two grandmothers in that little house in Carthage.

These are not your usual perfectly shaped biscuits. They are like clouds, all different shapes, with little crispy peaks and a delicious, soft, melt-in-your-mouth center.

2 cups plain flour

2 teaspoons baking powder

½ teaspoon baking soda

½ teaspoon salt

½ cup shortening (Crisco brand)

½ cup clabbered milk* (I now use buttermilk)

Melted butter

Preheat oven to 375 degrees. Grease an oblong baking pan or cookie sheet and set aside.

Put dry ingredients in a sifter while holding it over mixing bowl, and sift into bowl. Add shortening to dry ingredients and mix with your fingers until mixture is the texture of cornmeal. Push flour mixture to the sides of the bowl and add the milk into the center, stirring flour into milk with your fingers. Keep stirring with fingers until the flour is incorporated into the milk. It should be just firm enough to form a rough ball, not too sticky. Add more milk or flour to get the right consistency. Don't over-handle.

Hold dough in your hand and squeeze to make a fist, letting about ⅛ of the dough squeeze out above your thumb. Place dough in pan, and continue squeezing until you have eight biscuits. Don't pat or smooth them. Brush with melted butter and bake for about 15 minutes, or until beginning to turn golden on top.

* Clabbered milk was unpasteurized milk that had soured naturally. All I can remember for sure is that Mama Frye kept a jar in the refrigerator that she used only for her biscuits, and when it was nearly empty, she would refill it with more milk and I suppose it would turn sour from the sour milk left in the jar.

YIELD: About 8 biscuits

SWEET MEMORIES

Amy Rogers

In 1994, I got in my car and criss-crossed North Carolina to interview dozens of the state's award-winning cooks for my book, *Red Pepper Fudge and Blue Ribbon Biscuits*. Everywhere I went, generous people shared their recipes with me, including Raleigh's Rose Hampton, one of North Carolina's best bakers and candy-makers. Her sweet potato biscuits are truly memorable, and with their lovely orange color, they always remind me of autumn. I've modified Rose's recipe a little since then, and you can, too, adjusting the spices to your taste.

ROSE HAMPTON'S SWEET POTATO BISCUITS

2 to 2¼ cups sifted all-purpose flour, plus extra for rolling out biscuits

⅔ cup sugar

2 tablespoons baking powder

1 ½ teaspoons salt

½ teaspoon cinnamon

¼ teaspoon nutmeg

½ cup vegetable shortening

2 cups sweet potatoes; baked until soft, peeled and mashed

¼ cup milk

Preheat oven to 450 degrees. Grease a baking sheet and set aside.

Sift dry ingredients together. Make a well in the center. Add the shortening, potatoes and milk. Mix until a soft dough forms. Add more flour a little at a time if dough is sticky.

Roll out the dough on a floured board and cut with a biscuit cutter. Place on baking sheet and bake for 12 to 15 minutes. Be careful; these biscuits don't brown as easily as others. Watch near the end of the baking time to make sure they don't burn.

YIELD: About 15

MANGO BREAD

KARYN JOYNER

Lila Ponder, the 97-year-old mother of my close friend Lila Friday (sister-in-law of former UNC President Bill Friday), is from Florida and loves mangoes. She was poring over the memorabilia of her life and came across a faded scrap of paper on which was a recipe for mango bread. She gave it to me, and it is one of the most delicious things I've ever eaten. Thank you, Mrs. Ponder.

2 cups flour
2 cups sugar
2½ teaspoons cinnamon
2 teaspoons baking soda
½ teaspoon salt
1 cup oil
1 teaspoon lemon juice
1 teaspoon vanilla
3 eggs
2 cups mango, peeled and diced
½ cup nuts, chopped
½ cup shredded coconut

Preheat oven to 350 degrees. Grease two loaf pans and set aside.

Sift together flour, sugar, cinnamon, baking soda, salt. Separately mix oil, lemon juice, vanilla and eggs. Mix with dry ingredients and add mango, chopped nuts and coconut. Bake for one hour, or until a toothpick inserted into the center comes out clean.

YIELD: 2 loaves

SAUSAGE BREAD

SALLY OLIN

This has been a family favorite for years, especially popular during TV sporting events. You can add other ingredients such as green peppers and onions, just not so many as to overstuff the "jelly-roll."

1 pound of Italian sausage (medium or hot)
1 package of pizza dough
16 ounces Mozzarella cheese
Grated Parmesan cheese to taste
1 egg white

Preheat oven to 350 degrees. Lightly grease a cookie sheet and set aside.

Fry sausage, chop and drain well. Spread out pizza dough into rectangle. Spread sausage over dough. Sprinkle mozzarella cheese and grated cheese over sausage. Roll up jelly-roll style. Place on the prepared cookie sheet. Beat the egg white and brush over dough.

Bake until golden brown, about 20 minutes.

YIELD: 6 to 8 servings

OLD TIMEY MIX BREAD

JOY NETTLES

My mother's people came from West Columbia, South Carolina, and this recipe has been made and taken to countless church covered-dish suppers in that area and beyond. It may have developed from trial and error during the Depression or World War II. My grandmother used to make it quite often. I think the official name (if it has one) is Mixed Bread, but everyone just called it "mix" bread, and it was always a welcome treat.

It is coarse yeast bread made with cold grits and when served warm with butter it is absolutely fantastic. It hardly ever had time to "sit," but it's not bad served cold either. I lost the recipe for a while, but recently came across it again, and it immediately evoked warm memories for the people and times I remember. This recipe has traveled, via my mom, from South Carolina to Ohio to Texas—and now through me back to South Carolina.

1 cup water, lukewarm
1 package fresh yeast
1 teaspoon sugar
1 tablespoon cooking oil
2 teaspoons sugar
3 cups all purpose flour
2 teaspoons salt
1 cup grits, cooked according to directions and cooled
⅓ cup water (if needed)
Butter or margarine

Preheat oven to 375 degrees. Grease 2 bread pans and set aside.

Combine 1 cup of water, yeast and 1 teaspoon of sugar. Let stand 5 to 10 minutes. When yeast foams, combine with oil, additional sugar, flour, salt and grits. Mix with hands. (Add last ⅓ cup of water if dough is too stiff.) Mix thoroughly and place into the bread pans. Let rise until double. Bake 30 minutes, then grease top with butter or margarine. Bake an additional 20 to 30 minutes until top is golden brown. Cool and remove from pans.

YIELD: 2 loaves

CHALLAH BREAD

DEVORAH LEAH GORDON

"Of the first of your dough ye shall give the L-rd a portion for a gift throughout your generations." (Numbers 15:21)

Challah, freshly baked from the oven, fills the air with the fragrance of *Shabbat*. Throughout the generations, Jewish women have cherished the tradition of baking challah.

One of the gifts the Jewish people were commanded to give to the priestly tribe, who served in the Holy Temple in Jerusalem, was a portion of their dough. This is known as Challah, from which the name of the loaves we eat each Sabbath is derived. In remembrance of this gift and in anticipation of the future Redemption and the third Holy Temple, we still observe this ritual.

The baking of challah is special to me because it is entrusted to the Jewish woman. As the foundation of the home, the woman not only prepares the physical sustenance for the family, but by observing this commandment, she imparts a spiritual message as well: that all of our sustenance truly comes to us through G-d's hand, and that a portion of our livelihood is always reserved for charity. The woman, so influential in shaping the values and attitudes of her family members, brings blessings upon her home and family through this commandment and instills faith in G-d within those around her.

FOR THE BREAD:

2 ounces fresh yeast or 4 packages dry yeast

3 ½ cups warm water

¾ cup sugar

1 ½ tablespoons salt

13 to 14 cups flour, plus more for kneading

6 eggs, slightly beaten

1 cup oil

Shabbat means Sabbath in Hebrew. In this story, where the author has omitted letters, she has done so in a reverent style of writing which acknowledges the unknowable.

HINT
You can let the dough rise overnight in the fridge covered with a towel; mix all ingredients together at once, no need to knead.

HUNGRY FOR HOME

FOR THE GLAZE:

1 egg, beaten
Poppy or sesame seeds

Dissolve yeast in warm water in a large bowl. When dissolved, add sugar, salt and half of the flour. Mix well.

Add eggs and oil, then slowly stir in most of the remaining flour—dough will become quite thick. (Until the kneading stage, dough can be mixed in an electric mixer.)

When dough begins to pull away from sides of bowl, turn onto floured board and knead for about 10 minutes. Add only enough flour to make dough manageable. Knead until dough is smooth and elastic and springs back when pressed lightly with fingertip.

Place dough in a large oiled bowl. Turn it so the top is oiled as well. Cover with a damp towel and let rise in a warm place for 2 hours, punching down in four or five places every 20 minutes.

Grease several baking sheets or 4 to 6 large loaf pans and set aside.

Separate challah with the blessing.* Divide into 4 to 6 parts and shape into loaves; place in the prepared pans or on baking sheets. Let rise until double in bulk.

Preheat oven to 375 degrees. Brush tops of loaves with beaten egg and sprinkle with poppy or sesame seeds. Bake for 30 to 45 minutes or until browned. Remove from pans and cool on racks.

YIELDS: 4 to 6 loaves

VARIATIONS: Substitute 1 cup whole-wheat flour and ½ cup wheat germ for equal amounts of regular flour; add 2 teaspoons vanilla extract to dough before kneading; make smaller loaves and bake for less time.

* Separating the challah portion before baking bread is easy to do, but an understanding of the criteria involved is necessary; you should consult a rabbi for specifics.

SARITA'S CHEESY GARLIC PIZZA BREAD

SARITA OSBORNE

I found a recipe for spaghetti bread in a magazine and it was very good. It got me to thinking that you could also make a pizza bread. I don't care for meat on my pizza and I love the garlic cheese bread that they serve at pizza restaurants, so I came up with this version. Our family really enjoys it.

1 cup warm water
1 ½ tablespoons olive oil, plus more to oil the pan
½ teaspoon salt
1 ½ cups all-purpose flour
1 ½ cups whole wheat flour
1 ½ teaspoons yeast
⅓ cup grated Parmesan cheese
¼ teaspoon oregano
⅛ teaspoon each of basil, sage and slightly crushed rosemary

Place above ingredients in bread machine on dough cycle.

TOPPING:
2 large cloves of garlic, peeled
1 to 2 tablespoons olive oil
¼ teaspoon sea salt
1 cup or more of shredded mozzarella

Preheat oven to 500 degrees. Oil a pizza pan and set aside.

Dice garlic into small pieces. Place in small bowl and cover with olive oil. Add salt; stir and mash with the garlic and oil. Set aside for 10 to 20 minutes. When dough is ready, spread into prepared pan and brush with garlic oil. Top with cheese and bake for about 10 minutes or until cheese is bubbly and lightly browned.

YIELD: 6 to 8 servings

There are as many additions to cornbread recipes—peppers, cheese, onions, cracklings—as there are cooks. But most agree on one thing: "Real" cornbread does not contain sugar!

MEXICAN CORNBREAD

GRETCHEN RHODES

My husband and I are both retired from Stokes County Schools. For the past two years, we have been restoring a two-story log house that is more than 150 years old. Years ago, my sister gave me this recipe. It was a favorite at our school staff luncheons. It is easy to prepare and goes well with a variety of foods.

1 ½ cups self-rising cornmeal
2 eggs
½ cup onions, chopped
1 cup buttermilk
¾ cup mild cheese, grated
½ cup oil
1 teaspoon sugar
Pinch of salt
1 small can cream style corn
1 or 2 jalapeño peppers, chopped and seeded

Preheat over to 350 degrees. Grease whichever kind of pan you prefer—square, loaf or cast-iron frying pan—and set aside.

Mix all ingredients. Bake for 50 to 60 minutes or until done.

YIELD: 6 to 8 servings

PEACE-ON-EARTH-AND-AT-OUR-DINNER-TABLE CORNBREAD

HELEN LLOYD MONTGOMERY

My mother's dinner table was bound by the restrictions of finicky eaters. No meal was served without the ubiquitous bowl of creamed potatoes which were my brother's solitary form of sustenance. My preference was for peanut-butter-and-jelly sandwiches. My dad had military tastes—sausages, sauerkraut, chipped beef and gravy—chow that sent my brother and me reeling from the table in horror.

It therefore follows that my mother's cooking was severely limited to little more than meat, potatoes, and cornbread. But what cornbread that woman could cook! She'd pour a shimmering pool of Crisco into a cast-iron frying pan and set it in the oven to heat almost to smoking temperature. Meanwhile, she'd mix a bowl of cornmeal batter to add to the pan. It would sizzle and bubble mightily as it hit the hot grease and as it baked, it would fill the kitchen with an earthy, primordial fragrance and a sincere promise of good eating.

Twenty minutes later it emerged from the oven a fat, domed cornmeal cake, crispy-dark on the bottom, crinkled and gold on top. Cut into thick wedges, this was hearty peasant-fare at its finest, its coarse goodness guaranteed to satisfy even the pickiest eater. My brother liked his with creamed potatoes. I liked mine smeared with butter. My dad crumbled his into an ice-cold glass of milk and ate it with a spoon. And my mother enjoyed hers with a tremendous sense of relief that she'd found something that we would all eat.

2 cups yellow cornmeal
1 tablespoon baking powder
¼ teaspoon baking soda
¼ teaspoon salt

1 ¼ cups whole milk, or you might like buttermilk

1 egg

1 tablespoon Texas Pete brand sauce (don't argue, just do it)

1 tablespoon Crisco brand shortening, plus more for the pan

Preheat oven to 375 degrees. Combine dry ingredients in one bowl, wet ingredients in another. Put enough Crisco into a 10-inch cast iron skillet to coat the bottom. (You can use some equivalent of the cast iron pan; it won't be quite as good but it won't be anything to sneer at, either.) Heat skillet in oven until quite hot. Combine the wet and dry ingredients into a batter, pour into the hot skillet, and bake the whole thing for 20 minutes, maybe a tad more.

This is wonderful smeared with butter and washed down with a glass of really cold milk, but equally good with chunky winter soups or pinto beans with ham.

YIELD: About 8 servings

SOUTHWEST CORNBREAD

JANET CULLEY OYLER

My husband and I enjoy traveling and have a keen interest in foods of many kinds. This interest developed during tours of Air Force duty in a wide variety of places in this country and abroad. However, there is nothing better to me than a well-prepared Southern meal shared with family and friends.

This recipe combines a classic Southern comfort food, cornbread, with the vibrant flavors of the Southwest. During the eighteen years I lived in San Antonio, I developed a taste for these robust flavors. I combined some of those flavors into this moist cornbread recipe so that I can still enjoy them here in North Carolina. This bread has plenty of flavor but is not "hot." To raise the heat level, add more jalapeños.

1 ½ cups self-rising cornmeal
3 eggs lightly beaten
1 cup buttermilk
½ cup vegetable oil
1 cup shredded sharp cheddar cheese
¼ cup picante sauce
1 small onion, diced
½ medium green bell pepper, diced

1 jalapeño, seeded, deveined, and diced finely
1 cup cream style corn
A 4-ounce can diced green chilies
½ teaspoon garlic powder
1 teaspoon chili powder
1 teaspoon ground cumin

Preheat oven to 400 degrees. Grease a 9 x 13" casserole dish and set aside.

In a large bowl, mix together the cornmeal, eggs, buttermilk and oil, just until incorporated. Then stir in the remaining ingredients until they are evenly blended. Pour mixture into the prepared pan. Bake for 35 to 45 minutes, or until the top is nicely browned.

YIELD: 8 servings

CRACKLING CORN BREAD

DEBE JONES

I grew up on a farm below Tater Hill in Silverstone, North Carolina. We always raised a pig which we killed in the fall. We would take the fat scraps from the pig and cook it down for the lard. The pieces that were left are called cracklings. Mom would make crackling corn bread for supper. My brother, Doug, loved it so much he thought he was in hog heaven when Mom made it. Crackling corn bread is really good with tenderloin, mashed potatoes and shelly beans.

Oil for the skillet
2 cups cornmeal
¾ cup flour
1 tablespoon sugar
1 cup milk
Water, if needed to thin mixture
1 cup cracklings

Preheat oven to 375 degrees. Pour oil into a heavy skillet and heat until hot.

Mix and sift together cornmeal, flour and sugar. Add milk and water, then pour into the hot skillet. Sprinkle cracklings over top and press them into mixture. Bake for 30 minutes or until brown on top.

YIELD: 6 to 8 servings

GERTRUDE'S ROLLS

ALICE E. SINK

Gertrude, the African-American woman who cleaned, cooked, and ironed for our family in the '50s, earned fifty cents an hour. She came to our house one day a week, arriving early and staying late. With Gertrude in our kitchen, we had crusty fried chicken, homemade yeast rolls, buttery peach cobblers, and fried apple pies. We also had a clean and polished two-bedroom house with starched white organdy curtains and waxed kitchen linoleum. When I married in 1958, Gertrude's gift to me was teaching me how to make her rolls. There was no written recipe. Everything was in her head. I had to watch carefully and take good notes. I have been making and serving Gertrude's rolls for almost 45 years.

> 3 heaping cups plain flour
> ½ teaspoon salt
> 1 tablespoon sugar
> 1 heaping tablespoon shortening.
> 1 cup warm water + ¼ cup additional
> 1 package yeast
> 1 egg, beaten
> 1 stick butter (not margarine or other spreads)

Preheat oven to 400 degrees. Grease a baking sheet and set aside.

Mix together the flour, salt and sugar. Blend in the shortening.

In a separate bowl, stir together 1 cup warm water and yeast. Add to flour mixture. Add about ¼ cup more warm water, then add the beaten egg. Cover with waxed paper. Let rise one hour or until doubled in size.

Melt the butter and set aside. Knead batter and roll ¼" thin on floured board. Cut with floured jelly glass, then roll each piece in the melted butter. Fold each roll in half, and place on the baking sheet, just touching. Let rise one hour. Bake until light brown, about 15 minutes.

YIELD: About 2 dozen

HOMAGE TO FRIED BREAD

DOT JACKSON

Down below the garden, when I was a little kid, there was a thicket of briars and scrub with a couple of wallowed-out places where wayfarers often bedded down. The proximity of both the open road and unguarded crops of strawberries and watermelons and tomatoes—with the henhouse close at hand—offered more of the good life than many a brick home of the time.

The bed and breakfast part was all right with our mother. She could not bear for anyone who was tired and hungry to pass on by; that is why the seating at her dinner table nearly always included the piano stool and several crates turned on end, and at night one tiptoed with care among quilt pallets on the floor.

But she was watchful about her children rubbing shoulders with such carefree tourists as those sleeping in the woods. They might be escapees from the chain gang, or dope fiends. Some talked like Yankees.

She told a story about the time her first-born visited the thicket when he was not yet two years old. He was a very dainty eater—partly because our mother was at that time so devoted to the Experts' rules of good nutrition and sanitation that a good appetite didn't stand a chance.

One morning Brother smelled the coffee and toddled off to find excitement with the hoboes. They welcomed him to their sooty little fireside. When our mother swooped down on him, mortified, he was sitting with them on the ground in his diaper, chewing away on a gritty hunk of fried bread and grinning like a 'possum. Nothing he had eaten in his protected little life had ever tasted half that good.

By the time I came along, it was 1932 and wise folks had pretty well decided that whatever the Lord saw fit to provide was good, and good for you. Cookbooks counted calories, and the more the better when it came to the good old Southern holy trinity of sugar, salt and grease. Mae West was idolized in part because she was round; the tycoon's pot-belly symbolized the hope that somewhere down the road, there was Plenty.

Dot Jackson, beloved former columnist for the *Charlotte Observer,* now writes from the mountains of South Carolina.

Not many in that generation dawdled with their dinner. There were always other forks at the table ready to reach and spear what lingered on a sibling's plate. So it is amazing to survivors of that time to be told, in this day, "Oh, don't expect Tiny Tim to eat roasted goose and pudding with us. We have to microwave a frozen pizza for him. That's all he will eat."

Not long ago at a family gathering a chubby, Big Mac-nurtured little boy scowled disdainfully as platters and bowls were brought to the table. "I am a picky eater," he warned. I wanted to pick him (and his parents) to tee-tiny little pieces.

No—I wanted to put him out in the woods, and at the moment of collapse, for him to come across a piece of good fried bread.

It may be that this is a genetic need, in America. It may be that something in us remembers when we came into woods that then belonged to someone else, already out of whatever poor eats had made the journey with us, and at the brink of starvation we came upon a camp where people were frying bread. And kindly, they gave us some — and soon wished they hadn't.

These were the Native American people who gave us nearly everything else we have that was supremely fit to eat—squashes, corn, potatoes, native beans. We wonder without much enthusiasm what we lived on before we came here—mutton, oats and pea soup nine days old?

Cherokees and other tribes are still the masters of fry bread. Their young when far from home yearn for it; Indian festival-goers of every ethnicity stand in line for it. They make it much as we have learned to, sort of like biscuit dough patted out and fried lightly brown on both sides, in lots of grease.

The texture of its substance comes from using very little leavening—fry bread was never meant to be light eating—and scant if any shortening added to the dough of flour, a goodly pinch of salt and milk enough to knead with floured hands, and shape. Biscuit mix will pass in an emergency; even canned biscuits patted thin are better than nothing. Any clean cooking grease heated to small bubbles will do—shortening, lard, bacon grease or oil. In fact, old cold biscuits split and fried crisp and brown in butter are God's gift with hot coffee of a morning.

What to serve with fried bread? Bear grease; crisp fatback; molasses; honey; apple butter; jam. It all depends on how far up or down the scale we want to go.

The other day at a party in a gilded tea room the hostess brought out, with china cups of Earl Grey, a tray of doily-nested golden ovals, centered by bowls of crème fraîche, lemon curd, raspberry preserves and English marmalade.

Yeah. Fried bread. And in a flash it disappeared, with murmurs of decorous ladies' joy, like goose grease down a hot rock.

Everybody who makes fried bread makes it up as he or she goes, depending on what we have. Try this:

3 cups all-purpose flour
1 tablespoon baking powder
1 teaspoon salt
1 cup lukewarm milk, buttermilk or water, more or less, to make
    workable dough
Oil or melted shortening, lard or bacon grease an inch or two deep in
    an iron skillet

Stir flour, baking powder and salt together in a bowl. Add milk or water a little at a time to make dough stiff enough to be easy to shape. Amount varies with flour and humidity. Flour hands, knead a few times; let dough rest for a few minutes. Then pinch off pieces, small handfuls, pat out to ovals about half an inch thick. Let pieces rest on a floured plate or paper while the oil heats to about 375 degrees. Drop one at a time into hot grease; keep grease bubbling; do not crowd. Fry till light brown on bottom and turn to brown other side. (Check center of first one to be sure it is cooked through. If not, let others brown a little more.) Lift out onto paper towels or brown paper to drain. Good with soup, stew, honey, molasses, jam or jelly or just plain.

YIELD: About 10

WHOLE WHEAT BLUEBERRY MUFFINS

MARY ANN ROGERS

We are fortunate in Columbia to have the Rising High bakery, where we can buy fresh milled, whole wheat flour each Saturday. They grind Montana Red wheat for their customers. Up the road in Chapin, we have Collins Blueberry Farm, and between the two, it's very nearly a marriage made in heaven!

We gather blueberries in summer and freeze them so we can enjoy muffins all year long. I like to use local honey when available, and sometimes add walnuts and cranberries to this recipe, which was passed along to me from my friend, Cindy, who got it from another friend.

Not only are these muffins tasty, they have lots of fiber and fruit, so we feel good about serving them to our families and friends.

2 cups whole wheat flour
1 teaspoon salt
1 teaspoon baking soda
1 teaspoon baking powder
1 cup buttermilk
1 egg, beaten
½ cup vegetable oil
½ cup honey, plus ½ cup sugar (optional)
2 cups blueberries

Preheat oven to 400 degrees. Grease a muffin pan and set aside.

Combine dry ingredients in a large bowl and set aside. In a separate bowl, blend together the buttermilk, beaten egg, oil, honey and sugar, if you are using it. Pour the wet ingredients into the dry and blend just until moistened. Gently fold in the blueberries. Pour into prepared muffin pan and bake about 20 to 25 minutes, or until a toothpick inserted into the center comes out clean.

YIELD: About 12 muffins

DEE PUFPAFF: A CAJUN COOK COMES TO NORTH CAROLINA

Amy Rogers

Her family were true Cajuns—the French who settled in Acadia, then migrated south from Nova Scotia to Louisiana. But Raleigh resident Dee Pufpaff has journeyed farther than her ancestors could ever have imagined. Here is her story in her own words:

"I'm Deborah Ann Victoria DuPont Pufpaff. I was born in 'Morevill,' Louisiana. And I lived in Big Bend. No. Spell that M-O-R-E-A-U-V-I-L-L-E. Moreauville, Louisiana.

"My grandmother still lives in Big Bend. She taught me how to make biscuits for 4-H when I was nine. Well, I won, and she let me make biscuits every Saturday after that. We've offered her to come up here and visit, but she says, 'Oh, no, honey.' I don't think but maybe one time she's ever been out of the state of Louisiana.

"My family made boudin sausage—there's a white and a red kind—and they'd send me off so I wouldn't be too distressed when they went out there with the guns. Let me tell you, you get a real good respect for meat.

"Now, I like to tell my daughter, Mattie, stories about those days, instead of those bedtime things, you know? My grandmother would always tell us, 'No, no—you don't speak French—you speak English.' Back then you only went as far as the sixth grade, then you went to work in the fields.

"She made fried dough, something like what they call 'beignets' now, only we called them 'crêpes.' I can remember looking down at the table and there'd be seven cakes that my grandmother had baked all day. Peanut butter and chocolate and pineapple and coconut. That place, it's kind of lost in time. Now, the young kids when they grow up, they move off to the cities because there's nothing there. No job opportunities.

"For me, cooking just comes natural. I believe in those old iron skillets. I've got eight of them. Two or three belonged to my husband Mike's grandmother. I have one just for bread. See this one? It's as slick as a baby's bottom. Never cook meat or potatoes or anything else in a bread skillet. It absorbs the odor.

"Here's how to cure a skillet. Wash it, grease it, then put it in the sun, outside in the summertime when it's hot. Let it sit in the sun. Bring it in, wash it, grease it again, put it in the oven for the night. Next day, do it all again. Keep doing that till you get it right.

"We lived in Australia for two years. The first year, it was really tough adjusting. I had a real time getting my cooking to turn out. The ingredients are just different. They don't use a lot of preservatives. Where we feed our cattle on grain, theirs graze on grass. So the meat even smells and tastes different. And the temperatures are in Celsius. The measurements, too, so you need a little chart.

"I helped at Mattie's school, making morning tea for the teachers—that's something they do over there at least once a week. After breakfast, about nine, ten o'clock. Mostly pastries, sometimes little sandwiches. I love that custom.

"The stores? They're not like grocery stores here. In Australia, you've got big malls with department stores, plus they have food stores. You've got the fruit market, the fish market, then there's the bread store—all in the mall. It's wonderful.

"Here, we're so rushed to death. In Australia, things close up about 4 o'clock in the afternoon. Even most grocery stores. They really believe in family life.

"Not only were the scenery and the landscape different, but the people and the accents too. But it's just like in Louisiana—people will always have names for others who are different. But I think it makes life more interesting. I like it. I'd do it again. My feet are itching."

Asked what she believes to be important, Dee replies, "Well, my grandmother taught us to believe in these things: loyalty, honor, tradition, family. And she said, 'Always cook an extra chicken leg in case someone drops in.'"

BEIGNETS (LOUISIANA-STYLE CRÊPES)

½ cup warm water, about 115 degrees

2 packages dry yeast

¾ cup lukewarm milk

½ cup sugar

2 teaspoons salt

¼ cup shortening

2 eggs

5 cups all-purpose flour

Peanut oil for frying

HINT:
You can serve these with jam and confectioners sugar, or with butter and syrup.

Sprinkle the yeast in the warm water and stir. Set aside for 5 minutes.

Combine the milk, sugar and salt in a large bowl. Stir to dissolve. Using a mixer, beat in the shortening, eggs, yeast mixture and 2 cups of flour. Mix until smooth.

Add remaining flour and mix until the dough leaves the sides of the bowl. Turn out onto a lightly floured bowl and knead until smooth, elastic and no longer sticky. Place in a greased bowl and cover with a clean cloth or towel. Let rise in a warm place, away from draft, until doubled in size, about an hour.

Punch down dough. Divide into 2 equal portions. (At this point, one half may be frozen for later use.)

Fill a large iron skillet halfway with oil. Heat over medium flame, but do not allow the oil to smoke. Pinch off flat pieces of dough about 2" in diameter and lower into the hot oil. Do not crowd. Turn to brown evenly on both sides, then remove and drain on paper towels.

YIELD: About 2 dozen

SUPER EASY CREAM SCONES

4 cups self-rising flour

1 ¼ cups cream

1 ¼ cups 7-up

Preheat oven to 400 degrees. Grease a cookie sheet and set aside.

Combine all ingredients and mix till moist. Spoon onto prepared cookie sheet. Bake for 12 to 14 minutes.

YIELD: About 18

THE BEST-LAID PLANS

Amy Rogers

Everything was ready for the bakery's grand opening. Floors polished, counters gleaming, store-room stocked with fresh Montana wheat, bins filled with just-ground flour. Vats of honey, smell of cinnamon, mixers making dough. Families flying in from Chicago. Janet and Jeff Ganoung could hardly wait for the open house when everyone would celebrate.

Late that night, a winter storm pummeled the Carolinas. It toppled trees, ripped loose power lines and left millions cold and in the dark—including the Great Harvest Bread Company and its owners.

"We delayed a week and just kept going," remembers Jeff.

Janet, who grew up in Hickory, has a master's degree in nutrition and had been baking manager for a caterer. Jeff had been a food scientist. Married 24 years, they left jobs in Chicago and were moving closer to family in North Carolina when the timing seemed right to open the bakery.

A baker's day starts early. Here, it's at 4:30 a.m., when dough mixing begins. The loaves must rise before going in the oven. The store opens at 7, and fresh bread is ready around 10. The Ganoungs vary their offerings, but always supplement their breads with cookies, tea cakes, cinnamon rolls—and "scuffins," a sweet and chewy hybrid of a scone and muffin.

The wheat arrives in 60-pound sacks. It's ground on-site in an electric stone mill, a modern-day version of the old technology used to grind wheat for 10,000 years, explains Jeff. Each of the "stones" in this grinder is the size of a manhole cover. The store uses the flour within 24 hours to maintain its nutrient level.

Their goal is to provide bread that's consistently outstanding, and service to match. "We want to create jobs, product and nutrition," says Jeff.

"This fits me so well," says Janet. "I'm an immediate gratification person. We see the end product, and the joy of feeding people."

GREAT HARVEST LOW-FAT WHOLE-WHEAT BRAN MUFFINS

Here is a recipe that will feed a crowd:

1 gallon unprocessed wheat
  bran flakes

1 ½ gallons fresh-ground whole
  wheat flour

5 tablespoons plus 1 teaspoon
  baking powder

5 tablespoons plus 1 teaspoon
  baking soda

1 gallon raisins

12 cups milk

4 cups molasses

4 cups honey

3 cups canola oil

12 cups applesauce

16 eggs, beaten

Or if this is a bit much, try the following proportions:

1 cup unprocessed wheat bran
  flakes

1 ½ cups fresh-ground whole
  wheat flour

1 teaspoon baking powder

1 teaspoon baking soda

1 cup raisins

¾ cup milk

¼ cup molasses

¼ cup honey

3 tablespoons canola oil

¾ cup applesauce

1 egg, beaten

Preheat oven to 400 degrees. Grease or spray muffin tin(s) and set aside.

Combine the bran, whole wheat flour, baking powder and baking soda. Stir in raisins and set aside.

In a separate bowl, mix together remaining ingredients until well blended. Stir into dry ingredients just until moistened. Spoon batter into prepared tins, about ⅔ full. Bake for 15 minutes or just until done. Do not overbake. Muffins will be done when tops spring back to the touch. Enjoy!

YIELD: About 192 muffins for the larger recipe, about 12 for the smaller

5

Sweet Treats:

DESSERTS

MY LIFE AS A BAKER: FROM BASHFUL TO BRAVE

Amy Rogers

I admit it. For most of my life, I was baking-impaired. Faking a recipe for stir-fry or stew was easy enough: Just add enough wine and garlic, serve with rice, and you could hardly go wrong.

But baking was altogether different, like learning another language. "Beat until blended," the recipe would say. But for how long? Two minutes or 20?

"Put yeast dough in a warm place to rise." How warm? Where I live, it's awfully drafty in the winter, right when we're craving a crusty hunk of homemade bread. The only warm place in my house is the bathroom with the shower running—or under the cat.

And the science of baking scared me, too. All those chemical reactions, so carefully timed. Worse, you had to actually measure things! When I opened the *Joy of Cooking* and picked a simple recipe, say, for quick coffee cake, I could usually produce something edible. But I had no confidence. Worse, I wasn't having any fun.

Then I got lucky. In 1994, I heard that Jerry Bledsoe, the owner of Down Home Press, was looking for someone to write a book about the North Carolina State Fair and the people who enter their baked goods and win ribbons. I had been a freelance writer for a while and was eager to try my hand at a book-length project. Never mind that I knew practically nothing about baking. What I did know how to do was interview folks and get them talking. I tracked down dozens of them, spent a year of weekends on the road, and when I was done, I had nearly 100 recipes that had been proven to work. And to win.

I tested the recipes. Bread, biscuits, fudge, peanut brittle and pound cakes flowed from the tiny kitchen of the apartment where I was living. It

This recipe is fool-proof because you can do almost anything to it and it will still be delicious. You can double it or half it. Peel the fruit or not. Omit the ginger if you like, use light or dark brown sugar, use a deep or shallow baking dish. Add a little more butter for flavor. Or a little maple syrup. Or lemon juice. Just remember: If you use a tart fruit such as cranberries, increase the sugar.

was like visiting another country and being understood in a foreign tongue for the very first time.

After a while, I became brazen enough to try a few recipe modifications. If you stray too far from the recipe for blueberry pie, you'll get blueberry soup, I learned. But plenty of times, with some practice and creativity, you can improve on a dish, just a little, by making it your own. Here's an easy recipe that you can adapt as you like.

FOOLPROOF FRUIT CRUMBLE

3 cups fresh fruit: apples, berries, peaches or any combination
6 tablespoons butter
1 cup flour
1 cup brown sugar, packed
½ to 1 cup oats, quick or regular (not instant)
3 tablespoons candied ginger, chopped
1 teaspoon cinnamon
½ teaspoon nutmeg
¼ teaspoon salt

Preheat oven to 350 degrees. Grease an ovenproof baking dish and set aside.

Wash fruit and peel if desired; place in the dish. In a microwave-safe bowl, melt the butter, then mix with the flour, sugar, oats and candied ginger. Use your hands. Mixture should be crumbly; if it becomes too wet, add a little more oats.

Crumble the mixture over the fruit, then sprinkle with the cinnamon, nutmeg and salt. Bake uncovered for about 40 minutes, or until the berries pop and you see the juice bubbling.

Careful—crumble will be hot! The best way to cool it is by serving it over ice cream.

YIELD: 6 hearty servings

GRACIE'S ORANGE FUDGE

GAY R. SMALL

My Aunt Eva Grace arrived every summer in a cloud of tea rose perfume with presents in her suitcase. We weren't allowed to bother her on the first day of her visit. She was tired, probably because she was the only fairy god-mother who traveled each June by bus to North Carolina.

The most boring days of my life were spent waiting for the creak of the stairs, for Gracie to come smiling in to us, to pinch our cheeks and read us the new books she brought. *Charlotte's Web* was a special favorite, and I always hear her voice in its pages.

Gracie's dark eyes flashed with mischief as she taught us to play Rook and watched us running about, trying to solve a clue in a treasure hunt. "You're getting warm," she would yell. The prize was always a big square of orange fudge.

It was impossible to list all of the things she did for us, the real magic she brought to our lives, the family history she gave us. Mostly, I re-member laughing with her. My brother and I laughed until we lay help-less on the floor, showing her with our pure glee how much we adored her.

2 cups granulated sugar
½ cup half-and-half
3 tablespoons light Karo brand syrup
1 orange peel, grated
1 teaspoon vanilla
Pinch of salt
2 cups of chopped pecans or walnuts

Grease or butter a cookie sheet or shallow pan and set aside.

In a 2-quart saucepan, bring to a boil the sugar, half-and-half and Karo syrup. Stir gently until the sugar melts. Boil until it reaches the soft ball stage (234 degrees on a candy thermometer).

Remove from heat and drop in the grated orange peel. Add vanilla and a pinch of salt. Let cool to room temperature, then beat with a wooden spoon until glossy. It will begin to thicken. Then add the chopped nuts and spread onto the cookie sheet about ½" thick; let cool. When firm, cut into pieces with a warm knife.

YIELD: About 20 squares

GRANDMA SADIE'S MARBLE CAKE

MICHAEL PLATNICK

"Grandma Sadie" was always known for her baking, and her marble cake was a fixture in the community. From births to weddings to holidays, everyone counted on Grandma Sadie to have one or more marble cakes ready and waiting.

Although our grandmother passed on years ago, our memories of her live on forever, and to this day, seeing a marble cake made from her recipe brings back those special times.

3 cups sifted all-purpose flour
2 teaspoons double-acting baking powder
½ teaspoon salt
1 cup butter or margarine
2 cups sugar
3 unbeaten eggs

1 cup milk
½ teaspoon vanilla
¾ cup chocolate syrup
¼ teaspoon baking soda
¼ teaspoon peppermint extract
Aluminum foil

Preheat oven to 350 degrees. Grease a 10" tube pan and set aside.

Sift flour, baking powder, and salt together into a bowl and set aside. In a large bowl, cream butter thoroughly. Gradually add sugar to the butter; cream until light and fluffy. One at a time, add the eggs to the butter mixture, beating well after each egg.

In a small bowl, combine the milk and vanilla. Use an electric mixer on low speed to add the milk and the dry ingredients alternately to the butter mixture. Blend thoroughly after each addition.

Pour ⅔ of the batter into the prepared pan. Blend the chocolate syrup into the remaining ⅓ of cake batter, then add the baking soda and peppermint extract.

Pour the chocolate batter over the white batter in the pan. Do not mix the two batters! Bake for 45 minutes, then place a sheet of aluminum foil on top of the pan and bake another 20 to 25 minutes, or until a toothpick inserted into the center comes out clean. Cool in pan.

YIELD: 12 to 16 servings

MAMMAW'S COLD OVEN POUND CAKE

LYNDA F. CRISP

This recipe came from my grandmother, Mary McBride. She was a strong yet sweet Southern Baptist lady who raised me and instilled in me her strength and her faith. She worked second shift for Cannon Mills in Kannapolis, North Carolina, worked her garden, and raised cows, pigs, chickens, ducks and me! Her church family and neighbors knew they could depend on her for a "cold oven pound cake" anytime they needed it. She loved baking and giving.

As a child I remember she would line the cake pan with waxed paper, bake the cake, and when she took it out of the pan, she immediately put it in a Tupperware cake keeper and closed the lid. The cake would sweat as it cooled. She would cut me a piece to eat while it was still warm. I guess the best part was that as it baked, it filled our house with that wonderful smell of Grandma's love. I loved her dearly and have fond memories of this recipe as I pass it on to my girls.

3 cups cake flour	½ cup shortening
1 teaspoon baking powder	6 eggs
3 cups sugar	1 cup milk
½ pound butter (2 sticks)	1 ½ teaspoons vanilla

Do NOT preheat oven! Line the bottom of a tube pan with waxed paper, then grease and flour it. Set aside.

Sift together the flour and baking powder and set aside. In a large bowl, cream together the sugar, butter and shortening. Then add eggs one at a time, alternately with the milk, and the sifted dry ingredients. Mix well, then stir in the vanilla. Pour into the prepared pan and place in a cold oven. Turn to 350 degrees for 1 ½ hours. No peeping!

YIELD: 12 servings

EDNA'S OLD-FASHIONED POUND CAKE

Amy Rogers

She'd heard the story her whole life, and no one could say it wasn't true. Her grandfather, Lafayette Coble, was the first black man to own land in Alamance County. As a boy, he'd been a slave, carrying water for the Confederate troops during the war. When the Union army came through, Lafayette's mother hid him in a nearby thicket until the soldiers passed. It was a few years later, after the war was over, that a man named Mr. Cooper sold an 88-acre piece of land to Lafayette.

It was on that land that Edna Foust grew up. Her story is a different one: Edna never married or had children. An adopted brother was killed many years ago. So it might have seemed natural for Edna to cling to her family's land. But she thought there was more to life than that. She "got the wish" when she was little to become a nurse, and she made that wish come true. She went to school in Richmond, but returned home to North Carolina to practice.

With no one to keep the family farm going, the land was sold many years ago, but Edna's decision served her well regardless. Her career took her through 46 years at a half-dozen hospitals, and after that, she was ready to retire—or so she thought.

"I was miserable!" she exclaims. "I couldn't sit still." So in spite of foot surgery, she went back to work, part-time at Durham County Hospital. She enjoyed the patients and staff too much to stay away. Her work, however, didn't keep her from baking, something it took her a while to learn.

As a young girl, she tried to make a cake by imitating her mother. "It fell," she says. "I carried it to the pig pen and fed it to the hogs." Laughing, Edna has to stop and catch her breath before she continues, "Then I cleaned up, washed up everything before my parents came in from the fields."

Over the years, however, she got a lot of practice. Birthdays, anniversaries and weddings sparked her to fire her oven, but she didn't need a special occasion to bake for others. She remembers a cake she baked for her dentist. She took it over on a Wednesday afternoon, and first thing Thursday morning the phone rang.

"Edna—the cake is gone already!" the dentist groaned.

She hasn't any secrets, just an old-fashioned attitude about what works: lots of careful mixing and simple ingredients. So it was only right that Edna would win a blue ribbon, and she did, the first time she entered the North Carolina State Fair in 1992.

Her home of 20 years is full of special touches. The drapes and sofa match the silk flowers she has specially arranged. She's got her Kitchen-Aid mixer, her big-screen TV and a nice, comfortable chair, but she'll never forget an earlier time.

The little girl who picked cotton and attended a one-room schoolhouse has seen a lot of things change, but she knows what ought to stay the same. "Wash clean, don't make a mess, follow the rules, sweep under the bed—and in the corners." And she offers one more piece of advice that she's always carried with her, one that has served her especially well in her baking: "Whatever you do, do it well."

1 cup butter
1 cup vegetable shortening
3 cups sugar
6 eggs
4 cups cake flour
¼ teaspoon salt
1 teaspoon baking powder
1 cup milk
1 teaspoon almond flavoring or vanilla

Preheat oven to 300 degrees. Grease and flour a 10-inch tube pan. Set aside.

In a large bowl, cream butter and shortening until well-blended. Add sugar gradually until fluffy. Add eggs, one at a time, beating well after each addition.

In a separate bowl, sift then measure flour. Add salt and baking powder. Combine milk and flavoring in a measuring cup. With mixer on low speed, alternately add the flour mixture and milk to the butter mixture. Begin and end with flour. Pour batter into pan. Bake 1 ½ hours or until a tester inserted in cake comes out clean.

Remove from oven and cool in pan on wire rack before inverting on plate to serve.

YIELD: 12 to 16 servings

MY MAMMA'S PUMPKIN PIE

PAMELA K. HILDEBRAN

Within our large family, my mamma's pumpkin pie is considered the best in the world. As she did with all her recipes, Mamma always made it from scratch, minus measuring cups or other, more precise means. I attempted my first pumpkin pie while I was in college, but I wasn't sure how to proceed, so I called home for directions.

A pumpkin
Cinnamon
Vanilla
Sugar, ½ to 1 cup per pie
Eggs, one per pie
About 1 cup milk
Unbaked pie crusts (store-bought are fine)
Whipped cream or Cool Whip brand topping

*Ovens vary. So do cake batters. This pie can be baked in a moderate oven (350 to 375 degrees), or hot oven (400 to 425 degrees) if you like a pie that's not as moist.

Mamma said: "Peel the pumpkin, scoop out the seeds, cut up the pumpkin, put it in a big pot of water. Cook it until it's done. Drain off the extra water, mash the pumpkin, mix in cinnamon, vanilla, sugar, one egg (per pie), and milk until it tastes right. (Batter should be thinner than cake batter.) This will usually make about four pies; maybe six if the pumpkin is large. Fill the pie crusts with the pumpkin mixture.

"Put the pans in a *pre-heated oven and bake until the pies are done; use your finger to test the tops of the pies toward the middle. If the filling doesn't stick to your finger, the pie is done, usually in about 45 minutes. Let them cool. When ready to serve, put whipped cream on top of each piece."

I was worried. How would I know how much would be "enough?" How would I know "when it's done?" But I listened to Mamma, used my memories of watching her cook and tasting her pies, and I did what she told me.

Decades later, when I was teaching composition to first-year college students, they would ask how they could know when they'd done enough research, or how long a paragraph should be, or when an essay was complete. One day, these words came out of my mouth: "It's like my mamma's pumpkin pie," and I shared Mamma's directions. This may be a too-obvious metaphor, but it works: Pay attention; practice without too much fear of failure; recognize your limitations, and trust yourself to know "when it's done."

YIELD: 4 to 6 pies

HINT
Mamma made her pie crusts from scratch; I tried, but eventually relied on Pillsbury frozen pie crusts because some skills aren't mine to cultivate. You can "fancy up" the recipe by adding brown sugar, nutmeg, pecans, heavy cream, etc., but you *never use canned pumpkin pie filling.*

GRANDMA STANTON'S APPLESAUCE CAKE AND BROWN SUGAR FROSTING

LESLIE STANTON COUICK

This recipe came from my grandmother, Eliza Faries Stanton. She was born on January 23, 1890 in Clover, South Carolina, and lived until February 2, 1978. Throughout her life she was one of the hardest-working women in York County. She gave birth to twelve children; as a widow she raised ten of them when her husband, Minot Earl Stanton, died at forty.

My father told me stories of a beautiful young woman who was as tough as nails. Her skin was smooth as silk and the color of light brown sugar. Her hands were the only reflection of the toil of farm work. She could out-pick anybody when it came to picking cotton; some people said she could pick up to 350 pounds in a day. And when that was done she had to cook, tend the farm animals and look after all those children.

My father waited expectantly each year for his mother to make an applesauce cake for his birthday. She covered it with warm brown sugar frosting and decorated the top with walnut halves from the trees on her farm. She baked a cake for each one of her children's birthdays. All the ingredients came from her farm. Grandma would dry apples from her own apple trees, outside in the sun, on a table covered with brown paper. The butter she used in the frosting came from the cream she churned.

My grandmother was a resourceful, ingenious lady. I am proud to share a small part of her life, and this recipe made by her hands out of love for her children. When you slice a piece of Grandma's cake, you are taking a slice out of history.

1 cup water
2½ cups dried apples, chopped
1 cup shortening
2 cups brown sugar
4 cups plain flour
1 teaspoon cinnamon

1 teaspoon nutmeg

3 teaspoons soda

⅔ cup buttermilk

1 cup unsweetened applesauce

1 tablespoon vanilla extract

1 box dark raisins

1 cup black walnuts, chopped

Preheat oven to 325 degrees. Grease and flour a 10" tube pan and set aside.

Bring water to a boil and pour over dried apples in a heat-proof bowl. Soak for one hour, then drain off excess water. In a large bowl, cream together the shortening and sugar. In another bowl, sift together the dry ingredients. Alternately add the dry ingredients and buttermilk into the shortening/sugar mixture.

Add the chopped apples, applesauce and vanilla extract and mix until well blended. Fold in raisins and nuts. Pour into prepared pan. Bake for 1 ½ hours, but check after 1 hour and 10 minutes as ovens vary. Cake should be golden brown on top, and is done when a toothpick comes out clean. Remove from oven and cool, then turn out onto cake plate. Frost with the following frosting:

HINT
This cake is delicious right from the oven, but even better after a few days.

BROWN SUGAR FROSTING

1 ½ cups brown sugar

1 stick butter

⅔ cup canned evaporated milk

Mix above ingredients in a saucepan. Stir constantly over low heat until butter melts. Turn up heat to medium and stir until mixture comes to a boil. Continue stirring for 3 minutes over medium heat. Remove from burner, set pan over some ice in the sink and stir until thick, about 5 minutes. Pour over cake. Decorate top with walnut halves.

YIELD: 12 servings

COTTA BADERTSCHER'S MULE EAR COOKIES

LESLIE B. RINDOKS

HINT
If cookies are too sticky use a little more flour. Don't overbake or they'll get very hard.

My dad, one of six children, was raised on a farm in the heart of Ohio. He couldn't wait to get out of there. And he did: He raised two well-groomed girls in a perfectly groomed quarter-acre of a freshly scrubbed subdivision, which I couldn't wait to get out of.

Now I live somewhere in between, not the country, but not the city either. On those early spring days when farmers are preparing their fields, much to the dismay of my urban born-and-bred spouse, I roll my windows down as we drive out of town. City folk don't generally appreciate the earthy smell of freshly fertilized fields. It's more than manure; it's the warmth of the barn and the cows and the baby lambs. Breathing a little deeper, I can catch the hint of crabapples, maybe elderberry blossoms, too.

Growing up, we made regular visits to my grandparents' farm. In the spring I fed new lambs from baby bottles and pumped icy cold water from the well. In the summer, I helped milk the dairy cows and popped tar bubbles in the old farm road. The fall meant picking crabapples and grapes for jellies and jams, and crushing apples—cores, peels, seeds and all—in a loud, jangling apparatus that somehow transformed the slimy, lumpy mass into applesauce and apple butter. Cooking was practical, and baking was not for show. Mule Ears, grandma's molasses cookies, were as fancy as it got. They're not for the chocoholic. They won't provide you with a sugar high. They're an acquired taste, kind of like the springtime perfume of freshly fertilized fields.

1 ½ cups white sugar

½ cup margarine

1 egg

1 cup molasses

1 teaspoon soda
4 cups flour
½ teaspoon ginger
½ teaspoon nutmeg
1 teaspoon cinnamon
½ teaspoon salt

Preheat oven to 350 degrees. Grease a cookie sheet and set aside.

In a large bowl, cream together the sugar and margarine, add egg, then ½ of molasses. Dissolve the soda in the other half of the molasses and set aside. Combine the flour, spices and salt; blend into the sugar mixture. Then stir in the molasses/baking soda mixture.

Flour hands and pinch off enough dough to roll in a little sausage shape. Place on greased cookie sheet, not too close together. Press them flat with a spatula till they are about 1 ½" long and not too thick. Sprinkle with sugar. Bake 8 to 9 minutes.

YIELD: About 3 dozen

'NANAS FROM HEAVEN

RON RASH

Novelist Ron Rash, best-known for his national best-seller *One Foot in Eden,* is also an award-winning poet.

I heard the story when I was a child, so the details are blurred by the passing of four decades. What I *know* is that my grandparents and father were living in Asheville, North Carolina, in the late 1930s, and that like most people during the Depression they were poor. The mill where my grandparents worked paid little enough when it was open, but in these times it was often shut down. What passed for culinary luxury was, according to my grandmother, a chunk of fatback for the beans that, along with cornbread, made up most of the meals.

So when the produce truck hauling bananas turned over one Saturday afternoon in downtown Asheville, it must have seemed like manna from heaven. My grandfather evidently had no moral scruples about grabbing a huge stalk of bananas that did not belong to him and carrying them home. Or if he did, his doubts were outweighed by a hunger for something other than cornbread and beans. The writer in me would like to think he voiced some justification to his wife and son: "If God was good enough to turn that truck over and throw a stalk of bananas at my feet, who am I to question His wisdom?" What I know for a fact is that my grandparents and my father splurged for one of the few times during those hard years. My grandfather went to the store and bought the vanilla wafers and other ingredients, and the family ate banana pudding for dessert three days in a row – even after breakfast, according to my grandmother.

During my childhood, we always ate our Thanksgiving lunch at my grandmother's. We didn't have to wait anymore for a banana truck to overturn to have dessert. My grandmother by then could buy her bananas at the local A&P, but her pudding was a well-established tradition. What better food for our family to eat on a day when we gave thanks for all manner of blessings, even the unexpected ones.

2 boxes vanilla pudding (not instant)

Box of vanilla wafers

4 to 6 very ripe bananas, sliced

FOR MERINGUE:

4 eggs whites

½ teaspoon cream of tartar

6 tablespoons sugar

1 teaspoon vanilla

Preheat oven to 350. Prepare pudding according to package directions.

The key is the layering. In an oblong glass baking dish, put a layer of vanilla wafers on the bottom, then bananas, then pudding; repeat with wafers, bananas, pudding.

For meringue: In a separate bowl, beat the egg whites till frothy, then add cream of tartar and beat until peaks begin to form. Beat in the sugar, 1 tablespoon at a time until stiff, then add vanilla. Spread over the pudding and bake just until brown, about 15 minutes.

YIELD: 8 to 10 servings

SHORTBREAD

Amy Rogers

What could be easier than a dessert recipe with only three ingredients? It's simple, but with its buttery taste and texture, it's nice enough to serve company. Unlike most cookie recipes, it contains no leavening, so you can double or triple it as long as you maintain the proportions.

3 cups flour
2 cups butter
1 cup confectioners sugar

HINT
Don't use margarine. The taste of fresh, real butter is what makes shortbread special.

Preheat oven to 350 degrees. Grease a 9 x 13" baking dish and set aside.

Blend the ingredients together with a fork or with your fingers. Press into the prepared pan and bake for about 15 minutes, or until light brown. Watch carefully to avoid over-browning.

Remove from oven and slice into squares or bars while still warm.

YIELD: About 3 dozen squares

GRANDMA STEPHENS' CHESS PIE

WANDA STEPHENS BIRMINGHAM

When my brother, Brad, and I were children, it was the greatest treat to spend an occasional winter weekend, or better yet—part of every summer—at our grandparents' home in northern Mecklenburg County. The 1795 homeplace still stands, pristine in its condition and setting on the farm. My grandparents lived in the new house that was then only about 60 years old. No indoor plumbing, neither heat nor air, and minimal electricity were complemented by barns, corn cribs, chicken houses, cows, pigs, gardens—and meals cooked on the wood-burning stove.

Being city kids in the 1950s and '60s, we knew that these visits gave us a wonderful glimpse into our father's life before he left home. Brad and I loved our Grandma Stephens' cooking—especially her chess pie (vinegar pie), which she always made when we were visiting. When Brad was about 13, he asked her to bake the favorite pie for one of his friends. Our parents would have never allowed this, but when my grandmother called that the pie was ready, Brad got on his bike and rode all the way "up to the country" and then back, about 13 miles each way, holding the chess pie in one hand. And then his friend did not even like it because he said it was too rich!

HINT
This rich, country pie is very forgiving to make. You can use butter or margarine, brown sugar or white sugar, plain cornmeal or cornmeal mix. You can beat the egg whites separately and fold them in last, or just add eggs.

- 2 sticks of butter or non-whipped margarine
- 2½ cups sugar, equal amounts white and dark brown
- 2 tablespoons cornmeal
- 6 eggs
- 2 tablespoons vinegar
- ¼ teaspoon salt
- 2 teaspoons vanilla
- 2 pie shells or 1 deep dish shell (my preference)

Preheat oven to 350 degrees. Cream together the butter and sugar. Add the remaining ingredients and pour into the pie shell(s).

Bake for about 50 minutes. I usually start on the bottom rack then move it up halfway through baking.

YIELD: 8 servings

EFFIE'S LEMON PIE

MARIANNE LONDON

When I was growing up, my Grandma had an old Indian cook named Effie. This was back in the days when, in the deep South, people not only had a housekeeper, but a cook as well.

Effie was a raisin of a woman, her face pruned from years of hard work and steamy kitchens. When we grandchildren, or granchillun' as Effie called us, would come to visit, she always had lemon pies cooling in the pantry. At Grandma's, the midday meal was always referred to as dinner, not lunch; after dinner Effie would parade her pies out to the table. No one could beat a meringue like Effie. Her pies stood tall and proud, the meringue drifts having just the right tinge of brown to define their peaks. She would place them on the dinner table as if bestowing a gift to the queen.

My eyes would become big as saucers as Grandma cut hunks of yellow-and-white triangles and passed them down the table. So delicious!

Now some 30 years later, I make the same lemon pies for my own chillun', using Effie's recipe. They love the pies almost as much as I do!

1 cup of sugar
3½ tablespoons of flour
3 egg yolks
1 cup of milk
Juice and grated rind of 2
    lemons

A 9-inch pie shell, baked

FOR THE MERINGUE:

3 egg whites at room temperature
6 tablespoons of sugar

Preheat oven to 400 degrees. Blend sugar, flour, egg yolks and milk together in a heavy saucepan over medium heat. Stir often to keep from sticking. Add the lemon juice and rind, and cook until mixture thickens to a pudding-like texture. Pour filling into prepared crust.

Make the meringue by blending the egg whites with the sugar. Beat by hand with a wire whisk, or with an electric mixer until mixture is stiff and forms peaks. Spread over the top of the pie. Bake for 8 to 10 minutes or until top is golden brown. Remove from oven and cool before serving.

YIELD: 6 to 8 servings

PISTACHIO SURPRISE

SHIRLEY MADDALON

My family has been handing down recipes since the days of my great-grandmother. This three-layered dessert is one of our favorites.

2 cups of flour

2 sticks of butter

1 cup of chopped pecans

1 large container of Cool Whip brand topping, plus extra

Two 8-ounce packages of cream cheese

1 cup 10x powdered sugar

2 packages of instant pistachio pudding

Chopped nuts or cherries for decoration

Preheat oven to 350 degrees.

Mix together the flour, butter and pecans and press into the bottom of a 9 x 11" baking dish. Bake for 10 to 15 minutes until golden brown. Remove from oven and cool completely.

Combine the Cool Whip, cream cheese and powdered sugar and blend until creamy. Spread on top of cooled crust. Prepare the pudding according to package directions, then spread on top of the other ingredients. Top with additional Cool Whip, and sprinkle with nuts or cherries to decorate, if desired.

YIELD: 12 servings

HINT
You can substitute chocolate pudding for the pistachio, if you prefer.

PUMPKIN-OATMEAL BARS WITH CREAM CHEESE FROSTING

CORDELIA B. ANDERSON

The holiday season before my husband Ryan and I changed our eating habits, we immersed ourselves in food. Our offices at work overflowed with chocolate, cookies, chips and brownies. At home, I baked for families and friends. It sounds impossible, but I actually got sick of chocolate. By the new year, we were ready for a change.

Soon we realized we were living in a universe of sugary temptation. Ryan left his job to enter the police academy and I would bake cookies for his academy classmates, but we didn't eat any. We consoled ourselves with sugar-free and fat-free ice cream, but as another holiday season approached, our desire for baked goods returned. So I turned to pumpkin, a seasonal favorite, for inspiration.

I created these pumpkin bars to serve double duty as a snack or meal. You can freeze them and pack them in lunches, eat them as breakfast or dessert. Because they contain hearty ingredients, they are much more filling than you would expect.

⅓ cup sugar, or equivalent amount sugar substitute
½ cup canola oil
1 egg
¾ cup pumpkin, canned or fresh cooked
¼ cup apple sauce
½ cup orange juice
1 ½ cups whole wheat flour
¾ cup oatmeal (not instant)
1 teaspoon baking powder
½ teaspoon baking soda
2¼ teaspoons pumpkin pie spice
½ cups walnuts, chopped

An 8-ounce package cream cheese

¼ cup butter, softened but not melted

½ cup powdered sugar, or equivalent amount sugar substitute

2 teaspoons vanilla

Preheat oven to 350 degrees. Grease a 5 x 9" pan and set aside.

Cream first six ingredients together, then gradually add dry ingredients one at a time. Stir in nuts. Mix thoroughly. Spread batter into pan and bake for 25 to 30 minutes, or until inserted knife comes out clean. Let cool before frosting.

While bars are cooling, blend cream cheese and butter together, then add sugar and vanilla. Spread frosting on bars only after they are completely cooled. Store in a sealed container in a cool place.

YIELD: About 12 servings

HINT
Read labels carefully when using sugar substitutes. Some won't withstand the heat of cooking. And be sure to measure carefully. In most cases, you will use much less of artificial sweetener than sugar.

"KRISPY KREME" BREAD PUDDING

BRAD LEGRONE

I first heard of a restaurant that was serving a Krispy Kreme bread pudding from an article in the *Charlotte Observer*. On a drive home from Asheville, North Carolina, I became obsessed with thoughts of making this dessert. So, as soon as I got home, I found all the bread pudding recipes that I could get my hands on, and adapted them for doughnuts.

9 regular glazed Krispy Kreme brand doughnuts (day-old)
2 large eggs plus 2 egg yolks
½ cup plus 1 tablespoon sugar
1 teaspoon vanilla
½ teaspoon salt
½ teaspoon cinnamon
¼ teaspoon nutmeg
3 cups whole milk

Butter a 2-quart baking dish and set aside.

Cut the doughnuts into ½" cubes and spread evenly in the baking dish. In a bowl, whisk together the rest of the ingredients and pour over the doughnuts. Let rest for 1 hour.

Preheat oven to 350 degrees. Make a water bath for the pudding by placing the baking dish in a shallow, ovenproof pan. Then fill the pan with warm water. Place in the oven and bake for 70 to 75 minutes; the center should be firm. Serve warm or cold.

YIELD: 6 to 8 servings

Some cheesecake purists prefer to enjoy this rich, creamy dessert without the addition of fancy flavors. Others like to enhance their recipes with everything from coffee and chocolate to peanut butter and pumpkin!

CHEESECAKE

MEREDITH BRADY TRUNK

I came by this recipe in a fairly unusual way. My mother was an obstetrician/gynecologist who became friendly with some of her patients. One such friend, Sr. Kathleen, a Catholic nun, invited us to share dinner with her and served this cheesecake for dessert. My mother raved about the cake and had Sr. Kathleen write out the recipe for her.

My mom was a marvel in the operating room but her kitchen skills were less formidable, so she persuaded me to attempt to make the cheesecake. I'd never even heard of a springform pan before, so it was a challenge I reluctantly accepted. The original recipe called for crushed zwieback crackers to be used in the crust mixture. I tried crumbling the crackers using a plastic bag and a rubber mallet, but always ended up with more crumbs on the countertop and floor than in the mixing bowl. It wasn't long before I realized that using pre-crushed graham cracker crumbs did not alter the taste of the cheesecake at all, because the filling is the star.

I have been making this cheesecake for over 30 years and I've yet to meet a cheesecake fan who hasn't loved it.

FOR THE CRUST:

1 cup graham cracker crumbs
⅔ cup sugar
⅔ stick butter, melted

FOR THE FILLING:

16 ounces of cream cheese

8 ounces of cottage cheese

½ pint sour cream

1 cup sugar

5 eggs

1 tablespoon vanilla

1 teaspoon lemon juice

HINT

Using an electric mixer will make the batter smoother.

Preheat oven to 350 degrees. Grease an 8" or 9" springform pan and set aside.

For the crust, mix together the crumbs, sugar, and butter. Press into the bottom and sides of the prepared pan, reserving a bit for the topping.

For the filling, mix softened cream cheese with cottage cheese, then add sour cream and mix again. Add sugar and blend well. Then add eggs, one at a time, mixing after each addition. Stir in the vanilla and lemon juice. The batter is ready when it reaches a creamy consistency.

Pour batter into crust-ready pan. Sprinkle reserved crumbs over top. Bake for one hour. Turn off oven, but let cake stay in oven for two extra hours. This helps prevent cake from excessive falling. For best results, refrigerate overnight before serving.

YIELD: 8 to 10 servings

FUZZY NAVEL CHEESECAKE

SYLVIA LITTLE-SWEAT

I created this recipe for the Mattie Rigsbee Dessert Competition, named for Clyde Edgerton's character in *Walking Across Egypt*. The competition was a feature of the Fine Arts of Being Southern Symposium at Wingate University in 2001. The recipe won first place for the most unusual cheesecake.

What was most unusual to me, however, was that I made up the recipe one morning before going to school, did not test it; made it the day before the competition but did not sample it; and at the dessert bar which followed Clyde Edgerton's reading did not get a morsel to taste—because the five hundred other guests that evening got there first. Later, I made one for myself and was pleased that it tasted just like a Fuzzy Navel drink.

FOR THE CHEESECAKE:

Three 8-ounce packages of Philadelphia brand cream cheese
5 eggs, separated
1 cup sugar
½ teaspoon vanilla
2 tablespoons peach schnapps
2 tablespoons fresh orange juice
2 graham cracker crusts (Keebler brand 2-extra-servings size)

FOR THE TOPPING:

1 cup sour cream
¼ cup sugar
1 ¼ teaspoons vanilla

FOR THE GLAZE:

1 cup orange marmalade
½ cup peach schnapps

HINT
If you buy the Keebler brand crusts, you'll have plastic lids you can use to cover the cheesecakes while they chill.

Preheat oven to 300 degrees.

Beat the cheese and egg yolks together. Add 1 cup sugar, ½ teaspoon vanilla, 2 tablespoons schnapps and orange juice.

In a separate bowl, beat the egg whites until stiff, then fold into the cheese mixture. Pour equally into the two graham cracker crusts. Bake for one hour.

Meanwhile, mix sour cream, ¼ cup sugar and 1¼ teaspoons vanilla for the topping. Remove the cheesecakes from the oven and turn heat to 475 degrees. Spread the topping over the tops of the warm cheesecakes and bake for an additional 5 minutes.

Cool to room temperature, then mix the marmalade and schnapps; glaze the cakes with the mixture. Refrigerate overnight before serving.

YIELD: 2 cheesecakes, 6 to 8 servings each

LIFE WITHOUT SUGAR

Amy Rogers

A good friend returned from a trip to Italy a while back to learn he had diabetes. While he and his family had been making a thorough, if unscientific, study of the Italian ice cream called gelato, the doctor's office back home had been running tests and was waiting to give him the news.

Newly diagnosed diabetes patients get lots of instructions about how to exercise, plan their meals, and lower their blood sugar with medication. But what no one tells them is how to cope with giving up that daily Krispy Kreme doughnut, or those countless glasses of sweet iced tea served with every meal throughout the South.

Until learning he had diabetes, my friend was a confirmed waffles-and-syrup-for-breakfast man. At lunch, he would order his coconut pie for dessert at the same time he ordered his meal. After dinner, he'd have ice cream. He wasn't overweight, but something in his metabolism kicked in—and now he's in the club that has millions of members around the world.

Could you give up sweets and sugary snacks entirely? We celebrate so many of life's milestones and holidays with food. In plenty of those, sweets have a starring role. Imagine life without Easter Bunny candy, trick-or-treat goodies, Christmas cookies, or even wedding cake.

My friend with diabetes is no whiner, so when the doctor told him to quit sugar he did. He does a great job of sticking with the plan. When everybody "oohs" and "ahs" over the chocolate pound cake or peanut-butter pie being passed around the table, he seems content to nibble on a sugar-free cookie. But something continued to bother me. I wondered: Which is harder to give up—sweets, or the experience of enjoying them with others?

It's probably a little of both, but there was only one that I could do anything about, so I started trying my hand at low-sugar baking. On the Internet, I found some recipes but most seemed unappetizing, or they read like chemistry experiments. The results were pretty disappointing.

After a few false starts, it hit me. Sugar-free cookies could be crushed and mixed with melted butter for pie crust. Sugar-free pudding would work as pie filling. The health-food store had unsweetened coconut and fruit. Even whipped cream, if you make it from scratch, has almost no sugar in it.

Once I began working with these ingredients some interesting things started to happen. I discovered shortcuts that simplified those over-engineered recipes I'd first attempted. Other friends at my table started asking to taste the doctored-up desserts. Once or twice I served the low-sugar versions without telling anyone what they were, and people still remarked how good they tasted. Best of all, a serving of most of those desserts had only as much sugar as a slice of bread.

Diabetics need to watch their carbohydrates, too, and low-sugar desserts aren't a perfect solution. But they can satisfy, at least in part, one of the unfulfilled hungers that comes with diabetes: the appetite for enjoying sweet treats and delicious moments with loved ones. Given a choice, I would much rather help find a way to alleviate my friend's diabetes. But until that happens, I'll be in the kitchen.

NO-BAKE LOW-SUGAR COCONUT PIE

½ to ¾ cup unsweetened shredded coconut*
1 package sugar-free shortbread or oatmeal cookies
⅔ stick of margarine or butter, melted
2½ cups cold milk
1 package sugar-free instant vanilla pudding, 6-serving size
Light whipped cream or frozen non-dairy topping

*HINT
Very few supermarkets stock unsweetened coconut; try your local health food store for this product, as well as nuts and dried fruits prepared without sugar.

On a baking sheet, spread the coconut in a thin layer and toast just until it starts to brown. Remove from oven and let cool. (You can use a toaster oven for this step.)

Crush the cookies into fine crumbs, using a zippered food storage bag and a rolling pin. Combine the cookie crumbs with the melted butter and press into a greased 9" pie pan.

Pour the milk into a bowl, add the pudding, and stir with a wire whisk for 2 minutes. Reserving 2 tablespoons of the toasted coconut to use as topping, stir in the remainder, just until blended. Pudding will begin to thicken; pour into the pie crust quickly.

Refrigerate at least 1 hour, then top with whipped cream and sprinkle with the reserved coconut just before serving.

YIELD: 6 servings

SUGAR-FREE CHOCOLATE NO-BAKE TREATS

KAREN PROCTOR

This recipe began with a Hershey's Cocoa Powder box. I decided that as a diabetic, I was tired of not being able to have some chocolate every once in a while. So I improvised this recipe, which makes up quick. It's a good thing to have around for the holidays, or anytime the cravings strike.

HINT
All brands of artificial sweeteners are not the same. Many break down when heated. Check your recipe carefully.

2 cups of Splenda brand sweetener

½ cup margarine (1 stick)

½ cup skim milk

⅓ cup Hershey's brand cocoa powder

½ cup of crunchy peanut butter

3 cups quick-cooking oats

2 teaspoons vanilla

Line a cookie sheet with wax paper or foil.

Combine sweetener, margarine, milk and cocoa powder in a large saucepan. Cook over medium heat, stir constantly until mixture comes to a rolling boil. Remove from heat, add peanut butter, oats and vanilla, mixing well.

Immediately drop by teaspoonful onto the prepared cookies sheet. They are ready to eat within minutes.

YIELD: 25 to 30

EGG CUSTARD PIE

BETTY T. WILLIAMS

Approximately 41 years ago, I started observing my mother-in-law Dora Williams bake egg custard pies. She was always busy baking for someone, the same pie—egg custard—which was in great demand in our small community of Monroe in Union County, North Carolina. As a new bride and housewife, I wanted so badly to achieve this skill. I tried hard to learn exactly how Mrs. Williams made the pie crust from scratch and how the custard baked into a beautiful silky looking pie. My mother-in-law was very patient in showing me the steps, and what I could expect if I didn't follow the recipe carefully, along with her instructions.

Many years later, I entered the recipe in the North Carolina Egg Association Contest and won first prize. Over the years, I have probably baked 600 of these pies, sharing most of them as gifts. We have a joke about the pies when my husband or sons find one freshly baked in the kitchen. They always ask, "Who is this one for?" I especially feel grateful when I can offer a piece of egg custard in times of need—to a terminally ill patient, or an elderly person living alone, or over the holidays when someone has just lost a member of the family.

My mother-in-law and father-in-law both lost their lives due to a car accident in August 1972. I am thankful for the gift Mrs. Williams left me to pass on to others.

¾ stick margarine	6 large eggs, well-beaten
2½ cups milk	1 tablespoon vanilla
1½ cups sugar	An unbaked 10" pie shell

Preheat oven to 375 degrees.

Melt margarine into milk in a saucepan over low heat.

In a bowl, add sugar to beaten eggs, then add vanilla. Pour into margarine-milk mixture while still over heat; mix well. Pour into the pie shell. Bake for 10 minutes. Reduce heat to 325 degrees and continue baking for 20 minutes, or until custard is done. Hope you enjoy.

YIELD: 6 servings

BUTTER PECAN ICE CREAM

JANET CULLEY OYLER

Most Southerners love our native pecans in dishes of many types. I created this recipe to share at a church ice cream social. What could be more Southern! The ice cream is rich, creamy, and packs much more flavor than the standard supermarket brands. It is definitely worth the extra effort to share it with friends on a Sunday afternoon. Prepare and chill the mixture the day before to speed up the process.

A 14-ounce can sweetened condensed milk
A 12-ounce can evaporated milk
1 pint half-and-half
¼ cup dark brown sugar
¼ cup dark corn syrup
1 egg, lightly beaten (or ¼ cup egg substitute)
1 cup whipped topping, thawed
½ teaspoon salt
1 teaspoon vanilla
1 teaspoon caramel flavoring
1 teaspoon butter flavoring
1 ½ cups toasted pecans, chopped coarsely

Mix together in a large bowl all the ingredients except the pecans. Chill the mixture in the refrigerator for several hours or overnight. Then freeze it in an ice cream freezer according to the manufacturer's instructions. Toward the end of the freezing process, add in the chopped pecans and finish freezing. Place finished ice cream in a refrigerator freezer for a couple of hours to finish firming.

YIELD: About 2 quarts

FRIED APPLE PIES

JILL MCCORKLE

When I was growing up, I loved to sleep over at my Gramma's house as often as possible. She lived just on the other side of town and yet it was like traveling to a different place and time entirely. Her house was all about quiet comforts: featherbeds and a front porch glider and the best food I have ever eaten in my life.

My favorite memory is one my sister and I both lived many times. We lie snuggled in my Gramma's featherbed at dawn. She is already up and in the kitchen. I can smell coffee which she lets me—even at five—drink. I drink half coffee and half cream and I dip soft buttered toast down into it. But first I have to get from the bed across the cold floors to the kerosene heater in her breakfast room. There I will find my clothes hanging on a little rocking chair, all warmed up.

When the sun finally comes up, my Gramma has had her coffee and is busy in the kitchen. Her upright mixer whirrs nonstop. She whips cream and fills the glass refrigerator containers that we will sneak to all day long. She stirs up a pound cake, the red-and-white polka dot FireKing mixing bowl full of the best batter on earth. She rolls out thin strips of pastry to cook with chicken and she fries okra and country ham. All morning she is in there cooking what will make a huge Sunday dinner while my sister and I watch Sky King and Roy Rogers and try not to stuff ourselves with all the penny candy we always buy from the little store across the street: Kits and candy cigarettes, wax bottles filled with sugary syrup, Mary Janes and Squirrel Nut Zippers.

But we always saved room. Because of all the wonderful things my Gramma made, the very best was her fried apple pies. A pie or two and we were laid out for a nice long nap. The recipe is one I tried to figure out for the longest time—my Gramma had no real recipes it seemed; she just made things. I know that the pies were made with biscuit dough and then

Novelist Jill McCorkle, a native of Lumberton, N.C., wrote her first story, *The Night Santa Failed to Come*, when she was in the second grade.

225

she spooned in apples and cinnamon that she had cooked just that morning. Of course in a pinch, in the later years, she would also break open a can of biscuit dough and spoon in applesauce. Somehow whatever she touched was delicious.

If you can find Roy Rogers on television, you might enjoy watching while eating these pies, otherwise you should just eat—and eat.

FOR THE FILLING:

About 2 pounds of apples, peeled and diced
1 teaspoon cinnamon
¼ cup sugar
¼ cup brown sugar

FOR THE PASTRY:

3 cups flour, plus extra for rolling out the dough
2 teaspoons sugar
1 ½ teaspoons salt
¼ teaspoon baking powder
6 tablespoons lard
1 egg
¾ cup milk or less
Oil or shortening for frying

First, you want to boil the apples—any kind will do—with the cinnamon, sugar and brown sugar. Once boiling, simmer until apples are soft.

For the pastry, mix together the dry ingredients, then cut in the lard. In a separate bowl, mix the egg and milk together, then slowly blend into the dry ingredients. You will get a thick, sticky dough. Divide into twelve pieces. Use flour on rolling pin to roll it out as you would biscuits, then spoon in some of the filling, fold over and crimp the edges with a fork.

Heat oil or shortening in a frying pan and then fry the pies until golden brown, then drain on paper towels. They can be sprinkled with powdered sugar, or eaten with ice cream.

YIELD: 12 individual pies

FUDGY CHOCOLATE PIE ("PMS PIE")

GAYLE KELLY GARRISON

When you have to have some chocolate and have it quickly, this is the pie to make. It is intensely chocolate and can be made in a hurry. My daughter and I used to call it PMS Pie when, each month, we would crave chocolate. I have had the recipe for at least 35 years and have long forgotten where I found it, but I make the pie quite often and serve it with whipped topping and a few raspberries or strawberries. Because it is so rich, it serves 8.

1 stick of butter or margarine (butter preferred)
¾ cup sugar
⅓ cup cocoa powder
¼ cup flour
2 eggs
1 teaspoon vanilla
Whipped cream and berries for topping

Preheat oven to 350 degrees. Grease a 9" glass pie plate and set aside.

Melt butter, add sugar, cocoa and flour, then mix. Add eggs one at a time, beating after each egg. Add vanilla. Pour into prepared pie plate. Bake for 15 minutes. The center will not look firm, but will become firm after pie cools. Top with whipped cream and a few berries, if desired.

YIELD: 8 servings

GRANDMA'S CREAM PIE

SHEILA FREEZE

HINT

This recipe makes one perfect pie, but can be doubled without fear. The cream base accepts drained canned fruits, drained fresh fruits, coconut, and chocolate without failure.

Back before the Depression, my Grandma and Grandpa Copple owned and operated a small café in their hometown of Sedan, Kansas. The Copple Café, strategically located next to the corner drugstore on Main Street, was a common meeting place for town folks as well as travelers. Over a home cooked meal or dessert, men and women gossiped, traded crop information, and bartered and bought horses and cattle.

Tasty short order cooking was the forte of the Copples, and tongue tickling desserts were Grandma's specialty. Fresh fruit and berry pies and cobblers delighted summer appetites, and during the cold Midwestern winters cream pies warmed a diner's palate.

Grandma perfected her recipe for the ideal cream pie filling with the help of her five daughters, Meomia, Muriel, Menifee (my mother), Marjorie and Myrna. When they gave this version their "Clean Spoon Award," Grandma wrote the recipe in ink and glued it into her recipe book, never to be changed again. It has been a family favorite for five succeeding generations.

¾ cup sugar, heaping
⅛ teaspoon salt
⅓ cup flour, heaping
2 eggs, well-beaten
2 cups milk, scalded
2 tablespoons butter or margarine
½ teaspoon vanilla
Prepared pie shell
Whipped cream or meringue for topping

In a saucepan, combine sugar, salt, flour and eggs. Over medium heat, add milk slowly, stirring constantly until you reach a full boil. Reduce to a simmer and add butter and vanilla (*and chocolate, coconut, or other additions). Stir until just blended and pour immediately into any prepared pie shell. Chill at least two hours before serving. May be topped with either whipped cream or meringue.

YIELD: 8 servings

* For chocolate pie: Add two squares of your favorite semi-sweet.
For banana pie: Line crust with bananas and mix $1/2$ cup chopped bananas to the prepared cream filling. Add a touch of cinnamon or liqueur for added flavor.
For coconut pie: Add 1 cup shredded coconut; toast $1/4$ cup coconut in oven at 300 degrees for 5 to 7 minutes and sprinkle over topping.
For bowtie pie: Add 1 teaspoon rum, amaretto or your favorite liqueur to filling and 1 cup chocolate chips, stirring until just blended.

Southerners are particular about their peaches. Here are two favorite family recipes that have stood the test of time.

THE HOBSON FAMILY'S PEACH COBBLER

LINDA WHITNEY HOBSON

Peaches are native to China. Traders brought them west by way of Persia, where these fragrant and versatile fruits were known as Persian Apples!

Sometimes I drive down to Ferguson's fruit stand on Route 1 in Moore County, just over the line from Lee County to buy small, sweet peaches for this cobbler recipe.

The recipe was given to me by my former mother-in-law, Miriam Brevard Tuttle Hobson, on August 16, 1968, and was really part of my "cuisine trousseau." Miriam Hobson was the daughter of a revered Methodist minister, graduated from Greensboro College in the early 1930s, and became a marvelous, intuitive cook as she baked and cooked for church activities, three children, and a husband, Fred Hobson, in Yadkinville for sixty years before her death in February 1994. She was a great lady and a kind teacher of baking and cooking for this fish-out-of-water new bride in the late '60s and '70s. Miriam and Fred Hobson lived in town, but they kept up, on the lot behind their house, a half-acre garden of figs, apples, peaches, and more healthy, growing vegetables sprouting up out of fertile ground than I, a city girl from Ohio, had ever seen together in one place.

1 stick of butter
1 cup sugar
1 cup flour
1 cup milk

2 teaspoons baking powder

1 teaspoon salt

2 cups peaches, peeled, sliced and sprinkled with ¼ cup sugar

Preheat oven to 350 degrees.

Put the butter in a casserole dish and place in the oven until butter is melted. Remove from oven and let cool.

In a medium bowl, mix together the sugar, flour, milk, baking powder and salt. Batter will be slightly lumpy.

Put the peaches into the dish, then pour in the batter. Bake uncovered for 40 to 45 minutes, then increase heat to 400 and bake for 5 minutes more. Remove from oven and let cool until just warm. Then spoon into bowls, and pour milk or cream over the cobbler.

YIELD: 6 to 8 servings

HINT

Here's the change I made because of my busy, postmodern life: it is OK not to peel the peaches! Just wash about 6 peaches, then cut them up, and sugar them in a bowl—takes about 5 minutes. Now the rest is easy! Also, you can reduce the sugar to 3/4 cup, salt to 1/2 teaspoon, and butter to 1/2 stick if you like, but do not substitute margarine.

BETTY TERRES' PEACH COBBLER

BETTY BAKER TERRES

More than 50 years ago, a neighbor walked to my house down a road in Gaston County. Back then, houses weren't so close together and the roads were dirt.

She brought us a peach cobbler she had made. Later, I asked her for the recipe. I don't know where she got it, but she shared it with us, and I have been making this cobbler ever since—for my family, for church dinners, and for our senior citizens' meetings.

My husband and I, soon to be married 54 years, still live in the same house. I have copies of the recipe made that I give to anyone who asks. I think the secret to making this cobbler is the cup of boiling water. You can also make fresh strawberry or blueberry cobblers from this same recipe. If you try it, I think you'll agree.

A 1-pound, 13-ounce can of peaches, drained; or fresh
    peaches, peeled and sliced
3 tablespoons soft butter or margarine
¾ cup sugar for batter
1 cup self-rising flour
½ cup milk
½ cup sugar for topping
1 tablespoon cornstarch
1 cup boiling water

Preheat oven to 350 degrees. Butter or grease a square baking dish and set aside. Put the peaches in the dish (if you are using fresh peaches, use enough to cover the bottom of the dish).

In a bowl, cream together the butter and ¾ cup sugar, then blend in the flour and milk. Spread batter over fruit.

Combine the remaining ½ cup sugar and the cornstarch and sprinkle over the batter. Add 1 cup boiling water over top, then bake 1 hour or until brown.

YIELD: About 8 servings

CRYSTAL'S OATMEAL FRIENDSHIP COOKIES

AMY STALLINGS

Crystal was an African-American classmate of mine when we were in ninth grade at Kennedy Junior High in Charlotte, North Carolina. The year was 1971, and the kids in my neighborhood were bused to the formerly all-black school. I was scared. I had few friends anyway, and most of them were to remain at my old school.

Crystal and Wanda were the only two African Americans in my advanced English class. Thank goodness they chose to take me under their wings, because the three of us were assigned an English project that required time outside the classroom. My mother called both sets of parents to arrange a time for Crystal and Wanda to come to our house. We drove to Dalton Village, a public housing project, to pick them up. Crystal brought us these huge oatmeal cookies. Man, they were good. And this was the first "big cookie" I had ever seen. We spent a pleasant afternoon together and Wanda was particularly amused by my Siamese cat. She had never seen one.

When we drove the girls back down West Boulevard to Dalton Village, I noticed at a stoplight that the men in the car next to us were looking at us, staring fiercely. On the way back to our house, I asked Momma if she had noticed. She said yes, some people are ignorant and prejudiced. But she said we'd just had a good afternoon, because many parents and kids, black and white, would never want to visit each other—or be welcomed in each other's homes.

I've seen Crystal a few times since we've become adults. She's still radiant with a contagious laugh and bright smile. Her recipe for cookies is a reminder of those days in the 1970s, when the friendship she offered went against the tide. The lesson that Crystal and Wanda taught me is that ours is the most important kind of friendship to have.

1 cup shortening

2 cups brown sugar

2 eggs

2 cups all purpose flour

1 teaspoon baking soda

1 teaspoon salt

2 cups oatmeal (not instant)

Preheat oven to 350 degrees. Line baking sheet with aluminum foil, grease and set aside.

In a large bowl, combine the shortening, sugar and eggs. Blend until creamy. Then add the flour, baking soda, salt and oatmeal and mix until well blended. The dough will be thick.

For smaller cookies, roll into balls and place on the cookie sheet. For larger cookies, pat the dough flat. Allow space between the cookies. Bake on middle shelf of oven for 10 minutes for a chewier cookie, 12 minutes for a crisper cookie.

YIELD: About 2 dozen

ERNIE'S POUND CAKE

ANNE C. BARNHILL

My grandfather, Ernest Ballad of Lincolnton, North Carolina, died two months shy of his 101st birthday. Until his late nineties, he made a most delicious pound cake whenever family members came to visit. He and my grandmother, Gwen, lived for sixty years in the c.1930 house they built, and they had frequent guests—their three daughters, grandchildren, and great-grandchildren; neighbors and cousins. All were treated to a slice of "Ernie's Pound Cake" at each visit.

He would spend the whole day preparing his specialty, taking all the time he needed so the cake would turn out just right. I recall the ingredients had to be at room temperature, and I can still see him beating the batter by hand for what seemed like hours.

When he passed along his recipe to my mother, Virginia Clinard, she inherited the mantle with pride. He whispered a few of his secrets in her ear, and my mother is now the family pound-cake expert, though she keeps the secrets. She won a "Judge's Choice" award for the cake a couple of years ago and still gets rave reviews whenever she takes the cake to church socials.

I can still smell the light, lemony aroma of baking pound cake. Each slice is moist with a crunchy edge along the top, my favorite part. It's the kind of cake you eat with a fork because you don't want to miss even one savory crumb. I'm not much of a baker, but I suppose I'd better learn the secrets soon and start practicing.

1 stick butter
1 cup Crisco shortening
3 cups sugar
5 eggs
3 cups flour
1 teaspoon baking powder

1 cup milk
1 teaspoon vanilla extract
1 teaspoon lemon extract

Have all ingredients at room temperature. Preheat oven to 350 degrees. Grease a tube pan and set aside.

In a large bowl, cream together the butter, shortening and sugar until light and fluffy. Beat in the eggs, one at a time and blend well after each addition.

In a separate bowl, stir together the flour and baking powder. Add the flour mixture to the butter mixture, alternately with the milk, stirring well after each addition. Then stir in the vanilla and lemon extracts.

Pour into prepared pan and bake for about 1 hour and 5 minutes, or until a tester inserted into the center of the cake comes out clean. Remove from oven, cool on rack and invert pan to remove.

YIELD: About 12 servings

AUNT SUSIE'S RED AND GREEN JELL-O

LYNN VEACH SADLER

We never visited my Aunt Susie (Mrs. Andrew) Miller, who lived between Kenansville and Beulaville, near Hallsville, in Duplin County, North Carolina, without her serving red and green Jell-O for dessert. She made plain whipped cream for the children, and syllabub for the adults.

The word "syllabub" is Elizabethan. It originally referred to a drink made of wine and milk, with sugar and egg whites sometimes added.

- 1 package red Jell-O brand gelatin
- 1 package green Jell-O brand gelatin
- 1 carton of whipping cream
- Sugar to taste
- Sherry or homemade wine, optional

Prepare each package of gelatin according to the directions. Place in separate containers and chill until set. Whip the cream, adding sugar to taste. If it is to become syllabub, lace it with sherry or homemade wine.

Serve spoonfuls of red and green Jell-O side by side in champagne flutes or cut-glass bowls. Spoon the whipped cream or syllabub over the top.

YIELD: 6 to 8 servings

LEMON SHERBET

REBECCA SCHENCK

"Sorbet" isn't just a fancy way of saying "sherbet." Both are made of frozen fruit or juice, but sherbet can contain milk. Sorbet doesn't.

I can't reproduce my mother's roll dough or, therefore, the cinnamon buns that even my eighth-grade boyfriend still remembers; but I can and do make the lemon sherbet that Mother made in a deep ice tray in our refrigerator. Because Mother died long before her older sister, I wrote to see whether Aunt Mary could give me the sherbet recipe. The yellowed index card marked with brown spots is in Aunt Mary's handwriting, and she offered on the reverse side of the card another Lemon Milk Sherbet recipe with a notation, "Found this too, but it sounds like work!"

The recipe we use is easy except for the stirring, which should be done often—yes, to keep the sherbet from being icy.

    1 quart sweet milk
    1 ¼ cups sugar
    ½ cup lemon juice
    Grated rind of 1 lemon
    Pinch of salt

Combine all ingredients, stir well and pour into old-fashioned ice trays or a metal loaf pan.

"Mix and put in freezing compartment. Take out and beat when partially frozen and return. This keeps it from being icy, (I think)."

—Aunt Mary

YIELD: About 8 servings

MORAVIAN SUGAR CAKE

RICK MCDANIEL

The Moravians are a German-Protestant church whose members settled in Bethabara, near present day Winston-Salem, North Carolina. This is a favorite food gift throughout the state.

1 package dry yeast	1 teaspoon salt
½ cup warm water	2 eggs, beaten
1 cup hot, unseasoned mashed potatoes	5 to 6 cups sifted flour
1 cup sugar	Brown sugar
½ cup shortening	Butter
¼ cup butter, softened	Cinnamon

Dissolve yeast in warm water and set aside. In a large bowl, mix together the mashed potatoes, sugar, shortening, butter, and salt. Add yeast mixture and stir until blended. Cover mixing bowl and set aside to rise in a warm place until spongy.

Stir in eggs and enough sifted flour to make a soft dough. Shape dough into a ball and place in a greased bowl, turning to grease the top. Cover and allow to rise until doubled in bulk, about 2 hours.

Grease 2 baking pans, 13 x 9 x 2" and set aside.

Turn dough onto a lightly floured surface and knead 5 minutes or until smooth and elastic. Divide dough in half and spread evenly in the prepared pans. Set aside to rise again.

Preheat oven to 375 degrees. When dough has doubled in bulk, use your fingers to make holes 1 ½" to 2" apart all over the dough. Fill holes with brown sugar and generous pieces of butter. Sprinkle cinnamon over entire cake. Bake for 20 minutes or until golden brown.

YIELD: 2 cakes

HINT
Because of the size of the cake, it is usually cut in halves to wrap for giving. Cakes can be frozen and reheated for serving.

THE BEST BLUEBERRY DESSERT

Amy Rogers

Of the countless meals and memories we share throughout our lives, those we cherish most are often remarkable not for their extravagance, but for their simplicity. My mother, Elaine Rogers, knew this.

Back before gelato or Godiva entered our lives, we had full-fat milk in frosty bottles delivered to our doorsteps. Butter was so luminous that nothing else could even approximate its color. Fruit so endearing in its variations, no two pears or apples or berries were alike in size, shape, or hue.

Now, of course, the too-small peaches never make it to the market. Thin-skinned, green-spotted oranges full of sweet juice are passed over so we can purchase their bright, pulpy cousins. And all the grapes have become seedless.

Still, there are ways to recapture the pleasure of biting into the first Early Girl or the last Macintosh of the season. Each summer when I was a child, my mother prepared a rich yet effortless blueberry dessert that remains my favorite to this day. I can still picture her in the kitchen of our little split-level house on Long Island. She's wearing her summer ensemble of white slacks, a sleeveless top, and sunglasses on top of her head, where she's left them after coming home from shopping at the farm stand nearby.

    1 pint of blueberries, chilled
    1 small container of sour cream
    1 handful or more of brown sugar

Wash and drain the blueberries. Put them into a pretty glass bowl, or divide them into individual serving bowls. Top the berries with sour cream, then sprinkle generously with the brown sugar.

YIELD: 2 servings, enough for one mother and daughter

MARLOW SQUARES

LIANE CROWE DAVENPORT

I have been cooking practically since I was able to reach the counter, thanks to my mother, who wanted me to feel comfortable in the kitchen, no matter how messy it would be in the beginning. I felt comfortable pretty quickly, but I've never really overcome the messy part—oh well.

Growing up, I must have eaten hundreds of Marlow Squares at my dad's mom's house. My grandmother finally wrote the recipe down in December, 1982, so I could make them, too.

The name of this dessert is a play on words from one of the ingredients: marsh-mallows.

- 1 packet graham crackers
- 1 package miniature marshmallows
- 1 package dates, chopped
- 1 large package pecans, chopped (about 4 cups)
- 2 cups evaporated milk
- 1 large container candied cherries, chopped

Grease a 9 x 12" baking dish. Crush graham crackers into very fine crumbs. Sprinkle a coating of crumbs into the bottom of the dish; reserve the rest.

Combine the remaining ingredients, mixing well. Pour the mixture on top of graham cracker crumbs. Top mixture with remaining crumbs. Refrigerate for several hours before serving.

YIELD: 12 to 15

Warning: These are very rich!

BISCUIT-PAN CAKE WITH FUDGE ICING

DEBORAH CUTSHALL

My mother-in-law Mary Sanders Cutshall, born in 1915 in the Madison County mountains of North Carolina, was the mother of ten children and a terrific cook. This recipe is a homemade cake she put together. It was made in a biscuit pan and the hot chocolate icing she poured over it would run into the cracks and deep into the corners. Everyone wanted a corner with its thick, fudge-like candy icing.

Mrs. Cutshall baked this cake for everyday, and always on special occasions. She passed on before I had the pleasure to know her, but her daughters gave me the recipes she used to make. Now I bake her same delicious cakes on special occasions and always on my husband's birthday. And as always, people still hurry to get a corner piece.

FOR THE CAKE:

1 stick margarine	1 cup milk
2 cups self-rising flour	2 eggs
1 cup sugar	1 teaspoon vanilla

Preheat oven to 350 degrees. Melt margarine in a 9 x 13" pan. In a bowl, mix together the other ingredients. Pour the melted margarine into batter and blend in. Pour into pan. Bake for 20 minutes or until done.

FOR THE ICING:

2 cups sugar	½ stick margarine
6 tablespoons cocoa	1 teaspoon vanilla
½ cup milk	

Combine the sugar, cocoa and milk in a saucepan and bring to a boil. Cook until it reaches the soft ball stage (234 degrees on a candy thermometer). Remove from heat. Add the margarine and vanilla; stir about 5 minutes or until it starts to thicken, then pour over cake after it has cooled about 20 to 30 minutes.

YIELD: About 12 servings

PECAN CHIFFON PIE

HELEN S. MOORE

It was a hot August afternoon in 1975, and my kitchen was awash in freshly made pecan chiffon pies. The tempting fragrance of toasted pecans and bubbling dark brown sugar was still in the air. Some of the pies had fillings that were too soft or not made with enough pecans and the recipe was adjusted a bit more.

Smoothing whipped cream over the last of the light, nutty pies, retired baker, Dolores Stowe of Charlotte, nodded her approval.

"This looks like my old pies," she said with a smile. Stowe, who could make desserts in her sleep, had not made a pecan chiffon pie since her retirement in 1972 after working 26 years as S.H. Kress's pie baker. (Long-time area residents remember the S.H. Kress, a large variety store on the square at South Tryon and East Trade streets, where The Omni Charlotte hotel now stands.) The melt-in-the-mouth pecan chiffon pie at the Kress lunch counter brought in hordes of steady customers. Many wanted to know how to make the pie.

"A lot of times people asked for the recipe, but we weren't allowed to give it out," recalled Stowe in my 1975 *Charlotte Observer* article. "They offered to pay us so much if we'd slip it to them, but we thought our job was worth more than that little bit of money."

The pie, made from a closely guarded secret recipe, was an institution for years with S. H. Kress and with customers all over both Carolinas who were almost addicted to the meringue-type dessert.

Gradually, over the years the price of the pie climbed and sales slumped. Finally the company dropped the dessert from their menu in 1972. But memory of the delicious meringue-type pie still lived on with former customers and their families.

The pie-making episode with Stowe was the result of a Tell-It Line request that came into the newspaper while I was out of town on a two-week vacation. In my absence, Kress's regional headquarters in Atlanta was contacted by another *Observer* reporter who asked for the recipe. The company agreed to share the pie recipe with the public for the first time and it was printed. However, when the ingredients were downsized from 30 pies to two pies, the proportions were skewed. Adjusting quantity recipes can be tricky.

The first day back after vacation I walked into the newsroom and was surprised when two editors rushed toward me. Handing me a sheet of paper, one said, "Here—find out what's wrong with this recipe. We have had 125 calls about it."

That was my introduction to pecan chiffon pie. Since I had never tasted the pie, I felt it was necessary to locate one of the original cooks who could reconstruct the pie proportions the way it was meant to be made. Stowe was a delightful lady who graciously agreed to help and the result was gratefully applauded. Pecan chiffon pie is a delicious and most unusual dessert, possibly developed from a very old recipe. After all the work, I was happy we could offer the corrected, original recipe to readers. Over the years the recipe has appeared in many community cookbooks.

In the 1970s, no one worried about using raw eggs or partially cooked eggs in dishes. Since then, the possibility of salmonella in raw eggs and egg whites brings a sense of caution. To be on the safe side, use pasteurized egg whites in this pie, especially if it is served to the young, the elderly or anyone with a compromised immune system.

And as one well-known radio personality always adds, "Now you know the rest of the story."

1 cup coarsely chopped pecans, toasted
1 cup dark brown sugar
1 ⅓ cups plus 2 tablespoons water
4 tablespoons cornstarch
¼ cup water
⅔ cup egg whites, at room temperature
¼ cup granulated sugar
Two 8" or 9" baked pie shells
½ pint chilled whipping cream
¼ teaspoon vanilla, optional

To toast, spread pecans on a baking sheet and bake at 250 to 275 degrees for 10 to 15 minutes or until nuts barely begin to brown. (Take out a few, let them cool and taste them. The toasted nuts should have a richer, more pronounced nutty flavor.) Watch nuts carefully so they don't burn.

Combine brown sugar and 1⅓ cups plus 2 tablespoons water. Bring to a boil.

Mix together cornstarch and ¼ cup water and stir with a whisk, into the boiling brown sugar mixture. Stir constantly and cook until the mixture becomes clear and is the consistency of a thick pudding. Remove mixture from heat.

Whip egg whites at high speed of electric mixer until peaks form. Slowly add ¼ cup sugar and beat until peaks are stiff. Reduce mixer speed to low and gently add the hot brown sugar mixture and nuts. As soon as everything is blended, cut off mixer. Do not overmix.

Pile filling lightly into baked pie shells. (You will have higher, prettier pies if you use 8" pie shells for this recipe.)

Whip cream until stiff. The original recipe doesn't call for it, but you might want to add a ¼ teaspoon of vanilla. Divide whipped cream and spread over both pies. If desired, sprinkle a few additional finely chopped nuts over top for garnish. Refrigerate for 1 to 2 hours.

YIELD: 2 pies, 6 to 8 servings each

HINT
This pie is best served the same day it is made, but it can be kept overnight in the refrigerator.

Carolinians are particular about their persimmons. Here are two recipes, one that contains eggs and one without. Both are family favorites.

PERSIMMON PUDDING

VICKI WHITE-LAWRENCE

Don't try to snack on an under-ripe persimmon. It will make your mouth "pucker!"

This recipe has been passed down from my father's side of the family and is a compilation of several recipes. I remember enjoying it as a child at our annual family reunions in the fall. My two sons have obviously inherited my appreciation for this fine southern delicacy.

As they each were old enough to realize what could be created by the luscious fruit they helped pick up from the ground, they would beg me to tell them when we'd do it again. My youngest even took a sample of persimmon pudding for each of his classmates for his "Show and Tell" project in his first grade class. He told me he was sure they'd want a lot of money for it at the grocery store, and he was amazed when I told him I'd never seen it for sale in a grocery store!

Every time we have persimmon pudding, my mind is flooded with memories of warm fall afternoons picking up persimmons with my son after meeting him at his bus stop.

1 quart persimmons
3 tablespoons butter, melted
1 ½ cups sugar
3 whole eggs, beaten
2 cups plain flour
½ teaspoon baking soda
1 teaspoon nutmeg
1 teaspoon cinnamon
1 ¾ cups sweet milk
1 teaspoon vanilla

Preheat oven to 325 degrees. Grease a 13 x 9 x 2" baking dish and set aside.

Wash persimmons and pulp them through a colander. Seeds and skins will come off.

In a large bowl, mix together the butter and sugar; add eggs. In another bowl, combine the dry ingredients. To the butter-sugar mixture, alternately add the dry ingredients, milk and pulp. Beat slowly, then stir in the vanilla. Pour into the prepared pan, a little over ½ to ⅔ full. Bake about 1 hour or until a tester comes out clean and the center is firm.

YIELD: About 10 servings

GRANDMA'S PERSIMMON PUDDING

PEGGY J. RIDDLE

This recipe was handed down from my Grandmother Rosa Riddle to her daughter-in-law, Gertrude Riddle. My grandmother baked it in a wood stove. The home place had a very small kitchen and a large dining room where we ate home-cooked meals together. Most of the things my grandmother cooked were from handwritten notes. At the onset of fall, a tree in the backyard blossomed with orange orbs that would produce this golden delicacy. Thanks to Grandma Riddle, this pudding is one of our favorite desserts and has been enjoyed by five generations.

2½ cups all-purpose flour	1 cup butter
1 teaspoon baking soda	2 cups sugar
½ teaspoon baking powder	2 cups persimmon pulp
1 teaspoon cinnamon	1 cup sweet milk
1 teaspoon ginger	1 cup buttermilk
½ teaspoon ground allspice	

Preheat oven to 350 degrees. For thin squares, use a 12 x 17" jellyroll pan; for thicker squares, use a 9 x 12" inch pan.

Sift together flour, baking soda, baking powder, cinnamon, ginger and allspice; set aside. Melt butter in the pan you will use for baking; be sure the pan is coated.

Put the sugar into a large bowl, then pour in the butter that you melted in the baking pan. Add the persimmon pulp. Alternately add the flour mixture and milks to the persimmon mixture. Pour batter into prepared pan. Bake 1 hour. Will be nice and brown and pull away from edge of pan. Cool before cutting into squares.

YIELD: Depending on pan size, 12 to 20 squares

ONE-BOWL BUTTER-SCOTCH BROWNIES

Amy Rogers

These are so easy, they're dangerous. You can add peanut butter chips, chocolate chips, coconut or anything else you crave.

- 4 squares unsweetened baker's chocolate
- ¾ cup butter or margarine, but not low-fat spreads
- 2 cups sugar
- 3 eggs
- 1 teaspoon vanilla extract
- 1 cup all-purpose flour
- 1 ½ cups coarsely chopped walnuts or pecans
- 2 cups mini-marshmallows
- 1 cup butterscotch morsels

Preheat oven to 350 degrees. Grease an oblong baking dish (the one I use is 9 x 13") and set aside.

In a large saucepan on low heat, melt together the unsweetened baker's chocolate and the butter or margarine. Turn off the heat, but leave the pan on the stove while you stir in the sugar, then the eggs and vanilla extract. Stir in the flour and half of the nuts. Spread mixture into the pan and bake for 35 minutes. Remove from oven and resist the temptation to dig in—we're not finished yet!

Immediately sprinkle with the rest of the nuts, the marshmallows and the butterscotch morsels. Return the pan to the oven and bake for 3 to 5 minutes, and watch until you see the toppings start to melt. Remove from oven and cool before slicing.

YIELD: 15 large squares or 24 little ones

MUR'S CHOCOLATE CAKE

CAREN MCNELLY MCCORMACK

If a recipe calls for buttermilk, you can substitute sour milk. To make 1 cup, put 1 tablespoon of white vinegar or lemon juice in a measuring cup, then fill to the 1-cup mark with milk.

"If there ever were to be a feud in this family, it would be started over a cake pan," my Aunt Kitty once quipped in a moment of family insight. My aunt probably never realized her perceptiveness. *The* cake pan, and *the* recipe for the fudgy cake that goes with it, are as much a source of family definition as our Scottish roots. We bake this cake in the same pan for almost every special occasion.

The family treasure is a deep, silvery hunk, slightly larger than a regular sheet pan. Originally sold as an aluminum griddle, it weighs two to three times what today's pans weigh. No wonder it lends stability and continuity to the family. So far the pan has slipped from my great-grandmother, to my grandmother, whom we called Mur, to my mother (an only daughter). And since I'm the only daughter, I'm hoping that someday this pan will pass to me without incident. Maybe my aunt was right about the power of this pan. If my brothers want to get their hands on it, I'll say, "Let the feud begin."

FOR THE CAKE:

½ cup vegetable shortening (such as Crisco brand)

1 ¾ cups sugar

2 eggs

8 tablespoons cocoa, mixed with about 7 tablespoons hot coffee (or instant coffee and hot water); the mixture should have the consistency of toothpaste

2 cups + 2 tablespoons cake flour

¼ teaspoon salt

1 teaspoon baking soda

1 cup buttermilk or sour milk

1 teaspoon vanilla

Preheat oven to 325 degrees. Grease a 9 x 11 x 2" baking pan and set aside.

Using an electric mixer on medium speed, cream shortening and sugar. Then add eggs, one at a time, beating until smooth after each egg. Add the cocoa-coffee paste to the creamed mixture, beating until combined.

In a separate bowl, sift together the flour, salt and soda. Add the dry ingredients to the wet mixture, mixing alternately with sour milk. Stir in vanilla.

Bake for 25 minutes or until cake feels firm and springy to the touch. Cool cake completely on a wire rack.

HINT
Use a heavy or air-bake pan if possible. A thinner pan will result in a dry cake.

FOR THE ICING:

2 cups sugar
1 stick butter
2 heaping tablespoons cocoa
½ cup milk
1 teaspoon vanilla

In a medium saucepan, mix all ingredients and bring to full rolling boil. Boil for exactly 1 minute. Remove from heat and pour into mixing bowl. Beat at high speed for 4 to 5 minutes. Pour the icing on the cooled cake. It will be thin at this point but will harden to a fudge-like consistency once it cools.

YIELD: About 12 servings

CHOCOLATE-FILLED COOKIES FROM MARY MORINA'S KITCHEN

GILDA MORINA SYVERSON

My Italian mother is known for the variety of cookies that she makes. They have names like Mom's Plain White cookies, Chocolate Roll Ups, Almond Paste, Seven-Layer, Anise, and Snowball Dainties. When I go home to Syracuse at Christmas, I always return to North Carolina with a batch or two of her cookies. You could find some in my freezer today.

Although I've periodically made some of my mother's cookies, I don't do so as often as she does. They take a lot of time and energy. I guess I put that creative vigor into my artwork. My mother's creativity and mine came together when I had my first one-person art exhibit. My mother offered to do my reception, and I was delighted when she showed up with at least twelve types of cookies. My large wall hangings were a backdrop to an assortment of sweets that people swooned over.

When I proudly told her that I'd loved sharing my first opening with her, she shied back into the kitchen. There she whipped up another batch of cookies like an artist creating a commission for her patrons.

FOR THE COOKIES:

5 cups flour

1 ¾ cups sugar

4 heaping teaspoons baking powder

1 ¼ cups shortening

4 eggs

1 ¼ teaspoons vanilla

¼ cup milk

FOR THE FILLING:

1 can sweetened condensed milk
12 ounces chocolate chips
Confectioners sugar

Preheat oven to 350 degrees. Grease a 10 x 15" cookie sheet and set aside.

In a large bowl, mix together first three ingredients; cut in shortening. In a separate bowl, combine the eggs, vanilla and milk. Make a well the middle of the dry ingredients, add the wet and mix well. Divide in two. Roll out one into an oblong shape and place on the cookie sheet.

Warm the condensed milk in a saucepan but don't let it boil. Add the chocolate chips. Heat just until melted, then spread over the rolled out dough. Then roll out the remaining dough and place over the first layer.

Bake for 30 minutes. When cooled, sprinkle with confectioners sugar. Cut into squares.

YIELD: About 5 dozen

A CRAVING FOR SOMETHING SWEET

Amy Rogers

An Englishman who lived in North Carolina was spending the summer working with his American wife in Tuscany. On his birthday, he became homesick for a favorite dessert. His friends in the States knew this, so when they traveled to see him they packed into their suitcase a can of condensed milk and a plastic, lime-shaped container of juice.

When the friends arrived, they bought cookies and butter and cream at the local grocery store. When no one was looking, the friends mixed up the pie filling, crushed the cookies, melted the butter and whipped the cream by hand. They assembled a pie and hid it in the tiny refrigerator at the house they all shared.

That night, after a dinner of pan-roasted vegetables and pasta, they made espresso and served the Key lime pie. "*Felice compleanno*," they exclaimed. Although the cream had begun to separate and the crust was much too crumbly, everyone agreed—it was one of the best meals they had ever enjoyed together.

NO-BAKE KEY LIME PIE OR PARFAITS

2 cups crushed graham cracker crumbs, plus 1 stick butter, melted; or 1 prepared graham cracker pie crust

1 can sweetened condensed milk
½ cup Key lime juice
Whipped cream
Fresh raspberries for garnish

If you are making the crust, combine the graham cracker crumbs and butter and press into the bottom of a pie pan.

In a bowl, mix the condensed milk with the Key lime juice until well-blended. It will begin to thicken; pour into the pie shell. Chill several hours before serving, then slice and top with whipped cream and garnish with raspberries.

YIELD: 6 servings

Key limes are yellow, not green. Found mostly in Florida, they are small and round. Real Key lime pie should be yellow, too. The large, elongated green limes are called Persian limes.

HINT
If you are in a hurry—or if the crust crumbles—just press a handful of crumbs into the bottom of a parfait glass or wine goblet. Then proceed with the recipe as above.

HUNGRY FOR HOME

OLD SOUTH FRUITCAKE

REBECCA ADAMS FRY

My mother has used this recipe all my life. My godmother shared it with her from the Civil War times. My godmother died at 98 years old in 1961. Mom and I have carried this recipe on and we bake it just after Thanksgiving. We give it as gifts or share with the family. It's moist and good—better than any I've ever tasted.

½ pound flour	½ pound green candied pineapple
1 teaspoon cinnamon	½ pound mixed candied citron
1 teaspoon ground cloves	½ pound almonds, chopped
1 teaspoon allspice	½ pound pecans, chopped
½ pound butter	½ pound English walnuts, chopped
½ pound sugar	½ pound Brazil nuts, chopped
6 eggs	1 pound crystallized red cherries
1 pound raisins	1 pound thick strawberry preserves

Preheat oven to 250 degrees. Line 6 loaf pans or 1 large tube pan and 2 loaf pans with foil. Set aside.

Sift flour and spices together. Remove ½ cup of flour and spice mix and set aside.

In a separate bowl, cream butter and sugar. Add one egg at a time, mixing well after each addition. Add flour and spice mix to make a thick batter.

In a very large bowl, mix together raisins, pineapple, citron, almonds, pecans, walnuts, Brazil nuts and cherries. Sift flour that was reserved over the fruits and nuts and mix well. Pour cake batter over the fruits and nuts. Add strawberry preserves. Mix well with two spoons or with hands. Pour batter into pans. Decorate tops with red and green fruits if desired.

Cover completely with foil and bake for 3 hours. Then uncover and bake at 325 degrees for 1 hour. Let cakes cool in pans for 30 minutes. Remove from pans, wrap and store in a cool place for up to one month.

YIELD: This recipe makes 15 pounds of cake

OATMEAL CHOCOLATE-CHIP HEAVEN

LAUREN FAULKENBERRY

I learned a lot of things in art school that have helped me later in life: super glue will bond anything with the exception of roommates, and it's never a good idea to smoke around oil painters; but one of the most useful things I learned was how to make the world's most enchanting chocolate chip cookie. It was born on a cold Saturday night, in a tiny dormitory apartment, when my New Jersey friend declared a Girls' Night In. She'd decided that the ideal remedy for a hard week in the studio was a 5:1 ratio of homemade cookies to sappy movies. I don't generally like such movies, but a starving artist-in-training can often be influenced by decadent promises of chocolate and savory visions of fresh baked goods.

Neither of us could remember our mothers' recipes, so we made one up as we went along, using fragments of childhood memories and scrambled gleanings from cooking shows. We gleefully added a dash of this and a pinch of that, guessing on the flour and salt, and concentrating more on the delicate balance of oatmeal and chocolate chunks. Our sub-gourmet ingredients should have doomed us from the start—a puddle of butter that was nuked in the oven, a brick of brown sugar, and milk that had expired sometime around the last snowfall—but someone in culinary heaven was smiling down on us. We took turns haphazardly tossing things in the bowl, like a couple of mad scientists with a chocolate-chip jones. I laughed, but my friend swore that the secret of the beguiling cookies was to stir with a wooden spoon.

When the cookies were done (baked for exactly eight minutes to preserve the gooey center, yet prevent the spread of salmonella) and the movie had started, there was a knock at the door. We offered the caller a taste of chocolate oatmeal heaven, and before the guy could get the girl and live happily ever after, we'd met every student on the hall, none of whom apparently had eaten that day. We finally left the door ajar in sugary surrender, and by the start of the second movie, the cookies had vanished.

Since then, I've used the bewitching cookies on several occasions when I found myself wanting an ally or needing to cheer up a friend, or when circumstances were so dire that the only antidote involved oatmeal and chocolate chips. Since that cold Saturday night, they've systematically charmed a floor full of freshmen, a roomful of art majors, and countless employers; innumerable teachers, neighbors, and co-workers, and one archaeological field crew. No longer reserved for special occasions, but used for everyday purposes of spreading caloric cheer, they're famous in at least eight states, on both sides of the Mississippi. They've ended fights, started conversations, and prompted two marriage proposals—but everyone knows that relationships based on intense confectionary delight never last.

My New Jersey friend and I still keep each other posted on the latest enchantments of the last great homemade cookie, and this recipe remains, along with its birth among two hapless culinary alchemists, one of my fondest art school memories. Now and then, when no one is watching and I'm overcome by the warm, fuzzy feeling of nostalgia, I pull out the recipe and make a chocolatey toast to the good old days of paints and brushes and sappy movies. I may not remember a lot of things about college, like who taught my English class or who spilled the ink on my project the night before it was due, but I remember the important things. I remember a certain New Jersey friend's guerilla strategies for reversing a bad day, and who was there to bring cookies and happily-ever-after movies when the cute guy from the painting class never called. And, of course, I always remember to stir with a wooden spoon.

1 stick of butter

1 cup brown sugar

½ teaspoon salt

1 teaspoon baking soda

½ teaspoon cinnamon

1 teaspoon vanilla

2 eggs

2½ cups plain flour

2 cups oatmeal

2 tablespoons milk

8 to 12 ounces semi-sweet chocolate chunks (trust me on this)

Preheat oven to 375 degrees. Grease 2 cookie sheets and set aside.

Mix ingredients in the order above, stir with a wooden spoon. The dough should be thick. For large (college-size) cookies, use at least a heaping tablespoon of dough for each cookie. Place on the prepared cookie sheets, about 2" apart, and bake for 8 minutes.

YIELD: 18 to 24 big cookies

WORKING POOR BUT RICH IN BLESSINGS

Amy Rogers

She still remembers her daddy's last words. "Don't let the streets take you over," he pleaded. Temika Black was 22 and pregnant with her second child when her father was shot. She held him in her arms and watched him die.

That was ten years ago, and since then Black has done her best to honor her father's final wishes. She got off the streets, got clean and sober, then found work and set out to make a better life for herself and her children. But as the head of a low-income family, Black understands that the odds are stacked against her, that some days life is "one step up, two steps back."

Today is one of those days. Before lunchtime she's got a bad headache on top of the leftover congestion from a cold. But her food stamp money has arrived, so it's time to do the once-a-month grocery shopping.

At the store, the baby, who's five, rides in the cart. She wants a fancy cake she sees near the store entrance. "Not today," her mother says. There's no price on the bin of loose apples, so Black passes them up and gets the ones that are pre-bagged and marked $2.99. Two large heads of cabbage, 33¢ a pound, go into the cart behind the baby, who can't decide if she wants to ride or walk next to her big sisters. Broccoli, lettuce, peppers. Three pounds of onions are $1.69. Black gets two bags. A $2.99 bag of Yukon gold potatoes is on special for 79¢ with the store's discount card. She puts a bag into her cart.

In denim and sneakers, she looks like all the other moms who are shopping with their kids at the suburban grocery store. She's wearing her hair cropped short. When she smiles, which isn't very often, she's got dimples in both cheeks.

Black reads labels, checks prices, considers which size can or carton is the best value. Plain rice is 69¢ a bag. Raisins, $1.39. Applesauce, fruit cocktail, pickles; baked beans in the family size, $2.79 for 55 ounces. That's just the first two aisles of the store, and by the time Black is finished with her shopping, she will have had to stretch $318 to buy all the food her family will need for the month.

Every low-wage family has its own story, but what the families often have in common is a pattern of poverty, further ingrained into their lives by lack of education, job skills and life skills, all of which get handed down from one generation to the next. Too many disadvantaged families who find employment and housing still can't become functionally self-sufficient. They join the growing numbers of families known as the "working poor."

Far from reluctant to work, Black has been employed for most of her life. At 14, she lied about her age and got a job at a cafeteria, where she worked until twelfth grade. Other low-wage jobs followed: Bi-Lo, Winn Dixie, Burger King, McDonald's.

Once the babies came, finding work that would accommodate the young family's needs only got harder. Even with those jobs that paid better—at a grocery store she earned $9 an hour—Black found it tough to get by. "You finally get stable, but day by day you fall further and further behind."

Regardless of how families get that way, there's no doubt that by definition, "working poor" means struggling for, and often doing without, many of life's essentials. A bus that's late can cost you your job. So can a sick child who needs a parent to care for him. The job-hopping that results isn't so much a choice as a product of those circumstances.

Over the years, Black had begun slipping away into a life on the streets. It got worse when her dad died. "Those were bad times," says Black. Three times she wound up at the shelter with her kids.

That's where she met the pastor of a church that fed families at the shelter the first Saturday of each month. He began to minister to her, and helped her find her way back to church, and to an apartment where church and family members paid the deposit. "I worked at the airport and got paid weekly," but it still wasn't enough to get by, says Black. "I got two months behind."

Just when there seemed to be no hope—when the bills were so badly overdue that utilities were getting turned off—there was a break. It was one Black had almost been afraid to hope for: a job in an office, with her own computer, phone line and work space where she wouldn't have to stand on her feet all day.

"That's always been my dream," she says. "I used to think there was nobody worse off than me. My pastor said, 'There's always somebody worse off. Whatever you're going through, somebody else is going through, too.'"

Even though it's been ten years since he died, Black still talks to her father. On his birthday, she visits the cemetery with her grandparents. Before they get in the car to go home, they put a piece of birthday cake on the grave. "I did exactly what he asked me to do," Black says. "He sees me *now*."

While she dreams of having her own place, for now she and her kids will stay in the apartment complex where they've lived for three years. There's no washer, dryer or dishwasher, but the apartment has air-conditioning and Black has hung lace curtains on the windows and family portraits on the walls.

Her rent is subsidized, but if her income continues to go up, so will her rent. With a recent pay raise, the food stamp money decreased from $436 a month to $318. Regardless, Black states firmly, "Everything is starting to balance out." She has a savings account, and a plastic Bank of America card to prove it. Just having the card in her wallet gives her a good feeling.

On her days off she catches up on her sleep, cleans house, and cooks big family-style Southern meals. Sometimes it's canned salmon fried into patties and served with grits; sometimes it's chicken, greens and potato salad. Last week's trip to the Family Dollar store for the paper goods, toiletries and cleaning supplies you can't buy with food stamps cost $74.80.

The total amount she spends on this grocery shopping trip is $262.96, which includes store discounts of $34.03. Without being told, the kids help unpack and put away the groceries. In the months when she has enough money left over, Black will ride with a friend to a store that sells a pre-priced, $126-package of assorted meats that the family can stretch to last for several weeks.

On this shopping day, it's 3:00 before Black can stop long enough to eat some lunch, and the headache she's had since morning finally starts to loosen its grip. Over a meal of sausage, eggs, potatoes and biscuits, she asks the blessing. "Father God, we thank You for this food…"

Black has no doubt her children can be anything they want when they grow up, and she has no patience for people who are "trifling." "I want my kids to have a better environment, and to know something besides poverty. I don't care if I have to sit on the corner and sell every inch of my body, my children will have what they need."

Asked if she has advice for anyone facing similar struggles, Black doesn't hesitate. The woman who feeds her spirit by placing birthday cake on her father's grave says, "Dry your tears. Put one foot in front of the other. Ask and you will receive. Pray—He is alive. Blessings do come every day." And she has one more word of practical encouragement:

"If you have a roof over your head and canned goods you can make it."

6

Celebrations:
HOLIDAYS AND
SPECIAL OCCASIONS

HAPPY CHANUKAH, Y'ALL

Amy Rogers

It should have been so simple. His family had their holiday traditions and mine had ours. All we would need to do is choose our favorite foods and festivities, blend them together, and there we'd have it: a new holiday tradition that honored both families and both religions.

My husband grew up in South Carolina with presents under the tree on Christmas morning, followed by a feast of turkey, dressing, green beans, and potatoes at noon.

I grew up in Michigan, where we grated potatoes into pancakes called *latkes,* which my mother fried in oil, then served with applesauce. At sundown we lit one Chanukah candle each night for eight nights, and opened one gift every evening in a drawn-out ritual that made plenty of Jewish kids envy their Christian friends who got to indulge in a one-day frenzy of presents.

It didn't get any easier when we moved to North Carolina. Here, the Smithfield ham and the peaches from the Farmers' Market—frozen at the end of summer and thawed later in the year—were too delicious to ignore. We'd have to find a way to include these local delicacies in our holiday, too.

And then there were our neighbors: a woman from New Jersey married to a man from St. Thomas. A grandmother from Louisiana who sometimes worked as a chef. A high-school teacher who's Jewish and from Manhattan. From Thanksgiving to New Year's, rather than traveling to spend every holiday with their families "back home," many stayed here and celebrated with friends.

Things were getting complicated.

Northerners were moving south. Southerners were moving north. "What can we do," we wondered, "to pay tribute to our families' traditions, even while we try to define our own?" So we looked up the word itself, *tradition.* It means cultural continuity, handing down beliefs and customs from one generation to another without written instructions.

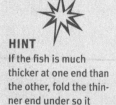

HINT

If the fish is much thicker at one end than the other, fold the thinner end under so it cooks more evenly.

That did it. We were stumped. My husband and I talked about what Christmas and Chanukah could possibly have in common, other than beginning with the letters "ch," and occurring in early winter. The foods and the faiths were completely different. It would take a miracle to find a way to observe both while honoring each. . .

Then it dawned on us. Both holidays commemorate real miracles: one, the birth of the Christian Savior; the other, the restoration of a sacred Jewish temple which invaders had desecrated. It wasn't a matter of Southern versus Northern cooking, and it wasn't a question of choosing only one moment in history to define our beliefs. What Christmas and Chanukah celebrate, in part, is our determination to remain connected to old traditions even as our lives move forward in new and unpredictable ways. That, by itself, can seem nearly miraculous.

Oh, and what we decided about the food is this: On the first night of Chanukah, we serve potato *latkes* and everyone gets one gift. On Christmas Day, we have a turkey and more gifts. Our friends from Alabama are getting accustomed to it. And when the two holidays fall on the same day? We have salmon.

MAPLE GINGER SALMON

¼ cup candied, crystallized ginger
½ cup maple syrup
½ cup brown sugar
Salmon fillet, ¾ to 1 pound

1 tablespoon chili oil, more or less to taste
2 tablespoons rice vinegar

Preheat the oven to 350 degrees. Grease a baking dish big enough to hold the fish and set aside.

Finely slice the ginger. Combine it with the maple syrup, brown sugar, chili oil and rice vinegar. Blend well.

Rinse the fish and pat dry; place in the baking dish and pour the sauce over it. Cover with foil and bake about 25 to 30 minutes, depending on thickness. Uncover and bake another 10 minutes or so until the fish flakes easily with a fork and is no longer translucent.

YIELD: 2 servings

ORANGE ROLLS

MAUREEN RYAN GRIFFIN

I actually enjoyed figuring out analogies on those standardized school tests. In the Ryan family, orange rolls were to Easter as stollen was to Christmas; it just wouldn't be Easter without orange rolls. I still use the recipe card my dad typed for me, complete with hand-written comments my mother added to be sure they would, as she would say, "turn out." The recipe card is dated 4/7/79, which was my first Easter after graduating from college.

FOR THE DOUGH:

2 packages dry active yeast
½ cup warm water
½ cup lukewarm milk
½ cup sugar
1 teaspoon salt
2 eggs
½ cup softened butter, plus extra for rolled-out dough
4½ to 5 cups flour

FOR THE FILLING:

1 ½ cups sugar
¾ cup orange juice, with pulp
3 tablespoons grated orange rind
¼ cup butter

The evening before: Combine yeast in warm water in a measuring cup for 5 minutes without stirring; then stir till yeast is dissolved. Pour into mixing bowl; stir in milk, sugar, salt, eggs and softened butter. Add flour in two additions (stir in 2 to 2½ cups, then add rest), first with a spoon, then with hands. Keep dough as soft as possible, as sticky as you're able to handle. Mix until smooth. When dough begins to leave the sides of the bowl, turn onto a lightly floured surface and knead for about 5 minutes, until smooth and elastic. Form into a ball and place in greased bowl, greased side up. Cover and let rise until double, 1 to 3 hours.

Prepare filling by mixing sugar, orange juice, grated orange rind and butter in a saucepan. Bring mixture to a boil; cook for 2 minutes on high heat, stirring constantly. Let cool.

Grease two 9 x 13" pans and set aside.

When dough has doubled, punch down and roll into a 9 x 18" oblong on a lightly floured surface, and, to quote my mother, "spread soft butter on rolled-out dough, then a little filling. This oozes out when you cut into slices."

Roll dough up tightly from the wide side, so that you have an 18"-long roll. Cut into 1" slices, place in the prepared pans, 9 rolls in each. Spoon half of the orange filling over the top of the rolls, dividing evenly between the two pans. Cover with foil and place in refrigerator. Cover the remaining filling, but do not refrigerate.

In the morning: Remove rolls from refrigerator. Place on stovetop while preheating oven to 375 degrees. Then, spoon on remaining orange filling, again dividing evenly between the two pans. When rolls have doubled in size (30 to 60 minutes), bake until golden brown, 25 to 30 minutes.

YIELD: 18 rolls

HOMEMADE RAVIOLI SCAPELLATO STYLE

SEAN A. SCAPELLATO

My father's family came to America in 1907. A second-generation Italian, he was raised on the cuisine of Naples and Sicily, a gentle, though sometimes harsh, mélange of customs and foods and drink.

Ever since I was old enough to remember, the ritual has been to make our Christmas Day meal from scratch—my great-grandmother's ravioli and sauce. The day before, we will break out the wine, put on the mood music, and take our spots at the large farm table in the kitchen. Dad makes the dough, Mom the filling; Sara, Ryan, and I man the pasta machine, ready to roll out the sheets. Despite our appointed roles, no one can resist plunging their hands into the mountain of flour and eggs, or rolling a sheet of dough, or stuffing each one with a dollop of cheese.

Amidst our assembly line, we smile at the curious eyes of my five- and two-year-olds waiting in the wings. We note how one day not long from now, they'll be mashing the raviolis tight with the fork, how they'll know about clamping the pasta machine to the table without scratching the top. There's something to learning the ritual, in passing it on. When I think of Christmas, I think of that.

6 cups unbleached flour
5 or 6 large eggs
1 cup of ice water
16 ounces Ricotta cheese
8 ounces grated Mozzarella cheese
8 ounces grated Parmesan cheese
About 1 cup canned breadcrumbs
2 or 3 eggs
An 8-ounce package of chopped spinach, thawed and squeezed dry
Salt and pepper, to taste
Extra flour for rolling out the dough

HINT
If you have one, a ravioli press works well to cut the dough.

Measure flour onto a clean counter-top and make small well in the center. Break 5 or 6 eggs into the center and using your hands, mix well. When dough begins to form, add tiny amounts of ice water, just enough to make the dough stick together. Knead dough until smooth, elastic, and a little shiny. Put in a large bowl and cover with a clean towel to rest.

In a separate bowl, mix together the 3 cheeses, breadcrumbs, 2 or 3 eggs, spinach, salt, and pepper. Adjust seasoning and mix until firm.

Use a pasta machine or rolling pin, and roll out a portion of dough onto a well-floured surface, making an oblong about 6 x 12" and ⅛" thick. Keep remaining dough covered.

Use a glass about two inches in diameter, dipped in flour, to cut circles from rolled dough. Place about 2 teaspoons of cheese mixture in center of each. Roll out another oblong of dough, cut into circles as before, and place one on top of each ravioli. Press all edges with a fork to seal the ravioli. Repeat until you have used all the dough and filling. Place on a pan lined with wax paper and allow to dry in the refrigerator for an hour before cooking.

To cook raviolis, add to boiling, salted water and simmer until tender, about 15 minutes or until raviolis begin to float. Serve with favorite sauce and fresh Parmesan cheese and pepper.

YIELD: About 12 servings

GRANDMOMMY'S CHICKEN AND DUMPLINGS

JULIE E. ADKISSON

Special occasions at my grandmother's were always marked by the same ritual: extending the dining room table, covering it in white cloth, setting each place with nice dishware, and filling every extra seat with mothers, brothers, twin sisters, husbands, cousins and even roommates. The final detail that marked these semi-annual family dinners was a pot of Grandmommy's chicken and dumplings (pronounced "dumplins'")—made from scratch and served hot right from the stove. Made right, they were an all-day affair.

As my grandmother got older, making this favorite dish became more of a group affair. What she was no longer able to do herself, the rest of us helped to get done. One winter, as we prepared for another family get-together, I was assigned a highly important task in the dumpling-making: documenting the process on paper. At age 11, I was finally old enough to help in the kitchen, not with the food, but with pencil and paper. Taking my job quite seriously, and quite literally, I recorded every single piece of dumpling-making instruction as dictated by my grandmother. The result is this play-by-play of her busy kitchen, which captured much more than this family recipe.

Whole chicken
Salted water for stewing
4 cups flour to start, plus more for kneading and rolling
½ teaspoon baking powder
⅔ cup shortening (we used Crisco brand)
1 ½ cups milk to start, plus 1 cup
1 tablespoon salt, or more to taste
Water, if needed

271

Stew whole chicken in a Dutch oven of salted water for about an hour. Once fully cooked, remove the chicken from bones and skin; place meat on a platter and keep warm. Save the stewing liquid.

In a large bowl, blend 4 cups flour, baking powder and shortening by hand or with a pastry blender. Add some milk slowly to the mixture, and continue blending until it is a semi-dry ball. Cover countertop with flour. Turn dough out onto floured work surface. Knead dough until workable.

Send Aunt Jo to get broth cooking. Prepare broth by adding about 4 cups water to every 3 cups broth, 1 cup milk and salt to taste to the water in the Dutch oven. Liquid should fill pot about halfway. Allow this to simmer on the stove while you prepare the dumplings. (Expect to have a layer of fat on top, about ⅛".)

Pinch off a fist-full of dough. Roll dough until very thin. (⅛"-thick dumplings are what my family prefers.) Cut dough into 2" strips with a sharp knife.

Bring the broth to boiling. Drop dumplings one at a time into the broth. Keep broth boiling, and stir. Don't let dumplings stick to bottom of pan. Tell Aunt Jo to keep stirring, while you add the dumplings.

Turn stove to low. Simmer until dumplings are cooked throughout. Aunt Jo will know when they are ready, about 20 minutes or so.

Place dumplings in a serving bowl. Have Aunt Jo carry them to the table with the warm chicken.

YIELD: 6 generous servings

HINT

If you do not have an Aunt Jo, any aunt will do. Or substitute another able-bodied assistant.

BLUE CHEESE AND SPINACH TIMBALES

HEIDI FLICK

I like to haul out Grandma's china and throw down with a big ol' Christmas-Chanukah dinner each December, serving up a multi-course meal so the night lingers for friends who can't make it home for the holidays. One year, it had to be done without meat, fish, shellfish, corn, tomatoes, beans, nuts, mushrooms or chocolate.

I panicked early, flinging aside the *Vegetarian Epicure*, the *Frugal Gourmet*, the *Moosewood Cookbook*—So many nuts! Too much curry! Where am I going to find whey?

Finally I sat down with a list of ingredients and came up with my own menu. It wasn't traditional holiday fare. The dinner started with a fresh, crisp salad, followed by pasta with a pureed roasted red-pepper sauce. Then came sweet potato latkes and the final course, spinach and blue cheese timbales, a suitably decadent holiday dish. The evening ended with baked apples drizzled with maple syrup.

My friends know that I hide my love and affection for them behind jokes. But when I feed them, I lay myself open, saying, "This was made with love. Stay a while, and let it make you happy."

That dinner was a great gift—to myself.

A 4-ounce package fresh baby spinach leaves
Olive oil
⅛ tsp nutmeg
¼ teaspoon white pepper
1 cup half-and-half
1 cup heavy cream
8 ounces of Maytag or Clemson blue cheese, crumbled
6 eggs, lightly beaten

Mixing a little hot cream into the eggs before combining completely keeps the eggs from curdling. Also, if the ramekins won't stay put in the water bath, you can line the pan with a wet dish towel.

Preheat oven to 350 degrees. Coat 8 ramekins with cooking spray and set them on a large roasting pan. Set aside.

In a large frying pan, sauté spinach leaves in a little olive oil until leaves are thoroughly wilted. Stir in nutmeg and pepper. Roll spinach in paper towels and press gently to remove as much moisture as possible.

Heat half-and-half and cream in a saucepan until first bubbles appear along edges. Do not boil. Divide blue cheese and spinach into ramekins. Pour a little of the cream mixture into beaten eggs and whisk. Then add the rest of the cream to the eggs, whisk briefly and pour into the ramekins. Place roasting pan on oven rack and pour in enough hot tap water to come halfway up the sides of the ramekins. Slide pan carefully into oven and bake for 35 to 40 minutes. Let timbales cool for 10 to 15 minutes, then slide a knife around edges and invert onto serving plate.

YIELD: 8 servings

SMOKED OYSTER BALL

SCOTTIE KAREN ASH

I've made this recipe many, many times and it's always a favorite. If you roll the chilled ball in the parsley/paprika mixture, the red-and-green color looks very festive during Christmas holidays.

An 8-ounce package of cream cheese, softened
2 tablespoons sour cream
¼ to ½ teaspoon chopped parsley
Dash salt
Dash pepper
2 cans of smoked oysters, drained and chopped
Chopped pecans, or additional chopped parsley mixed with paprika

In a bowl, cream together the cream cheese and sour cream. Add the parsley, salt, pepper and oysters, and mix until well-combined.

Form the mixture into a ball shape and refrigerate several hours. Just before serving, roll the ball to coat it in either the chopped pecans or the parsley/paprika mixture.

YIELD: About 24 canapé servings

VALENTINE CHERRY CAKE

MAUREEN RYAN GRIFFIN

My mother celebrated every holiday by baking. For Valentine's Day, it was this delicious and appropriately pink maraschino cherry cake. When I was young, this cake, along with the slew of Valentine's cards from schoolmates, was all I needed to have a happy Valentine's Day. Then came the years of hoping for a Valentine from that special someone. Mother, determined to raise all five of her children "right," watched the romantic goings-on of her children with an eagle eye. Not only did she have stringent requirements about dating, she also frequently warned me that men were only after one thing, even before I was savvy enough to understand what that "one thing" might be.

These memories came flooding back when I found a "Dear Abby" clipping Mother had enclosed in a letter she sent me when I was in my early twenties. A young girl had written in to ask what she could do about her kitten who "isn't even a year old and he keeps running off to be with a girl cat." Dear Abby's advice contained the question, "How would YOU like to be 'fenced in' so you couldn't mingle with boys during your teen years?" And right underneath, in Mother's scrawl, was the comment, "It could have been worse!"

Yes indeed. For whatever the state of my love life on Valentine's Day, I have always enjoyed a slice of Mother's Valentine cherry cake.

FOR THE CAKE:

3 cups cake flour or 2¾ cups all-purpose flour

1¾ cups sugar

4 teaspoons baking powder

1 teaspoon salt

⅓ cup shortening

⅓ cup butter, at room temperature

⅓ cup cherry juice

⅔ cup milk

5 egg whites, unbeaten

1 teaspoon vanilla

1 teaspoon almond extract

16 diced maraschino cherries

½ cup walnuts, chopped

FOR THE FROSTING:

3 cups confectioners sugar

2 tablespoons evaporated milk

2 tablespoons cherry juice

⅓ cup softened butter

A few drops red food coloring

1 teaspoon vanilla

Preheat oven to 350 degrees. Grease and flour two 9" cake pans and set aside.

Sift together flour, sugar, baking powder, and salt. Add shortening, ⅓ cup butter, ⅓ cup cherry juice and milk. Beat until blended. Add egg whites and beat 2 minutes. Add 1 teaspoon each of the vanilla and almond extracts. Fold in cherries and nuts.

Pour the batter into the prepared pans. Bake for 30 to 35 minutes. Cool.

For the frosting, combine confectioners sugar, evaporated milk, 2 tablespoons cherry juice, ⅓ cup butter, red food coloring and 1 teaspoon vanilla and mix until smooth. Add more evaporated milk, if needed, until desired consistency. Frost and assemble the cooled layers.

YIELD: 12 servings

JULY BIRTHDAY CREAM
(PEACH ICE CREAM)

JULIE E. ADKISSON

In North Carolina, late July is the time of year when the heat is intense, days last forever and peaches are at their prime. These hot, long, prolific days are also the time of year when I was born. So instead of traditional cake and candles, for many years I've had something different at birthday celebrations. Something smooth and sweet. Something cooling on a sweltering summer day. I chose homemade peach ice cream. A perfect reward for enduring the heat, and a heavenly transformation of those baskets of ripening fruit that can't be eaten fast enough.

I can remember helping my mother mix together the ingredients inside while hearing my father preparing the old, wooden ice cream maker outside. While we were blending fruit and milk, he was churning salt and ice. This churning part was the most difficult for me. Not because it required any manual labor, but because at this point 30 minutes seemed to take longer than it did each year for my birthday to arrive. The ice cream is so good, it's hard to wait, but definitely worth it. Plus at my house, the leftovers always went faster than cake. Here's our family's recipe:

*For a gallon freezer, you will need about 20 pounds of crushed ice and 3 to 4 cups of rock salt.

3 whole eggs

2½ cups sugar

1 large can evaporated milk

1-pint carton half-and-half

1 can sweetened condensed milk (I use Eagle Brand)

2 teaspoons vanilla extract

½ teaspoon salt

1 quart ripe fresh peaches, peeled, mashed and sweetened with ½ cup sugar

1 quart whole milk

*Crushed ice

*Rock salt

Beat the eggs and sugar until the mixture is thick and light yellow in color. Gradually add the evaporated milk, half-and-half and condensed milk. Mix in the vanilla and salt. Continue beating until the mixture is well blended. Pour mixture into the freezer container and chill in the refrigerator at least 4 hours. Remove container from the refrigerator and add the fruit and whole milk to the fill line on the container. Follow the manufacturer's directions for your ice cream maker, and freeze until the mixture is hard.

YIELD: About a gallon

CAROLINA CRAB AND MUSHROOM BISQUE

TERRANCE ZEPKE

Christmas is a big deal in my family, particularly Christmas Eve. The family attends Christmas Eve church service and then we congregate at my aunt's spacious, yet cozy, Gibsonville farmhouse. We are a family that honors traditions, although we often change them! At one time, everyone was allowed to open one gift during our Christmas Eve party. Now, we open most of the presents that night. We also used to have dinner before the church service. Now, we forego that tradition, opting instead to eat "party food." Each of us is responsible for bringing a special dish for the night's festivities. I think every year about 95 percent of the food on the dining room table and kitchen counter are sweets. My contribution, to ensure we eat something of substance, is one of my favorite recipes, Carolina crab and mushroom bisque.

Besides being so delicious, I like it because the rich, creamy concoction is a perfect appetizer or entree for most occasions.

½ cup butter (not margarine)
½ cup onion, chopped
1 large spring onion, finely chopped
½ cup bell pepper, color of your choice, chopped
1 cup fresh mushrooms, chopped
¼ cup all-purpose flour
2 cups whole milk
*1 tablespoon lemon blend
3 cups half-and-half
½ teaspoon hot sauce
1 pound lump crabmeat, drained
¼ cup parsley, chopped
¼ cup dry sherry

In a large saucepan, melt half the butter over medium heat, then add onions, bell pepper and mushrooms. Cook for five minutes or until tender, stirring frequently. Remove mixture from saucepan.

Over low heat, melt the rest of the butter in the saucepan. Slowly stir in flour until smooth, cooking and stirring constantly for about one minute. Add milk. Slowly increase heat to medium and stir constantly until mixture becomes thickened. Stir in lemon blend, half-and-half and hot sauce. When it comes to a boil, reduce heat to medium-low heat. Stir in crabmeat, vegetables and parsley; simmer for about four or five minutes. Add sherry and serve. I usually double this recipe to feed my hungry crowd.

YIELD: About 9 servings

*TO MAKE LEMON BLEND:

3 tablespoons grated lemon rind
1 tablespoon salt
1 bay leaf
1 teaspoon celery seeds
1 teaspoon ground coriander
1 teaspoon black pepper

Combine ingredients and blend until finely chopped—a food processor works best.

Is it stuffing or dressing where you live? With or without giblets, oysters, cornbread or nuts? It seems each cook, whether native or new to the South, has a favorite recipe—and story.

OYSTER STUFFING

TAMMY WILSON

Oyster stuffing has been part of Thanksgiving since I was a child, though it sounds terribly New England for a family living in the cornbelt.

The first time I remember it was at my aunt's farmhouse fifteen miles further into nowhere than where we lived, in Shelby County, Illinois. As usual, we gathered around the Horn of Plenty and little pilgrim candles as the adults passed around turkey, mashed potatoes, sweet potatoes with marshmallows, green bean casserole, cranberries, pickles, deviled eggs and a bread-like concoction with black things buried in it.

The concoction, I learned, was oyster stuffing. I spit out my first bite, but over the years I came to like it. I remember watching Mom make that stuffing, something she learned from watching her mother.

"Don't use selects for stuffing," she said. "The standards are expensive enough."

I've served oyster stuffing in my own home, splurging with an extra can of standards. Friends in North Carolina are amazed that this recipe hails from Illinois, 800 miles from the nearest salt water.

2 sticks margarine	2½ cups water
1 onion, chopped	2 cans standard oysters,
½ cup celery, chopped	undrained and chopped
2 bags herbed bread-crumb stuffing	Sage to taste

Preheat oven to 350 degrees. Grease 2-quart baking dish and set aside.

Sauté onion and celery in margarine; then in a large bowl, combine with the bread crumbs and water. Mix in the oysters and sage. Add enough water to moisten the bread crumbs well. Bake at least 1 hour, or until top is well browned.

YIELD: 12 to 16 servings

OYSTER DRESSING

KAREN S. COBB

Oyster dressing has been part of my family's Thanksgiving for at least 20 years. My mother, Anne Shue of Concord, North Carolina, gave me the recipe. She is not certain, but believes she got the recipe at a grocery store more than 40 years ago.

When I married in 1982, she asked me to begin making dressing and bring it to our family's Thanksgiving meal. I found the recipe she gave me many years prior, made the dish and took it to our family dinner.

My younger brother, Randy Shue, is a picky eater. He asked what the dark pieces of meat in the dressing were. Knowing he hated oysters, I replied, "Giblets." My mother and I just looked at each other and he continued eating. He enjoyed the dressing so much that the next year, he asked me to make a pan of dressing especially for him.

Every Thanksgiving since, I have willingly accommodated him with his personal pan of dressing. For 20 years, he has believed he is eating giblet dressing. My mother and I secretly get a good belly-laugh every Thanksgiving when Randy or his wife, Tammy, whom he married in 1997, calls to request that I bring the dressing, and to please make a pan exclusively for them. Little do they know that for 20 years, Randy has been eating one of the foods he hates the most—oysters!

Like eggs, oysters are graded according to size.

- 2 tablespoons butter
- 1 cup onion, chopped
- 1 ½ cups celery, chopped
- 9 cups bread crumbs
- 1 teaspoon salt
- 1 ½ teaspoons crushed sage leaves
- 1 teaspoon thyme leaves
- ½ teaspoon black pepper
- ¼ cup fresh parsley, chopped
- 1 pint oysters, chopped
- 2 eggs
- Oyster liquor, plus enough milk to make 1 ¾ cups liquid

Preheat oven to 400 degrees. Grease a large casserole dish and set aside.

Melt butter in saucepan. Stir in onions and celery, cooking until translucent. Remove from heat.

In a large mixing bowl, combine bread crumbs, salt, sage, thyme, black pepper and parsley. Stir in oysters. Beat eggs into the milk/oyster liquor. Pour into the bread crumb mixture, then add the sautéed onions and celery; toss to coat. Spread in baking pan. Bake for 30 minutes.

YIELD: About 12 servings

MISS ARNETTA'S DRESSIN'

EVA L. DAWKINS

No one ever forgets the love that got away. This sentiment still applies when that love is food. I still miss my grandmother's flatbread scored into large squares on her old, warped, black baking sheet and her pancakes that were so good they were better without the Karo syrup.

One evening while in college, I sat in my apartment, hungry without cash (a recurring experience in college only compounded by my laziness that made cooking the food in the refrigerator a totally ridiculous solution to my predicament). As the evening went on and my stomach growled on, I fantasized about my favorite moments with food.

Thanksgiving, one of only three times a year when Mom cooked dressing, came to mind immediately. Then, in true college-student fashion, I called my mom collect. After 30 minutes of her listing ingredients and my repeatedly asking for the accompanying amounts, I hung up the phone satisfied that this love would not get away.

It would be another 10 years before I would use the recipe to prepare Thanksgiving dinner for my oldest daughter. Since then I have made adjustments and additions to suit my particular taste, but now 14 years later I still put my original copy of the recipe up on the refrigerator while I prepare Thanksgiving dinner. The gifts that mothers give their daughters are often not realized until the daughters are mothers themselves. Although daughters usually develop their own way of doing things, the foundation remains irrefutably a gift from Mom.

Leftover broth from turkey or chicken already baked or boiled
1 pan cornbread (use whatever scratch recipe or prepackaged mix you like)
2 eggs, hardboiled, chopped fine
½ cup onion, chopped fine
½ cup celery, chopped fine

½ cup giblets, liver; or turkey or chicken meat, chopped fine
8 ounces stuffing mix (I use Pepperidge Farm blue band)
Additional chicken broth, canned, if needed
1 ½ teaspoons sage
Salt and pepper

Prepare meat and save broth. Prepare cornbread. Boil eggs.

Preheat oven to 425 degrees. Chop onion, celery and meat finely. Combine the eggs, onion, celery, giblets, stuffing mix and cornbread in large bowl, crumbling cornbread until evenly mixed with large spoon or fork. Add leftover broth until mixture is sufficiently moist, but not soupy. If you run out of leftover broth before you get the right consistency, use canned chicken broth as needed until dressing mixture is sufficiently moist. Add sage up to 1 ½ teaspoons to taste, then salt and pepper to taste. Be careful not to oversalt especially if broth contained salt.

Bake in ungreased casserole dish or large baking pan for 30 minutes to 1 ½ hours. Length of time will depend on depth of baking dish; a deeper pan will take longer. Start checking at 30 minutes for doneness. Dressing is done when edges have started to brown and top starts to develop a crust all over. However, top should not brown. Allow to sit for 15 minutes before serving. Enjoy!

YIELD: 16 to 18 servings

HOPPIN' JOHN

RICK MCDANIEL

This is a traditional dish of the Carolinas. It is often eaten on New Year's Day, and the custom is to stir a dime into the pot just before serving. Whoever finds the dime is supposed to have plenty of luck and money in the coming year.

TO SOAK THE PEAS:

1 ½ cups dried black-eyed peas
3 cups cold water
1 tablespoon salt

TO COOK:

6 strips salt pork or bacon, diced
1 medium onion, chopped
Salt
2 cups water

¾ cup long-grain white rice and water to cover
Salt and pepper to taste
Dash of hot sauce
½ cup minced green onions, including tops

Like many foods believed to be identifiably American, the black-eyed peas that are part of Hoppin' John traveled to the U.S. from somewhere else. These legumes were most likely brought here during the era of African slave trading.

Rinse peas and pick them over. Cover with 3 cups of cold water; add 1 tablespoon salt and let stand overnight.

The next day, drain peas, discarding water, and place in a large pot.

In a separate pan, sauté salt pork or bacon until crisp; add it to the peas; reserve the drippings. Add onion, a little salt and water. Bring just to a boil, lower heat, and simmer until peas are tender, about 20 minutes. A small amount of cooking liquid should remain; if liquid is absorbed too quickly by cooking, add fresh water ¼ cup at a time.

Meanwhile, cover rice with cold water. Bring to a boil, stir once. Cover, lower heat and simmer rice for 20 minutes.

When peas are tender, add cooked rice to pot. Stir in 2 tablespoons reserved bacon drippings, salt, pepper and hot sauce to taste. Cover and simmer about 15 minutes longer so flavors combine and rice absorbs some of the remaining cooking liquid. To serve, garnish with green onions.

YIELD: 6 servings

BESSIE'S TURKEY HASH

RACHEL R. WRIGHT

Turkeys are native to the Americas, although early Spanish explorers brought the birds back to Europe. Then, colonists who came to the "New World" brought turkeys with them, back to the place from which the birds first came!

My mother, Bessie Clark Ray, first May Queen at Salem College and first public school music supervisor in our county, wasn't much of a cook. The day after Thanksgiving, however, she took leftover turkey and concocted a famous hash. My son George particularly loved Bessie's hash. One year he invited a few friends to our house for lunch and hash. Many years later, the final year, 34 showed up.

The day after Thanksgiving became Hash Bowl Day. After the meal, the boys played pickup football, the Hash Bowl Game. Later, a gilded "Hashman's Trophy" was presented! College students and married men argued like the three bears over who was sitting in their seats. Bessie sat at the head of the table. I cooked.

Instead of leftover turkey, we cut up 21-pound turkeys. Bessie and I got "turkey-tunnel" syndrome from using kitchen shears. We cleared the Stove Top Stuffing, cranberry sauce, frozen pumpkin pies, and sweet potatoes at Food Lion.

The hash parties lasted until George was overseas as a Naval Officer and Bessie had died at age 91. Twelve of the Hashmen came to Bessie's funeral, sitting together in homage to her and her special memory.

Butter	Salt and pepper
Celery, chopped	Worcestershire Sauce
Onions, chopped	Cooked turkey, cut up and re-
Flour, enough to thicken	moved from bones
Canned chicken broth, plus	
bouillon cubes if needed	

In a large sauté pan, melt the butter, then sauté the celery and onions. Add flour to thicken, then stir in the chicken broth. Add extra bouillon cubes if needed, then salt, pepper and Worcestershire Sauce to taste. Add the turkey, reduce heat and simmer, covered, for one hour. Add a little more flour mixed with water for thickening, if needed.
Serve on rice, stuffing, or toast.

YIELD: Depends on how much turkey you start with; allow about 1 cup
      per serving

AUNT ROSALEE'S CARAMEL ICING

KATHLEEN PURVIS

I can't cook like Aunt Rosalee Bass.

There. I've admitted it. In print.

Readers of the *Charlotte Observer* food section might gasp at that news. After all, I hold their literary hands and coax them through béarnaise sauce and backyard barbecue, a conquistador of the printed food world. It's my job to make cooking look as easy as following a path through a jungle.

But before you turn the page in disgust, take another look at that first sentence. I didn't type, "I can't cook." I typed, "I can't cook like Aunt Rosalee."

Not a Purvis in the world would disagree. They can't either. No one can. Aunt Rosalee Bass of Americus, Georgia, was one of those legendary cooks, a woman who made great cooking look as simple as a sigh and as natural as a long vowel.

One of my cousins said it best, and sadly, at a family reunion a couple of years after Aunt Rosalee passed, a picnic with markedly fewer casseroles and only the lesser desserts. Garrett had a polite slice of someone else's imitation of Aunt Rosalee's caramel cake as we took turns recalling her greatest hits. "Aunt Rosalee could stick her finger in a cow pie and I'd eat it," he said solemnly. Profane. But true.

And therein lies the problem with cooks like Aunt Rosalee. They make it look so easy. Their talents seem no more complex than pointing a finger—at a bowl or a cow pie. They wave off compliments and insist, "Oh, sugar, there's nothing to it."

Which leads to how I met my Waterloo in Aunt Rosalee's caramel cake. That cake was my aunt's crowning glory. The cake underneath was simple—your basic pound cake would be fine. The key to the thing was the caramel icing, a thick tan coating that held perfect ridges from the icing knife. It had the consistency of stiff fudge, a creamy richness that gave just a little resistance when you pressed a fork into it. She would make the cake for my father if he was at her home anytime within a month of his birthday. He would be stingy with slices, as was his right, but just a bite of something so delicious was all it took to imprint the memory in a child's mind for life.

Aunt Rosalee, Dad's doting older sister, had been one of the only family members at my parents' wedding, a simple civil ceremony in a judge's office in Georgia. She died a few years before their 50th wedding anniversary. So when my sister planned the menu for their golden anniversary dinner, she had a brilliant idea: If Aunt Rosalee couldn't be there in body, she should at least be there in spirit. Her caramel cake would be the dessert. And my sister knew just the cook for the job: Me. The newspaper food editor.

After all, I had the recipe. The fact that I had never actually made the icing didn't give my sister pause. The fact that penguins can't fly doesn't stop anyone from calling them birds. In my sister's small apartment on the morning of the party, I bravely set out to tackle my task. The cake was no problem. A simple 1-2-3-4 cake, available in every basic cookbook, fit the bill. Cream the butter, beat in the eggs, fold in the flour. By mid-morning, cooling layers were spread out on the dining table.

On to the caramel icing. My sister's kitchen is crammed with gadgets, except the one I really needed: A candy thermometer. No matter. Aunt Rosalee never fooled with such folderol and neither would I. I followed the instructions, dripping dabs of hot sugar into a glass of water, trying to remember from home ec class what the "soft-ball stage" looked like. I added butter and started beating the hot sugar.

And beating. And beating. And beating some more. Appreciating with every beat why my aunt had been able to hug us so tightly. Eventually, my forearms burning, I decided I had beaten enough. I spread the icing on the cake.

Where it promptly slid down the sides and puddled on the plate. For the next 30 minutes, my sister and I took turns trying to coax the icing back up the sides of the cake. We finally dubbed it "Vietnam"—the more you tried, the messier it got.

With many yards of golden ribbon, we managed to disguise the cake. My father insisted it tasted just like Aunt Rosalee's, but I knew better. It might have tasted a little like it, but it didn't look anything like it. Since then, I've discovered another caramel icing—a much simpler version that works every time. It's heresy to say it, but it tastes remarkably like the original. But this one has a snowball's chance of making people think you're a cook.

3 ½ cups sugar, divided
1 ¼ cups milk
½ cup (1 stick) butter
1 teaspoon vanilla

In a large pot, combine 3 cups sugar and milk. Bring to a rolling boil.

Meanwhile, melt ½ cup sugar in a small, heavy pan or skillet; don't stir. Cook until it just begins to turn brown. Stir the browned sugar into milk mixture; it will boil up. Cook until well into the soft-ball stage (234 to 240 degrees), but do not stir. Remove from heat. Add butter and vanilla.

Let stand until cool, then beat until spreading consistency. Don't just stir—you really have to beat it. It's at the right stage when it loses its gloss and starts to look a little grainy.

YIELD: Icing for one cake

EASIER CARAMEL ICING

I learned this version at a dessert contest at Wingate College several years ago, but I've tweaked the instructions since then. It's simpler and less temperamental than the cooked-sugar version. Hot sugar icings are also easiest to use on flat cakes like sheet cakes, or spread over the top of pound cakes, rather than trying to fill cake layers before it sets up.

1 cup (2 sticks) butter
1 pound light brown sugar
7 tablespoons evaporated milk
1 teaspoon baking powder
1 teaspoon vanilla

Melt butter over low heat in a saucepan. Add sugar and evaporated milk and blend well. Increase heat and bring to a rolling boil, stirring constantly. Reduce heat and cook 5 minutes. Remove from heat and add baking powder; it will foam up. Beat until the baking powder has blended in. Add vanilla and beat until icing is spreading consistency, but still warm, about 5 minutes.

YIELD: Icing for one cake

HAMANTASCHEN (A DAIRY DISH)

MELINDA FARBMAN

I started out a Northern *WASP*, but now I am a Southern Jew. The story of my conversion is geographical, spiritual and gastronomical; these three threads together make up who I am—but not like challah, the braided bread made for Shabbat, more like hamantaschen, those yummy cookies for Purim that start out as circles and end up triangles oozing with fruit.

One childhood afternoon in upstate New York, my 4-H leader, who was a lawyer, mother of three, and wife of a rabbi, rolled out a smooth sheaf of chilled hamantaschen dough and presented a riddle: How could we turn a circle into a triangle? With animated hands, she cut the dough into circles and dropped onto them spoonfuls of gooey stewed apricots and prunes. Her strong, flour-covered fingers pinched three places on each circle and folded their curved sides inward, making triangles.

Later I learned the Purim story: Hamantaschen represent the three-cornered hat of the evil ruler, Haman, whose voice is to be drowned out by raucous noise in the annual reading of the Book of Esther. My sister Sarah, who is also Jewish, a lawyer, and a mother, gave me this recipe for the springtime holiday treats. She reminded me that hamantaschen represent the pockets of Haman; in German, *tasch* means pocket.

Down here in North Carolina I do get drunk on Purim, listen to the "Whole Megillah" being read, and make hamantaschen with my daughter. Yet I know my roots. I may look like a triangle, but I am also a circle. Only the two together could taste so good.

FOR THE DOUGH:

1 cup sugar
½ to ¾ pound butter (2 or 3 sticks)
1 teaspoon vanilla or almond extract
2 eggs
3 cups flour, plus 1 cup for rolling out dough
6 teaspoons baking powder

FOR THE APRICOT FILLING:

1 cup dried apricots
1 cup water
½ cup sugar (optional)

FOR THE PRUNE FILLING:

1 box pitted prunes
Water to cover in pot

Preheat oven to 400 degrees. Grease a cookie sheet and set aside.

In a large bowl, cream together the butter, sugar and vanilla. Add eggs one at a time.

In a separate bowl, sift together flour and baking powder. Add to butter mixture and combine just until blended. Chill dough for several hours, but not overnight.

For homemade fruit fillings, cook fruit in water until soft. Mash the mixture thoroughly or process in a blender until the consistency of jam. Cool. (Canned fruit fillings may be purchased in the Kosher section of your supermarket.)

Roll out dough to about ¼" thickness on a well-floured surface, being careful not to over-handle the dough. Cut circles with a circular cookie cutter or the rim of a glass. Drop a large teaspoon of filling into the middle of each circle. Gather up the edges and pinch together at three angles, making a tri-cornered shape. Bake for 12 minutes, until light brown.

YIELD: 3 dozen

NANNY'S AMBROSIA

NANCY PATE

Three things I could always count on at holiday family dinners at my grandmother's in Lowcountry South Carolina.

First, there would be chilled ambrosia served in a cut-glass bowl. Because Nanny didn't have enough small fruit bowls to go around, she also set on the white tablecloth six stemmed and footed Depression glasses that gleamed as golden as the ambrosia.

Second, no sooner than grace had been said, everyone seated, and platters and dishes started being passed than Nanny would leap from her chair. "My stars!" she'd say, and we knew that either the rolls or the macaroni pie were still in the oven.

Third, I never, ever, got to sit at the grown-up table. This was fine when I was a kid: We were fed first, seated at card tables and TV trays in the living room, and were finished eating—"May I be excused, please?"—to go outside and play while the adults lingered over dinner. "Who has the gravy?" "I don't think there's enough celery in the dressing." "This roll's not so burned."

Still, as I grew older, I coveted the status of the dining room table, which, with extra leaves could sit as many as 16. The rude realization that sitting there was not a function of age came the year I graduated from college. My cousin Meg, two days my younger, and her new husband were proudly ushered to the grown-up table for Thanksgiving. I was again relegated to the living room with my younger brother and cousins.

And so it was that I, postponing marriage, never sat with the grown-ups. I thought the utter humiliation would come the year when my younger brother and his bride arrived for Christmas dinner. Keith, the only other unmarried cousin, couldn't come that year. I would be in the living room with Meg's children. "Here, Nancy, come get your plate." Sure enough, when the day arrived, Nanny directed me to the living room. But soon I was eating ambrosia and knocking knees at the card table not only with Meg's toddlers but also with Cousin Richard, who was three years older — and recently divorced.

    2 or 3 grapefruit
    6 to 8 oranges
    2 bananas (optional)
    1 coconut
    1 pineapple (optional)

Peel grapefruit and oranges, then section the fruit into a large bowl. Puncture the coconut and drain into separate container. Then crack the coconut into two pieces and grate the interior into fruit bowl. If desired, peel and slice bananas and/or pare and core pineapple, cutting it into small chunks. Add to fruit. Chill.

YIELD: 12 to 16 servings

CRANBERRY RELISH

IRENE GAMMON

I first made this relish when I was about 7 years old. It was my Brownie troop's project; we made loads of the stuff and put it into pretty little yuletide-y jars to give to our parents for Christmas. I was so proud of this, my first culinary offering to the family. They ate it up, and my heart was filled with joy.

The next year, I made my own cranberry relish at home. The meat grinder, which I hadn't clamped to the counter properly, fell to the floor. Cranberries stained the wallpaper and the grinder dented the linoleum, leaving marks to remind us all of that year's batch of holiday relish. Nevertheless, the family ate it up again.

My cranberry relish became quite the annual tradition for everyone, and a glorious winter ritual for me. I prepared it with the most earnest of Christmas cheer, eager to pass it along to all my loved ones at the holiday dinner table.

About 25 years later, I found out that a few of my family members don't really care for cranberries in any form, but they had always been kind enough to put some of my relish on their plates. What could be a better illustration of the true spirit of Christmas?

2 to 3 seedless oranges   ½ to 1 cup sugar
A 12-ounce bag of fresh cranberries

The preferred method of grinding up the cranberries and oranges is by using an old-style, manual meat grinder. In lieu of such a cool, retro apparatus, a food processor can be used quite successfully.

Peel the oranges "sloppily"; that is, leave about ¼ of the peel intact, and quarter them. Remove any seeds you might encounter. Set aside.

Grind or process the cranberries, alternating with the oranges, about ¼ of each at a time. Stir well. If preferred, add additional peeled orange, one quarter at a time. Then add ½ cup sugar, stir again, and let sit for at least an hour in the refrigerator. Taste for sweetness and add more sugar, if desired.

Relish will keep in refrigerator for at least a week.

YIELD: 2 to 3 cups

THE TASTE OF TRADITION

FRYE GAILLARD

Monty Branham thought he was losing his mind when he first saw the buffalo coming through the clouds. He was working as a carpenter, building a roof on a lake house in North Carolina, when he stopped for a moment to gaze at the sunset. It was a beautiful sight, full of reds and golds, as if the lake itself were on fire—and that was when the buffalo appeared and told him it was time to return to his people.

Branham was a young Catawba Indian who had never given much thought to his heritage. He had grown up wild in South Carolina, dabbling in alcohol and drugs, working for a while as a NASCAR mechanic before drifting from there to his job as a carpenter. He remembered the stories the old people told—how back in the days when the Indians were strong, when they roamed the forests and the broad riverbanks, visions were a part of their everyday life. But all of that was a long time ago, and by the time Monty Branham was coming of age, the Catawba Nation was almost gone. The reservation had shriveled to a single square mile, the people were poor, and nobody spoke the language anymore. There were those who feared they would soon be extinct.

By the 1990s, there were a handful of leaders trying to keep that from happening, and in the troubled introspections that followed his vision— his hallucinations on a lakeside rooftop—Branham found himself drawn to that cause. He started spending his days with the elders, especially the potters, who were keeping an ancient art form alive. He watched as they rolled and kneaded with their hands, bending the clay into intricate shapes, scraping, polishing, then burning each pot in a hardwood fire.

Branham soon became a potter himself, and it was about that time that he began to spend more time in the woods. Walking alone by the river, where the ferns rustled gently on the floor of the forest, he began to pay attention to the living things that had enabled the Catawba people to survive. There were roots and berries that the ancestors ate, or boiled into teas whenever an illness would descend on the village. There were animals, too,

Journalist Frye Gaillard is the author of 19 works of non-fiction, including three national award-winners.

The term "venison" includes not only meat from deer, but from other game with antlers, such as moose, elk and caribou.

the deer and the bear and the flocks of wild turkeys that added meat to the diet of a people who had farmed for longer than anybody could remember. The ancient ceremonies were tied to the food—the green corn dance in the season of the harvest, and the songs in honor of the deer and the bear. The deer, especially, were the cornerstone of life, an animal as important to the eastern tribes as the buffalo had been to the people of the plains.

As the 20th century was slipping toward an end, the deer were still abundant in the forests, still a staple in the diet of the Indians. Branham thought he saw a symmetry in that, a connection to the past. The men who hunted did it for the food, far more than the sport, and that was the way they knew it ought to be. There was also something about the venison itself: no preservatives, none of the cholesterol issues with beef; all in all for the Indian people, a healthy and instinctive expression of their identity.

Branham set out to make the people understand, to see as clearly as he was beginning to himself that the ways of the Indian had not disappeared. Today, he works as a teacher for the tribe, giving classes on the language, the pottery, the food, all of those ancient touchstones of culture. Among the Catawba adults, as well as the children, he finds a hungry audience for his views.

For many of the people who make up the tribe, the last decade has been a time of new pride. In 1994, the Catawba Nation won a century-old dispute with the federal government—a $50 million settlement for land that was stolen in the 19th century, and official federal recognition as a tribe. They have taken the money and bought new land to expand the reservation, and sturdy new houses for the people to live in, and every year at Thanksgiving—a holiday borrowed from the Indians by the Pilgrims—they invite their neighbors, black and white, to gather for a celebration near the river.

There are Indian dances, and the sound of drumbeats drifting through the woods, and the smell of venison cooking on the fire. It is a festive occasion, a time of thanksgiving that comes from the heart, as the Catawba people celebrate a renewal that many of them never thought they would see.

Here is a modern variation of a traditional Catawba recipe, offered by Monty Branham and his sister, B.J. Van Zant.

VENISON POT ROAST

A venison roast, 2 to 5 pounds
2 tablespoons salt
1 package dry onion soup mix (Monty and B.J. use Lipton brand)
Potatoes, as many as desired, chopped
Onions, as many as desired, chopped
½ to 1 cup raw rice
Garlic, chopped
Seasoning salt
Green bell peppers, chopped
Beer (optional)

HINT
If cooking on a stove instead of an open fire, cook over low to medium heat for 1-1/2 to 3 hours. No two roasts are ever the same.

Marinate a venison roast for at least a half-day in water with a little salt. This helps remove the wild flavor. Drain. Place meat in several cups of fresh water in a Dutch oven, add salt and pour in the onion soup mix. Add potatoes, onions, rice and "a whole bunch of garlic" to taste. Add seasoning salt and peppers. Let simmer over a fire of white coals for at least 3 hours. As liquid boils away, keep adding water, or if you prefer, beer, so meat and vegetables continue to simmer. After the first hour, using a spoon, taste the cooking liquid and add additional seasoning as needed. Meat is done when tender and falling off the bone. If unsure, cut into roast.

YIELD: 4 to 8 servings, depending on the size of the roast

SWEET POTATO PUDDING

REBECCA SCHENCK

Thanksgiving is a time to be grateful for ancestors who pass on recipes that become cherished traditions, reminding us of people as well as getting votes for the best taste of a holiday meal. My Aunt Myrtle's recipe for Sweet Potato Pudding is an example. Myrtle Hopson, who died just shy of 99 in 2001, was known for her cooking in the eastern North Carolina town of Fuquay-Varina.

Myrtle was a member of the Friendly Dozen luncheon club, twelve women who each entertained others once during the year, using their fine china and crystal, linens and favorite recipes. As members aged and times changed, the women sometimes ate at restaurants. Myrtle recruited my husband and me to help plan and serve meals in her month of August. She wanted a theme carried out from invitations to menu to program, and Gordon and I have fond memories of Crêpes Myrtle (both in vases and on plates), foods from the Bible another year (loaves and fishes with water turned into grape juice), and a political rally (with straw votes) in her living room—banners flying outside the house in which sweet potato pudding had been lovingly prepared.

1 cup raw sweet potato, grated	½ cup melted butter
½ cup white sugar	3 eggs
½ cup brown sugar	1 teaspoon vanilla
¼ teaspoon salt	½ teaspoon cinnamon
1 cup milk	½ teaspoon nutmeg

Preheat oven to 375 degrees.

Combine all ingredients in blender and mix well. Pour into an ungreased 9" pan or loaf pan and bake for one hour or until set.

YIELD: 6 to 8 servings

CHANUKAH LATKES (POTATO PANCAKES)

ELLYN BACHE

For a Southern Jewish mama whose friends and whose kids' friends were mostly Christians, the best thing about the potato latkes we urged them to try at Chanukah was that they were interestingly "ethnic" but tasted enough like hash browns not to frighten anyone away. Jewish families serve latkes ("pancakes" to the uninitiated) topped with sour cream, apple sauce, or occasionally sugar, but my Catholic husband, a hash brown fan, always doused them with ketchup.

Latkes are a traditional dish, fried in oil to remind us of the miracle of light and freedom this holiday celebrates. After defeating King Antiochus, who had ordered idol worship and despoiled the Jewish Temple in Jerusalem, the Jews re-kindled the Temple's "eternal light" but found only enough oil to last for one day. When the new supply arrived eight days later, the lamp was still burning. On each of the eight nights of Chanukah, Jews light one more candle in the menorah, until on the last night all are burning. Some families also exchange small gifts each night, but ours gave gifts only on the first night, when we also had our holiday dinner.

In addition to the traditional roast chicken and latkes, my kids always wished I'd make another fried-in-oil treat—the jelly doughnuts popular at Chanukah in Israel. But as a less-than-gifted cook, I declined. Latkes are easy enough if you remember to get the oil good and hot before you drop the potatoes in. Otherwise, they're likely to come out greasy. This is a good recipe that serves four.

6 medium potatoes	¼ teaspoon pepper
1 small onion	1 teaspoon salt
2 eggs, slightly beaten	½ teaspoon baking powder

Peel and grate potatoes and onion. Let stand ten minutes so liquid will rise to the top. Remove liquid. Stir in eggs. Add other ingredients. Drop by spoonfuls into a hot, well-oiled skillet. Brown on both sides. Drain on absorbent paper. Serve hot with apple sauce, sour cream, sugar—or ketchup.

YIELD: 4 servings

Ellyn Bache's novel *Safe Passage* was made into a movie starring Susan Sarandon.

There are many spellings of "Chanukah," some beginning with "Ch" and some with "H." That's because there is no English equivalent for the Hebrew letter—or sound—that starts this word.

LEMON SORBET

CAROLINE CASTLE HICKS

Every year, during that peculiar no-man's-land of time between Christmas and New Year's, I've been known to indulge in a rather unbecoming fit of post-holiday blues. The Christmas season has always been my favorite time of year. As an adult, I must confess that I have continued to succumb to that childlike after-Christmas melancholy, when after all those weeks of buildup and anticipation, I must accept the reality that the party is most definitely over. Each year, as I've walked listlessly from room to room, surveying a tree that is dropping an increasing number of needles, a Christmas tablecloth now decorated with cranberry stains, and tins upon tins of goodies that are tasting staler by the day, I have despaired that there is nothing left but to venture out into the bleak and barren wasteland that is January.

I might have continued this pathetic yearly tradition for the rest of my life if my 14-year-old daughter Mariclaire had not chosen to reveal herself as a philosopher—and perhaps, a budding psychologist and poet as well. Upon once again hearing my pitiful lament at having to box up all the decorations and toss our pretty tree on the curb, she cast me one of those fed-up, assessing glances at which teenagers are so adept.

"Mom," she said, "I know I'm *supposed* to be sad that Christmas is over, but I'm not. I *like* January. Christmas is great and everything, but it's kind of like eating cheesecake. The first few bites are really good, but then after a while, it starts tasting too rich and you just want to push it away and have something like lemon sorbet. To me, January is lemon sorbet."

Now, as a writer, I am always on the lookout for a good metaphor and a mother's bias notwithstanding, I had to admit that this was one of the best I'd heard in quite a while. Hers had the power to alter a whole way of thinking. Unwittingly, my wise daughter had given me the gift of a fresh perspective and I resolved then and there to quit whining and to begin viewing the entire "de-Christmassing" process in a new light. Rather than seeing it as a depressing chore, just maybe I could turn it into a kind of benediction to the old year and a path-clearing for the new one.

I made some lemon sorbet for the family, and although it's sometimes hard to tell with 14-year-olds, I think Mariclaire was pleased at my ability to come around. And as I stood there squeezing lemons in my newly-undecorated kitchen, their clean, citrus scent filled the room, infusing the air with freshness and the unmistakable tang of possibility.

HINT
Egg whites improve the texture. If you omit them the texture will be grainier, like a granita.

1 lemon, washed, quartered and seeded
Water
1⅓ cups sugar, divided
3 tablespoons fresh lemon juice
1 pasteurized egg white (or use dehydrated egg whites following directions on package)

Place quartered lemon in small saucepan with enough water to cover. Bring to a boil, then cover, reduce heat and simmer 10 minutes, or until lemon is tender when pierced with fork. Remove from heat and drain.

In a food processor or blender, process the lemon with ⅓ cup sugar just until blended. With machine running, gradually add ⅓ cup water. Pour mixture back into saucepan and bring to a slow simmer, stirring frequently until thick and syrupy, about 20 to 25 minutes. After removing from heat, stir in lemon juice. Chill.

While lemon mixture is chilling, combine 1 cup water and remaining 1 cup sugar in another small saucepan. Bring to a boil, stirring constantly. Remove from heat. Cool to room temperature; chill.

After chilling both lemon mixture and syrup, process together. Transfer to a metal pan or bowl and freeze until almost, but not completely, frozen. Process again adding pasteurized egg white. Refreeze.

YIELD: 6 servings

CHOCOLATE PECAN PIE

CHERYL SPAINHOUR

Over the years, there's been a lot of laughter in my kitchens, and with it most often, the smell of something burning. I've steamed broccoli without the water in the pot and sizzled spaghetti sauce until it stuck to the bottom of the skillet. I've blackened casseroles and corndogs in the oven, charred burgers and set fire to salmon on the broiler.

And I'm not limited just to burning food. Once, while trying to cook a "homemade" meal for a date, I caught my favorite shirt on fire as I stirred the goulash on the top of my gas stove. When he pointed out the flame rising up the front of my shirt, I casually patted out the fire with my oven mitt and kept right on stirring, as if it happened all the time. Because, in a way, it does.

What can I say, I'm a dreamer, not a chef. And while I don't often dream of becoming a good cook, I do love good cooks and their kitchens. I'm not envious (well, just a little bit) of their admirable abilities, just genuinely appreciative. Good food, cooked up at home, can't be beat, and despite my extended history of disasters, I occasionally try to fill my old farm kitchen with good smells. I figure the patient members of my family—who for the most part, have politely endured my fumbling about and fires and Frankenfood experiments—deserve a break now and then.

This recipe was passed along to me by a good Southern friend. I bake it for birthdays of people I dearly love—my mother-in-law is actually the only one—and at Thanksgiving and Christmas. There are actually a few dishes I've learned, through much practice, to cook fairly well. So what that boils down to is this: If I can make it, anyone can.

1 ½ cups sugar
3 tablespoons cocoa
½ teaspoon salt
1 egg, well beaten
½ stick margarine, melted

1 small can evaporated milk

1 teaspoon vanilla

1 cup pecans, chopped

1 unbaked pie shell

Preheat oven to 350 degrees.

Mix together sugar, cocoa and salt; set aside. In a separate bowl, mix together egg, margarine, milk and vanilla. Add to dry ingredients, mixing well. Stir in pecans. Pour into unbaked pie shell. Bake about 1 hour or until set; start checking at 45 minutes.

YIELD: About 8 servings

MOTHER'S CHOCOLATE FUDGE

LYNDA F. CRISP

This recipe came from my mother, Ruth Shoemaker. She became quite well known around Kannapolis, North Carolina, for her chocolate fudge. She was in an auto accident in 1960, was crushed from the waist down, eventually losing one leg, but she was still able to walk. She lived on disability and loved to keep children for extra income.

She began making the fudge for family at Christmas, but as years went on it became her special gift. Living on a fixed income, she gathered the ingredients during the year when the stores would have special sales. She would also buy decorative containers at clearance sales. Beginning the first of December, she would start making the fudge, filling the containers and delivering them to family, friends and three nursing homes. That was her gift and everyone loved it. Mother died and was not able to make fudge last Christmas, but her recipe—and her love of giving it—live on in all of us.

5 cups sugar

1 large can (12 ounces) evaporated milk

2 teaspoons vanilla extract

18 ounces chocolate chips

3 sticks butter or margarine

2 cups nuts, chopped (optional)

Grease or butter a large oblong pan or baking sheet with sides and set aside.

In a saucepan, mix together the sugar, milk and vanilla; bring to a boil and boil for 8 minutes. Meanwhile, put the chocolate chips and butter in a large bowl.

Pour the hot sugar mixture into the bowl. Beat with an electric mixer until the chocolate chips and butter are completely dissolved; pour into prepared pan. If using nuts, add them before pouring fudge into pan. Let cool, and enjoy giving it away!

YIELD: About 2 pounds

HINT

Mother used the Milnot brand. She said it made the fudge creamier.

HARVEST OF FIRST FRUITS

AHMAD DANIELS

Celebrated between December 26 and January 1, Kwanzaa is a joyous and deeply meaningful holiday which gives African Americans an opportunity to reunite with family and friends and to pay tribute to their rich cultural heritage.

The coming together of millions of African Americans at the close of every year to celebrate the very best they have to offer is what Dr. Maulana Karenga had in mind when he presented Kwanzaa to the world in 1966. According to Dr. Karenga, "the core principles of Kwanzaa..., which I developed and proposed during the Black Cultural Revolution of the '60s are a necessary minimum set of principles by which Black people must live in order to rescue our history and lives."

The core principles of Kwanzaa, the Nguzo Saba (the Seven Principles), are :
Umoja (unity)
Kujichagulia (self-determination)
Ujima (collective work and responsibility)
Ujamaa (cooperative economics)
Nia (purpose)
Kuumba (creativity)
Imani (faith).

There are seven symbols associated with Kwanzaa. They are also expressed in Kiswahili, a language spoken by Swahili people in the coastal regions of Kenya, Somalia and Tanzania. The symbols are:

mazao (fruits, vegetables, and nuts)
mkeka (place mat)
kinara (candleholder)
vibunzi (ear of corn)
zawadi (gifts)
kikombe cha umoja (unity cup)
mishumaa saba (seven candles).

All attendees to Kwanzaa celebrations are encouraged to participate in daily discussions on the principle of the day. It is on the sixth day of Kwanzaa following the exploring of the principle Kuumba (creativity) that a Karamu (feast) is held. Participants are encouraged to bring a covered dish of anything they desire except pork.

Whereas Dr. Karenga's originating of Kwanzaa may have been inspired by successful harvests in Africa, the harvest here in the U.S. is not focused on the "in gathering" of food but the bringing together of African American people to discuss issues and actions relating to their self-determination. The partaking of a sumptuous meal and engaging in provocative dialogue are meant to illuminate the way for the New Year while reminding all that the principles of Kwanzaa are to be practiced throughout the year.

Here is a favorite recipe:

KWANZAA SUCCOTASH

2 large onions, chopped
3 cups fresh corn kernels, taken from the cob (or frozen kernels)
3 tablespoons vegetable oil
8 ripe tomatoes, skinned, seeded, and chopped
1 pound fresh okra, sliced
Water, enough to cover the vegetables
Salt and freshly ground black pepper to taste

In a heavy saucepan, sauté the onions and corn kernels in the vegetable oil. Add the tomatoes and okra. Add enough water to cover. Season with salt and pepper to taste. Cover and simmer for one hour, adding more water if necessary.

YIELD: 8 servings

THE PASSOVER TABLE

Amy Rogers

There's an old joke about Jewish holidays, and what they signify. It goes like this: "They tried to kill us; they couldn't; let's eat."

This is an admittedly simplistic statement, but it fittingly describes Passover, the solemn yet joyous holiday that takes place each spring.

Passover commemorates historical events, but like any of our favorite holidays, it's the food that brings us together. More than mere tradition, the unusual assortment of foods on the oversized Passover plate, served at a dinner called a Seder, represent the struggles of Jews to win their freedom from enslavement more than 3,000 years ago.

A mixture of apples, nuts and wine – called haroset – reminds us of the mortar the slaves used when they were forced to build temples to pagan gods. Bitter herbs symbolize the hardships the slaves endured. A tiny bowl contains salt water, for their tears. A lamb shank-bone and a hard-cooked egg represent sacrifice.

But the Passover plate offers hope and optimism as well: Parsley or other greens signify the coming of spring and new life.

There is no bread served at this holiday dinner table, nor in the seven days that follow. The flat, cracker-like matzos remind us of the haste in which Jews fled their captors – into a desert Exodus – before the bread could rise. Along with the Passover meal, celebrants drink four cups of wine, as they pray and remember the sacrifices, tears, and triumphs of their ancestors.

Passover will be celebrated this year, as it has thousands of times before. At tables around the world, Jews will gather to remember their shared past. At modern-day dinners, you can find dishes as varied as the regions of the world where people observe the holiday. One cookbook gives a recipe for Moroccan chicken stewed with fruit and almonds; another offers a new American interpretation: chicken with sun-dried tomatoes and shiitake mushrooms. Even something as unique as the Passover haroset is interpreted differently from place to place. The apples we Americans chop and mix with wine, North African Jews replace with dates.

It may be naïve to think that the act of eating ceremonial foods could move us forward in our larger human struggle, but it somehow seems appropriate if the words of Rabbi Alfred Kolatch's opening prayer take on a new or deeper meaning: "May the problem of all who are downtrodden be our problem; may the concern of all who are afflicted be our concern; may the struggle of all who strive for liberty and equality be our struggle."

Whether we remember it with food, with prayer, with our actions in daily life or a combination of all three, the message couldn't be clearer. As Rabbi Kolatch says, "Truth, justice and loving-kindness are the enemies of slavery, tyranny and oppression. This is the power of Passover; this is the lesson of history; this is the story of freedom."

PASSOVER TZIMMES (CARROTS, POTATOES AND SWEET POTATOES)

10 to 12 large carrots

3 large sweet potatoes

2 large white potatoes

½ to 1 cup pitted prunes (optional)

⅔ cup honey

½ teaspoon cinnamon

2 teaspoons grated lemon or orange peel

1 cup warm water

2 tablespoons butter

Preheat oven to 350 degrees. Grease a 3-quart baking dish and set aside.

Bring a large pot of water to a boil. Peel and slice the carrots into 1" rounds, add to the boiling water and cook for 5 minutes. Meanwhile, peel and cut all the potatoes into 1" cubes, then add to the carrots and cook until the vegetables are just beginning to get tender. Remove from heat and drain.

In a large bowl, put the drained vegetables, and add the rest of the ingredients except the butter. Stir until just combined and place in the prepared baking dish. Dot with butter and bake for 30 minutes. Check at 20 minutes; if it is getting too brown, reduce heat to 325 and cover with foil for the remaining 10 minutes.

YIELD: About 8 servings

NONNA'S TORTA

ROXANE MARIA JAVID

As the holidays approach, my mind turns not to turkey but torta, a pie-like dessert prepared during the holidays by my Italian grandmother, Nonna. This isn't just an ordinary dessert, but an ancient recipe that's been uniquely my family's for generations. It's been passed through the hands of Tuscan mothers and daughters over the centuries, and according to Nonna, families in Italy have different versions of what is commonly called "torta."

Most Americans are taken aback when they hear what's in Nonna's torta. The filling consists of raisins, grated chocolate, eggs, bread, milk, sugar, vanilla and a little spinach. At times I keep the last ingredient secret, because most people won't even taste it when they hear that spinach is involved. The crust is a doughy biscotti crust, rolled into knobs that circle the outer rim. As a little girl, I'd watch Nonna's large, strong hands grate thick bars of chocolate, tear a large loaf of bread into small pieces, and knead the thick doughy crust. She'd spend the entire day in the kitchen, but the end result was well worth her effort—four tortas quickly consumed by her four grateful grandchildren.

One year, I decided it was time for me to tackle the making of torta. When I asked Nonna for the recipe she said, "There is no recipe," her Italian accent still pronounced despite more than 60 years of living in this country. "Each time I make it a little differently." This was bad news for a compulsive direction-follower like myself.

"Listen, Nonna," I said, "I'll just watch you make torta and measure what you do." Despite her grumbles that measurements were unnecessary, she seemed pleased that I was trying to learn how to make her trademark dessert.

Since that fated day about ten years ago, I have made torta for my family during the holiday season. When I stand in my kitchen surrounded by bowls of raisins, chocolate and bread, I feel a kinship with my Italian female ancestors who enjoyed preparing this special treat for their families. I have yet to approach the perfection that is Nonna's torta, but with each year that passes, I come closer. This year, I've decided that it's time for my two daughters to join me in its preparation. Who knows, this may finally be the year I nail it.

FOR THE FILLING:

9 ounces black raisins

1 cup lukewarm water

1 loaf day-old white bread, 1½ pounds

Hershey's brand thick milk chocolate bars, at least 21 ounces total, but feel free to experiment

9 ounces chopped frozen spinach

Handful of chopped parsley

1½ sticks butter or margarine

1 cup milk

6 eggs

2 cups sugar

2 tablespoons vanilla extract

2 tablespoons crème de cacao, optional; or ¼ cup sugar

FOR THE CRUST:

6 cups flour, plus more for kneading

2 sticks butter

6 eggs

1 cup sugar

2 tablespoons vanilla

HINT
Extra dough can be used to make biscotti cookies. Roll the excess dough into a long tube. Bake at 350 for 15 minutes, then brush with egg/sugar/water/milk mixture. Continue cooking until brown. Let cool and cut into sections.

Filling: Soak raisins in 1 cup lukewarm water for 30 minutes and set aside. Take bread, tear into small pieces, and place in a large bowl. Grate milk chocolate bars into slivers and add to the bowl of bread pieces. Reserve 1 cup or more of grated chocolate for topping. Reserve the residual clumps of chocolate that didn't completely grate.

Heat spinach and parsley together; drain. In a separate saucepan, combine butter and milk; add any leftover chocolate "clumps" and heat until chocolate and butter are melted. Set aside. Add raisins and their soaking water to the bread/chocolate mixture. Add parsley and spinach to bread/chocolate mixture and stir it all together. Add the unbeaten eggs, stirring after each addition. Add sugar and mix. Add the warm milk/butter mixture, vanilla extract and crème de cacao. If crème de cacao is not used, then add an extra ¼ cup of sugar. Stir all ingredients until well mixed. Set filling aside while you make the crust.

Crust: Preheat over to 350 degrees. Grease four 8" or 9" pie tins with butter and set aside.

Cream flour and butter in a large bowl. Beat eggs with sugar in a separate bowl. Add vanilla to the eggs and mix well. Combine egg mixture and flour mixture. As mixture becomes thicker, use your hands to knead dough. Add flour to the dough as necessary until dough no longer sticks to your hands.

Put a pastry cloth over a bread board and flour the rolling pin. Divide the dough into 4 equal balls. Roll each ball out in a circle approximately 12" in diameter. Roll completed circle around the rolling pin and transfer to a pie tin, making sure that 2" of dough extends over the side of the pie pan.

Repeat the above steps with the 3 other balls of dough, until you have 4 pies ready to be filled. Divide the filling among the pie pans.

To finish the pie crust and make the "knob" outer rim, take a sharp knife and make a diagonal slash in the pie dough from the edge of the pie pan to the outside of the crust. Roll the dough toward the pie plate and slash on the opposite side creating a knob, with the diagonal point up. Slash again, roll again, until the entire outside rim is covered with knobs. Periodically, it may be necessary to trim off extra dough if too much crust accumulates in the rolling process. The knobs should be about ½" in size.

Sprinkle the reserved grated chocolate on top of each pie. Bake for 45 to 60 minutes. After baking for 15 minutes, remove the pies and brush crust with a mixture of:

1 egg
1 tablespoon sugar
1 tablespoon water
1 teaspoon milk

Remove from oven and let cool. After 10 minutes remove pie from plate and let torta completely cool on a wire rack. Torta freezes well for later use when wrapped in aluminum foil.

YIELD: 4 pies

DIVINITY UNDER THE STAR-LIT MOON

CYDNE HORROCKS WATTERSON

Every Christmas, from the time I was two until five, my father and I made divinity under the star-lit moon. My memory is of my father heating the Karo syrup on the stove until it boiled vigorously. Then he would gather a large towel from the drawer, grab the pot at its broken handle and head outside.

It was a Utah December so I know it must have been cold, but I followed him without question. I remember the crunch of crisp snow under my feet as I crouched to sit next to him on the back stoop, the cool breeze on my cheeks that eventually ached. The tin roof of the garage reflected the glow of the moon. It was evening, winter white, quiet. He held the pot against his leg and stirred. "What color should we make it?" he would ask. Clutching the plastic McCormick vial of color kept hidden until now, I would open my chubby little child hand and reveal the color. One year we made it pink. I remember the delight on my father's face the year I selected green.

It was always the same silver pot, a wedding present, my parents said. The pan seemed irreplaceable with its worn-off coating and broken handle. The bottom was charred black, but scrubbed meticulously clean.

> 2 cups sugar
> 1 cup corn syrup (I use Karo brand)
> ½ cup water
> 2 egg whites
> 1 teaspoon vanilla
> Food coloring of your choice
> Nuts, if desired

In your favorite broken-handled pot stir together the sugar, corn syrup and water. Place candy thermometer in pot. Heat on high until it reaches 250 degrees; do not stir. Once the thermometer reads 225 degrees, begin beating the egg whites in a large bowl until stiff. When the syrup reaches between 245 and 250 degrees (or forms a ball when you drop it into a cold glass of water) SLOWLY pour the syrup into the eggs as you keep mixing the eggs on high.

Add vanilla, food coloring, and nuts if desired. Soon the mixture will become too stiff for the beaters to handle. This is when my Dad takes the bowl and heads outside. Using a wooden spoon, fold mixture until cool and desired stiffness. Come back inside and drop by spoonfuls onto wax paper.

My father has modified his techniques since my early memory when I was only two. "The key is to use a thermometer and pour the syrup SLOWLY into the egg while they are beating on high," he told me. Yes, he still heats his syrup with the same broken-handled pot.

YIELD: About 2 dozen

BERNICE'S SIDE DISH

LORRAINE STARK

It was my first Thanksgiving dinner as a newlywed. I was frantic. I had never prepared a dinner of this size that included such a variety of foods. What was a girl to do? So, I knocked on my neighbor Bernice's door, hoping she had a recipe or two to help complete my holiday dinner. Within minutes she wrote down two of her own very simple dishes. That moment marked the beginning of our beautiful friendship. A holiday cooking tradition began, simply from a knock on a neighbor's door.

Now, thirty years later, I still take out the same paper Bernice wrote the recipes on—the page with my favorite splattered cooking designs—and I think of that sweet encounter the day she helped rescue my first Thanksgiving.

Each Thanksgiving, I give her a call to say hello and express my love, and I thank her again. For as surely as Thanksgiving comes, so does the making of Bernice's recipes. Her recipes remain on paper, but most of all they remain in my heart.

2 packages black cherry gelatin dessert
1 can (16 ounces) jellied cranberry sauce
1 small can of crushed pineapple

In a large bowl, prepare the gelatin dessert according to package directions. In a separate bowl, mash the cranberry sauce until smooth. Drain the can of crushed pineapple.

Add the cranberry sauce and pineapple to the gelatin and blend well. Refrigerate until firm, then serve.

YIELD: 6 to 8 servings

GRANNY'S APPLE STACK CAKE

ANN H. HOWELL

I remember the first time Christmas meant more than what Santa's magic puffed through the straw-sized chimney of our mobile home. By noon we'd made our way across the graveyard of last summer's vegetable garden to Granny's. I rushed in, anxious to know what my other cousins had gotten for Christmas. A wall of scents halted me. Apples dominated.

My grandmother, (Mrs. Walter Hyatt of Leicester, North Carolina) stood in the kitchen, a scene from Norman Rockwell, from her bunned hair to the gingham apron that hugged her bowl-full-of-jelly middle. She held a mixing bowl tucked in one arm, and whipped up potatoes by hand. On the counter, her apple stack cake loomed, eight layers high. The pancake-thin teacakes had been soaking in the apple-spice mixture for three days in the refrigerator.

The last time I ate her apple stack cake, she'd run out of energy and used a cake mix. I remember the disappointing taste. Christmas evaporated right then. Between my memories of her original, family recollections, and piece-mealing recipes, I've come up with one. Dad gave me the greatest compliment last Christmas. "This is as close as I've tasted to Mommie's."

There are literally thousands of varieties of apples cultivated around the world. Hendersonville and Waynesville are among North Carolina cities that host apple festivals each year.

FOR THE FILLING:

1 ½ pounds dried apples
Water or cider to cover
1 teaspoon cinnamon
½ teaspoon allspice
½ teaspoon cloves
1 cup sugar (white, brown or mixed)
½ teaspoon salt

FOR THE CAKE:

½ cup shortening
½ cup sugar
1 cup molasses
2 eggs
4 to 5 cups self-rising flour, plus extra for rolling out the dough
1 teaspoon soda
1 teaspoon ginger
1 teaspoon nutmeg
1 teaspoon cinnamon
½ cup buttermilk
1 tablespoon vanilla

You can substitute applesauce for the soaked, dried apples; use about 2-1/2 cups and reduce the sugar to 1/2 cup. This cake freezes well.

The night before: Soak the dried apples at room temperature overnight in just enough water or apple cider to cover.

The next day: Cook apples on low until tender, then mash. Add spices (more or less to your taste), sugar and salt. Return to boil, being careful not to scorch. When sugar is dissolved and mixture thickens, remove from heat and cool.

Preheat oven to 350 degrees. Lightly grease as many 9" cake pans as you have (recipe makes 8 layers) and set aside.

In a large bowl, cream shortening and sugar until light and fluffy. Add molasses and mix well. Add eggs, beating well.

In a separate bowl, combine the dry ingredients; then add to creamed mixture, alternating with buttermilk, beating well after each addition. Stir in vanilla, blend well. Dough will be very stiff. Place on well-floured surface and work in enough flour for easy handling. Divide into 8 balls. Roll out each so it looks like a large cookie and press into prepared pans. Bake 12 to 15 minutes or until lightly browned. Remove from oven and cool.

Cover each layer, except the top one, with the apple mixture, spreading to the edges. Store in refrigerator at least overnight, but it's better after several days.

YIELD: 10 to 12 servings

TIPSEY CAKE FROM ALICE LENORA DUKE WOOTEN

MARILYN MEACHAM PRICE

Mealtimes at Grandmother Wooten's house in Statesville, North Carolina, were exciting times for a little girl. The pie safe (which I now have) held delicious pies and cakes, but the favorite was Grandma's Tipsey Cake, made as a special treat at Christmas, for a family of non-drinkers.

The big, black oak table was covered with a damask cloth and set with Aunts Miriam and Rachel's crystal and silverware. In the nearby kitchen, delicious food, cooked on an apple-green enameled wood stove, was being dished up. Later, no one would leave the table hungry.

Alice Duke was the youngest of six children of a Civil War soldier who was wounded at Antietam, Maryland. Alice later married Thomas Gaston Wooten. During that time, covered wagons rumbled down from the mountains, driving large herds of cattle, which Tom later butchered and sold in his meat market.

Grandpa Wooten died unexpectedly in 1923, and left Alice with six children, ages 7 to 20. With a garden, a cow and an orchard, they managed to eat well, canning and preserving what they needed. This family of gentle people showed a spirit of grace and survival through many challenging times.

Here is Alice Lenora Duke Wooten's recipe as she wrote it down in 1923:

6 eggs leaving out the whites from 3
2 cups of sugar
2 teaspoons of vanilla
2½ cups flour, with 1 level teaspoon of soda and 1 level teaspoon of cream of tarter sifted in

"Beat the yellow of eggs a little, add sugar and beat until light, then add the 3 beaten whites and a cup of boiling water. Then add the flour, flavor with vanilla and bake in 3 layers [in moderate oven].

"Then take 2 quarts of sweet milk, 8 eggs and 2 cups of sugar and make a boiled custard.

"Have a large glass bowl, put in this bowl 1 layer and saturate with some good white wine, then stick layer thickly with blanched almonds, then pour over some of the boiled custard, then add the rest of the layers and do them as the first was done. Serve with whipped cream which has had wine added to it; to a quart of rich cream add ¾ cup of sugar and ½ pint white wine, whip until stiff."

"Whipped topping: To one quart of rich cream add ¾ cup of sugar and ½ pint of whole cream which has been whipped until stiff."

MARILYN MEACHAM PRICE'S TIPSEY CAKE (EASY MODERN-DAY ADAPTATION)

1 angel food cake (I use sugar-free)
White wine or sherry for flavoring
2 packages French Vanilla instant pudding mix
1 package blanched slivered almonds
1 large carton whipped topping

In a large glass bowl, place a layer of cake pieces soaked in wine, then layer with pudding, almonds and whipped topping; repeat until finished. Top with whipped topping and refrigerate.

YIELD: About 12 servings

HINT
Either sugar-free or regular angel-food cake will work.

GRANDMA'S FLAPJACKS

CARRIE BARNES

Christmas Eve was the only time that my sister Brenda and I didn't have to be coaxed into going to bed, because we believed Santa Claus would not come if we stayed awake. Snuggled under the heavy quilts in the big double bed, long after the embers in the wood stove had died, we whispered secrets and speculated about what presents Santa would bring.

At dawn we tiptoed into the living room to search for our gifts among the piles of unwrapped items that lay under the tree and on the sofa. Satisfied with our presents, we dressed and prepared to make our favorite breakfast. Fruit, nuts and raisins were selected from our fruit sacks, and cut into small pieces. Brenda then set the dining room table with Grandma's bone china dessert plates. The warmth of the fire and the quiet of the early morning erased all memory of sibling squabbles and jealousy as we ate our special meal.

Many years have passed, but even now on Christmas morning I still wake at dawn and remember two sisters sitting at the dining room table sharing their special breakfast, flapjacks.

1 cup sifted all-purpose flour
3 teaspoons baking powder
½ teaspoon salt
2 teaspoons sugar
⅛ teaspoon cinnamon
3 eggs
½ cup buttermilk
2 teaspoons butter or margarine, melted
¼ cup apple, peeled and finely chopped
1 tablespoon pecans, finely chopped
2 teaspoons raisins
Oil and butter for the pan

Slowly heat griddle or heavy skillet over medium heat. In a small bowl sift flour, baking powder, salt, sugar and cinnamon. In a separate bowl, beat eggs until fluffy. Add dry ingredients. Beat until smooth. Stir in buttermilk and butter. Add apple, nuts and raisins. Stir until combined. Do not overmix.

Grease skillet with cooking oil and butter. Pour ¼ cup of batter onto hot skillet and cook until bubbles form on the surface and edges are cooked. Turn and cook until the underside is browned. Serve with syrup of choice.

YIELD: 6 to 8 generous-sized flapjacks

ICE BOX CAKE

JANIE W. BIRD

I grew up in North Carolina during the Depression. Sweets were a rarity. We made ice box cake every year either at Thanksgiving or at Christmas. This is exactly how my family made this holiday treat.

Standing high in the crotch of a pecan tree in our front yard, Daddy rocked back and forth. Pecans rained down onto the lawn. Brother and I gathered them in a bushel basket, hulled and diligently broke them into pieces until Mama would finally declare that we had enough pieces for the cake.

Mama, in her apron, melted a pound of marshmallows in a can of evaporated milk while Brother and I crushed a pound of graham crackers by placing a few crackers at a time between sheets of wax paper and pounding them with a rolling pin.

Mama broke more than one wooden spoon stirring the pecan pieces, the graham cracker crumbs and a pound of raisins into the cooled marshmallow mixture. We gladly took turns pressing the mixture into the heavy square glass dish that was always used. The mixture was sticky and finger licking was good.

This is how ice box cake is made today—go to the store and buy:

1 pound marshmallows (marshmallow crème will not work)
A 12-ounce can evaporated milk (not fat free)
1 pound fresh pecan pieces
1 pound graham cracker crumbs
1 pound raisins
Whipped cream

In a saucepan, melt the marshmallows in the evaporated milk. Combine the cooled mixture with the nuts, crumbs and raisins in the bowl of a heavy-duty mixer. Use the dough hook to mix thoroughly. Press firmly into 2 loaf pans, which may be lined with foil for easy removal. Refrigerate overnight. Recipe may be doubled. Slice and serve with whipped cream—and love.

Foolproof. No hurt fingers from hulling pecans by hand. No sticky fingers to lick. No great memories generated.

YIELD: 2 loaf pans

ILA'S MARSHMALLOW CREAM FUDGE

PHYLLIS H. LAMBERT

Today's marshmallows contain none of the plant, marshmallow root, for which the confection was originally named. Make a sandwich of marshmallow crème — or "fluff" — with peanut butter and you'll have a "fluffernutter."

My mother-in-law, Ila Lambert, who passed away in 2000, presented this recipe to me. She was a very dear person and a terrific cook. The dessert is special to me because it reminds me of Christmas, sitting around Ila's kitchen table.

Ila was a beautiful woman who demonstrated her love through her delicious meals. Most memorable to me were her desserts. Fancy salads, cakes, pies, and candy were the most wonderful delicacies I had ever tasted.

I remember her "golf balls," round spheres of candy with a *potato* filling and wrapped in chocolate. Her layered Christmas salad was unforgettable. It was made of cherry Jell-O, white cream cheese, lime Jell-O, and crowned with walnuts and homemade whipped cream.

Igloos, a frozen dessert, were another of her specialties. This concoction was made from cookies dipped in soft, coconut icing with a delectable filling of cherries and pecans. Sweet potato pie, fresh coconut cake (with coconut ground by hand), would literally melt in my mouth.

And of course there was the fudge…The smell, the flavor, the memories, the love is what I shall always cherish. Eat a piece of Ila's creamy fudge, but chew it slowly and savor the aroma, the texture, the significance of it. Enjoy!

1 large can Carnation brand evaporated milk

5 cups sugar

½ pound margarine (2 sticks)

2 packages semi-sweet chocolate chips

1 pint jar marshmallow crème or 1 large bag of marshmallows

A few drops of vanilla extract

Nuts (optional)

Grease a 10" square pan or small baking sheet with raised edges. Set aside.

Combine the milk, sugar and margarine in a large saucepan, bring to a boil and cook about 10 to 12 minutes, stirring constantly until thick. Remove from heat and add the chocolate chips, marshmallow crème (or marshmallows) and vanilla. Stir until everything is dissolved; stir in nuts if you are using them.

Pour into prepared pan and let cool before cutting. Fudge may be wrapped and stored in the refrigerator nearly indefinitely.

YIELD: 25 small, rich squares

WARTIME CAKE

STOWE B. COBB, JR.

This cake has been made by at least three—possibly four—generations of our family. My grandmother, the late Amy Setzer Cobb of Kannapolis, North Carolina, made what she called a Wartime Cake. I am not sure where she got the recipe, perhaps from her mother. She passed the recipe to my father, the late Stowe B. Cobb, Sr.

Sometimes he made the cake at Thanksgiving, but he always made the Wartime Cake at Christmas. I am now 67 years old. I remember having the cake when I was seven or eight years old. It became our family Christmas cake.

After my father died, my mother, Evelyn Sweatt Cobb, continued to make the cake at Christmas. Daddy had always made it and we missed him so much. The cake was our connection to him. I married after he died. My mother continued to have the five of us, our spouses and children at her house on Christmas Day for a covered-dish dinner. She made Wartime Cake until her death.

My wife, Karen, asked her for the recipe one year after she had the cake at our Christmas gathering. The Wartime Cake continues as a holiday tradition at our house.

2 cups brown sugar
2 cups hot water
2 tablespoons cinnamon
2 tablespoons shortening
1 box raisins
1 teaspoon baking soda
3 cups sifted flour
1 teaspoon hot water
2 cups sugar
Juice of 4 lemons

Preheat oven to 350 degrees. Grease a bundt pan and set aside.

In a large saucepan, combine the brown sugar, 2 cups hot water, cinnamon, shortening and raisins. Bring to a boil, reduce to a simmer and cook for 5 minutes. Remove from heat and let cool.

Then add the baking soda, flour and remaining teaspoon of hot water. Stir until combined. Pour into prepared pan and bake 50 to 60 minutes, or until a tester inserted into the middle comes out clean.

While cake is cooling, combine the remaining 2 cups of sugar with the lemon juice. After cake cools, spread it with the lemon glaze.

YIELD: About 8 servings

HUNDRED-YEAR-OLD WELSH CHRISTMAS PUDDING

LISA WILLIAMS KLINE

This traditional recipe calls for suet, a fat from beef or mutton. It's as familiar to British cooks as lard is to Americans.

The miseries of mining slate drove my ancestor, Owen Williams, from Caernarvon, Wales. I have heard the Williamses were discriminating people; during the winter they allowed the cow in the house but not the pig. My suspicion is that our family coped, not by leading strikes against mine-owners or freeing blind pit ponies, but by gathering 'round the peat fire in the stone cabin and seeing who could tell the best story.

My father's mother had a sly sense of humor. At a barn dance as a girl she once danced holes in her shoes. After her funeral, thirty relatives stuffed themselves into her tiny lace-doily living room. I had loved her, and steeled myself for an anguishing afternoon. But conversation grew lively, the men standing to compete in storytelling. Fortified by pound cake and coffee (our side of the family were tee-totalers but others may have had additional fortification), the men went on for hours, until our sides hurt from laughing and tears ran down our cheeks. My grandmother would have had such a good time.

My grandmother's recipe for Welsh Christmas pudding takes two weeks and is basically inedible. However, if you are listening to a great story while eating it, you might not notice. It's valuable for historical purposes so we can say, "Man, can you believe people used to eat this?"

1 pound sugar
1 pound suet
1 pound bread crumbs
1 pound flour
1 box raisins
1 box currants
4 ounces citron
1 tablespoon orange peel, finely chopped
1 tablespoon lemon peel, finely chopped
2 teaspoons baking powder

Pinch of salt
4 eggs, beaten
1 tablespoon lemon extract
Enough milk to make the ingredients stick together (about 1 cup)

In a large bowl, add the first 11 ingredients to the beaten eggs. Add the lemon extract. Add milk a little at a time and mix until ingredients are incorporated and stick together.

Tie the pudding in a wet cheesecloth that has been dredged in flour. Tie up, leaving a little room for the pudding to swell out.

Drop in boiling water and boil 4 hours in plenty of water. Then remove from water and without removing the cloth, place in a large bowl and shape into a flattened ball. Leave overnight.

The next day, remove from bowl but leave cloth in place. Allow to dry at room temperature for 10 to 15 days. Turn each day to dry all sides.

Serve with hard sauce made from sugar, butter, vanilla, eggs; and rum, brandy or whiskey. Cut thin. Warm when you serve to soften the pudding.

YIELD: 30 or more servings

"GIFT FOOD"

Amy Rogers

If it's better to give than to receive, then it is certainly better to give than to receive *gift food*. This is because gift food is rarely any sort of a gift, and sometimes barely even qualifies as food.

Let's clarify exactly what we mean. Here are some examples: Any food packaged at one Christmas and claiming still to be edible the next, is gift food.

Any food which comes packaged inside a toy, an ornament, or a tin that depicts happy families traveling over the river and through the woods, is gift food.

Any food which has been chemically altered to assure uniformity of size and eliminate the need for refrigeration, is gift food.

Any food packaged with a logo of a resort, a theme park, or bearing the phrase "a souvenir of," is gift food.

And so is any holiday-themed food where, upon opening it, you discover there's more package than product.

Why do we do this? Why do we spend good money on bad food? First, it seems to make sense. Everyone loves gifts and everyone loves food. But that's like saying everyone loves hotdogs and ice cream, so Ben & Jerry should put hotdog-flavored ice cream right next to Cherry Garcia.

Second, it seems thoughtful yet practical. Loved ones will use and enjoy your gift. Forget the cranberry relish that Grandma makes every year. This year you can send something pasteurized, bottled, and boxed. Overnight delivery is only $6.95 extra!

Third, it seems creative. Food is necessary, so why not dress it up a bit and let it have some fun? That's not a bad idea, it's just what happens in the attempt to mass-produce—and market—gift food where it all goes horribly wrong.

Let's say you have a friend who loves to play golf. He also has a sweet tooth. So you pick up the phone and order him a set of chocolate golf balls. Or maybe another friend likes coffee, so you dial the 800 number and send her those teeny bags of coffee, packaged in a handy, holiday tin.

Dear food-gifter, these are mistakes. Golfers don't want to put their mouths around a chocolate-ized version of a Titleist. Coffee connoisseurs don't savor squinty little bags of grounds that were packaged months—or years—before brewing. And they have no use for that cute, collectible tin that doesn't match the kitchen. It's just one more thing to wash, store, and remember to display when you come to visit.

What's that? You haven't visited in a while? Why is that? Before you log onto the web for faster gift-food service, stop and think. Your friends and family don't want any of that stuff. Oh, they want food: good food, fresh food, but not something out of a warehouse.

Actually, the sad truth is that almost anything you send them is sure to disappoint, because what they really want is you. They want you at the dinner table, telling Grandma how much you enjoy her relish. They want you out on the golf course with them, no matter how rusty your swing. And they want you drinking coffee at their kitchen table, not on the other end of a telephone somewhere.

Here is what to do: Find a cheap plane ticket, book a hotel if you need one, then go. Go see your sister or nephew or that classmate you email all the time. Take the train or get up early and drive. If you feel you must bring a gift, make cookies or bring bread from your neighborhood bakery. Stop at the farmer's market and pick up something that's in season.

Or invite a fellow food-gifter to visit you. If you hate to cook, go to the drive-in where you hung out as teenagers or check out the new Chinese restaurant that has dumplings on the buffet.

This is the gift that everyone wants: time spent together. And if that time is spent sharing food, preparing food and savoring food, the experience is all the more delicious.

PEPPERMINT BARK CANDY

Making this candy doesn't require using a thermometer.

FOR THE CANDY:

A box of peppermint candy canes (12)
A 12-ounce bag of dark chocolate chips
A 12-ounce bag of white chocolate chips

EQUIPMENT YOU'LL NEED:

A hammer (yes, a hammer)
Large, heavy-duty plastic zipper-lock bags
Wood or acrylic cutting board
Baking sheet
Aluminum foil
2 rubber scrapers or wooden spoons
2 microwave-safe bowls
Waxed paper
A clean linen towel
A sharp knife
Cute holiday candy bags or boxes

Don't you love a recipe that lets you smash something with a hammer? Even better, when you're finished, there's candy! No need to measure anything, and no candy thermometer required, either.

Unwrap the candy canes and place them in a zipper bag, seal it, then place the bag inside another one and seal, squeezing out as much air as you can each time. Put the double-bagged candy on the cutting board, take the hammer, and whack away on the candy until it splinters into little bite-sized bits. DO NOT under any circumstances try to crush the canes in their cellophane wrappers! The wrappers will shred into the candy and you will have to throw everything out and start over. This is the voice of experience speaking.

Line the baking sheet with foil. Do not grease it. Set aside.

This next part sounds a bit complicated, but it's so easy you won't believe it. Put the dark chocolate chips in one of the bowls and heat the chips until they begin to melt in the microwave, usually about 3 to 4 minutes. Do not let them melt completely; remove when they begin to melt and stir until smooth. Reheat a bit if needed. The idea is to melt the chocolate enough to spread it, but not much more than that.

Quickly spread the chocolate into the prepared pan, to a thickness of about ¼". Don't worry about making it smooth. It's really gooey at this point; when you're done, set the spoon down on waxed paper to keep things neat. Place pan in the refrigerator to cool slightly while you do the next step.

Put the while chocolate chips in the other bowl, microwave as above until chips begin to melt, stir with the clean spoon until smooth. Remove the pan from the fridge, and spread the melted white chocolate over the first layer, covering it completely.

Then sprinkle with the crushed candy and press in gently with your fingers. Don't worry about being neat. (By now you probably have bits of candy all over the place anyhow.) Put the pan back in the fridge and let it chill at least an hour while you lick the bowls—I mean, clean up.

When the bark is well chilled, remove from fridge, cover with the towel and turn upside down. Pull away the pan and peel off the foil; it should come off easily. Place right-side up on the cutting board and cut into pieces. Don't worry about the "splintery" look; the irregular shape and size is the hallmark of homemade candy. Oh—and the crumbs that break off are for you and your helpers, if you have them.

Put the bark into little holiday candy boxes or bags and watch it disappear.

YIELD: About 1 ½ pounds

HINT
How long it will take for the chips to melt depends on your microwave. After the first batch, you'll be able to approximate how long to set the timer. You can also make this candy in a double boiler; just heat until the chips begin to melt and follow the rest of the instructions from there.

AMITY'S ROASTED GARLIC MASHED POTATOES

LEE SMITH

Best-selling novelist Lee Smith, who now lives in Hillsborough, N.C., began writing in her hometown of Grundy, Virginia.

Like me, you probably receive a number of Christmas letters every year. You know the ones I mean—those long, chatty epistles mass-produced on Merry Christmas stationery, full of mostly good news. These letters used to come mimeographed—remember that fading purple ink? Then they were photocopied . . . now they are often typeset on a computer.

Maybe you just shake your head, and toss your Christmas letters into the trash. Maybe you really hate them: one of my friends refers to them as "brag and gag" letters.

Me, I have this compulsion to read them all, every word, several times, even if they are from a distant cousin I scarcely remember, or some couple I met on a trip to Gulf Shores in 1985 and have never laid eyes on since.

For every Christmas letter is the story of a life, and what story can be more interesting than the story of our lives? Often it is the life of an entire family. We get the big news—who died, who got married, who had a baby or moved off to Texas, all conveyed in that strangely perky tone peculiar to Christmas letters.

But there is always some news we don't read here, some equally big news which we are *not* being told, and this is perhaps the most fascinating thing about Christmas letters. Sometimes what is *not* said is even more important than what is on the page. I read every word and save every one, mulling them over and over.

Since I write Christmas letters myself, I know what's going on here. Denial is at work—that catch-all term for *not-knowing* or *not-admitting*. Psychologists are always trying to get us to give up denial; but I think it is often a good and useful thing, keeping us going, allowing us to do what has to be done in the world. Families run on denial—we have to! Actually, the term I prefer is "the saving lie." These "saving lies" are often the very stuff of Christmas letters. They're not even lies, not really. When we sit down to write a Christmas letter, we are constructing a story of our lives, and it *is* a true story, though we could write another, different story that would be equally true.

In my own family, my mother often ended her Christmas letters with a recipe, and I do, too. This Christmas, the next generation has gotten into the act; my stepdaughter Amity makes the best mashed potatoes in the world, so I'm sharing *her* recipe.

A giant clove of garlic
4 pounds Idaho potatoes, plus one sweet potato; peeled, quartered, boiled, and drained in a colander
4 teaspoons salt
2 sticks butter or margarine
1 cup heavy cream
Approximately 1 cup milk
Ground pepper

First, roast a giant clove of garlic, then mash it up. Add everything to the hot potatoes. Beat with a hand-held mixer. Taste to make sure seasonings are right. Amity leaves a lot of peel on, and does NOT whip them until they are super-smooth. The addition of one sweet potato gives them a lovely golden color and a very special taste.

YIELD: About 8 servings

Christmas letters are written as much for the writer, I believe, as for the recipient. Because Christmas can be dangerous, a scary season, full of loaded traditions and ideas. Writing a Christmas letter forces us to take stock: How do we really feel about our family? Who do we really want to keep in touch with? What part of the past do we want to forget? What part of the past do we want to claim? What is really important to us anyway? How do we feel about kids, faith, marriage, home? What does success mean? These are the traditional themes of the Christmas letter, and your correspondent is walking through an emotional minefield to get to you. It's hard. We've only got one page to get it right. Or at least to get it as right as we can, which is all anybody can ever do anyway, isn't it? For me, the underlying message of any Christmas letter is one of hope—written across the years, across the map. We're still here, and we hope you are. *Merry Christmas.*

IDA MAE MANER'S FRUITCAKE

PATSY B. KINSEY

As an eight- or nine-year-old child, nothing said "Christmas" to me more than my grandmother's fruitcake. I would know the exact day that she was baking, because walking home from school, I could smell the fruitcake a block away. This would be around Thanksgiving, but we would not cut the cake until nearer Christmas, after it had time to soak up the sherry sprinkled on it—the only alcohol kept in the house.

Years later when I tried my hand at my grandmother's recipe I discovered that not only did she not write down the exact measurements, she added extra ingredients according to what she had in the pantry. My first cakes were too dry. When I asked my mother what was missing she replied, "Did you add the fig and blackberry preserves?" I have baked this recipe many times since then and I have taken care to add my own homemade fig and blackberry preserves, obviously my grandmother's secret ingredients. Although I am extremely biased, I love fruitcake and this is without a doubt the best I have ever eaten.

½ cup flour to roll nuts and fruit in
¼ pound citron
½ pound crystallized pineapple
½ pound crystallized cherries
½ box raisins
½ box currants
1 box chopped dates
¼ pound almonds
¼ pound Brazil nuts
1 cup black walnuts
½ pound pecans
½ pound butter (2 sticks)
2 cups sugar

HINT
My grandmother did not give any directions, and since the preserves were her "secret" you can add them in any amount you like. If there's too much batter, you can just keep filling smaller pans until it's gone.

6 eggs

4 cups flour

½ teaspoon baking powder

½ teaspoon baking soda

½ teaspoon each cinnamon, allspice, ground cloves, ginger

½ teaspoon each vanilla, orange, lemon, black walnut extracts

1 cup buttermilk

A generous scoop of fig and blackberry preserves, optional

Sherry, optional

Preheat oven to 325 degrees. Grease and flour a large tube pan and a 9 x 5" loaf pan, or two medium-sized tube pans; set aside.

Roll nuts and fruit in ½ cup flour and set aside.

In a large bowl, cream together the butter and sugar and add eggs one at a time. Beat well.

In a separate bowl, sift together the dry ingredients. Add the dry ingredients to creamed mixture alternately with the buttermilk. Stir in nuts and fruit; batter will be stiff. If you are using preserves, stir in. Pour batter into prepared pans about ¾ full and bake about 60 to 75 minutes, or until a tester inserted into the center of the cakes comes out clean.

If you are using sherry, let cake cool, then sprinkle as lightly or heavily as you like. Wrap in foil and store in the refrigerator. Cake will keep a very long time.

YIELD: At least 30; the cake is very rich

TAKING COMFORT IN HERITAGE FOODS

AMANDA DEW MANNING

It seems like only yesterday that I dashed up the wisteria-lined lane that led to my grandmother's house, carefully avoiding the drunken bumblebees darting across my path. I scurried on, eagerly anticipating the Sunday dinner that would soon be laid out on the dining room table. I could hear the simmering pot of fresh turnip greens tapping out its own melody on the old white stove as the pungent odor drifted from the bubbling lid.

There was always a country ham waiting to be carved. Baked to perfection and garnished by pineapple slices studded with cloves, it created juices both sweet and fragrant. Depending on the season, there might also be roast venison, smothered quail, catfish stew, or fried chicken. Side dishes included pilaus, or just plain rice and gravy, grits, sweet potatoes, creamy corn pudding, or my favorite—macaroni pie.

In the summer, we could count on butter beans, fried okra, and sliced tomatoes still warm from the garden sun. Artichoke relish and scuppernong preserves, put up fresh each year, were served in the same elegant cut-glass bowls that graced my great-grandmother's table and now grace mine. A crisply ironed linen napkin lined the sterling silver bread tray piled high with hot and flaky scratch biscuits.

Soon the biscuits would cradle the sweet hand-churned butter that would eventually seep through to every layer. And then there were the desserts: lemon jelly cake, ambrosia, peach cobbler with dumplings, and pecan pie, among my favorites. As I close my eyes now, my senses are flooded with the sounds of the family gathering around the table, the tantalizing aromas wafting from the kitchen, and the memory-laden tastes of those Sunday dinners.

My heart embraces the memory of the warmth and love experienced in my grandmother's kitchen. My sister once told our mother "even a slice of bread tastes better at Grandmama's house." When I prepare these same foods today, I am instantly connected to the generations of my family that came before me.

History tells me that the recipes and techniques used by my grandmother had their genesis in the cookery of South Carolina's earliest settlers. I find that very comforting.

Daniel Webster once said, "Those who do not look upon themselves as a link connecting the past with the future do not perform their duty to the world." Knowing more about our family's food traditions will help to reconnect us with our heritage and, in turn, to pass along these traditions to our children and grandchildren.

Taking a journey through the history of some of my family's favorite foods has been enlightening. I learned that okra has been a valued and versatile vegetable in South Carolina kitchens since Colonial times. Culinary historians believe it to be native to Africa and brought by African slaves to South Carolina in the 17th century. It was originally used in pilaus (pronounced "pur-low"), a dish of rice cooked in one pot with other ingredients such as chicken, shrimp, or tomatoes, and in gumbos, soups, and stews. During the War Between the States, okra was used as a substitute for coffee, which was nearly impossible to obtain because of Northern shipping blockades. The seeds, when mature and slightly roasted, made an acceptable brew. Today, okra is still enjoyed in pilaus, gumbos, soups, and stews.

Summer would not be summer without our beloved peaches. We grew up with a small, but sufficient, peach orchard on our farm. There are many recipes for peach cobbler, but few that have the delicate dumplings produced by Grandmother's expert touch.

Recipes for peach sherbet, peach marmalade, peach leather, pickled peaches, preserved peaches, brandy peaches, and peach chips can be found in several of South Carolina's earliest cookbooks. Today, South Carolina is known as "The *Tastier* Peach State" and is the second largest producer of peaches in the country after California. During peach season, cooks across the state frequent farmer's markets, roadside stands, orchards and packing sheds to buy just-picked peaches at their peak ripeness.

Natives take artichoke relish for granted, but newcomers often don't know that our favorite condiment is made from the Jerusalem artichoke, a nondescript tuber with little taste of its own. It is native to North America and grew wild along the eastern seaboard from Georgia to Nova Scotia. Often called a "sunchoke," it is a relative of the sunflower. Native Americans ate the crunchy tubers, but South Carolinians prized it as the main ingredient in condiments, such as artichoke relish and artichoke pickles.

As early as 1847, the cookbook, *The Carolina Housewife by a Lady of Charleston*, contained instructions for pickling artichokes.

For two days each year, the women in our family assembled in my grandmother's kitchen for the ritual of making the cherished artichoke relish. First, the tubers were scrubbed clean and chopped, then soaked overnight in cold salted water, along with the rest of the vegetables, to keep them crisp. The second day was devoted to cooking the "sauce" that bound the relish, sterilizing the jars and lids, and filling them with relish that was heated so hot the kitchen windows steamed over, even though it was still mild fall weather. Everyone in the kitchen was rewarded with a share of the glistening Ball jars filled with the bright yellow relish.

Few who have breathed in the fruity, musky odor of muscadine grapes will ever forget it. As children, my sister and I stood in the shade of the old grape arbor at Grandmother's house, picking and eating the divine fruit until we could eat no more. The grapes grow in clusters of four or more fruits which, when ripe, can be harvested easily by shaking the vine. Our father made a special stick that was long enough for us to use.

The muscadine grape is native to the Southeastern United States and was found growing wild by the early colonists along the coasts of Georgia, North and South Carolina. However, Native Americans preserved muscadines as dried fruit long before the Europeans arrived on this continent. Although muscadines can be grown successfully in most parts of South Carolina, they adapted best between the Piedmont and the Coastal Plain. Because of their unique fruity, musky odor and flavor, muscadines and scuppernongs have been used to make jams and wine since the 17th century. They are still used today in much the same way.

No Thanksgiving dinner at my grandmother's house was complete without a dish of sweet potatoes. Because they are as wonderfully sweet as "most any dessert," the children lobbied her to cook them for Sunday dinners, too. I think she agreed because, even then, she knew them to be nutritious. Whether served baked, stewed, in pies, pones, in butters, or in soufflés, sweet potatoes have nourished generations of South Carolinians.

In Colonial days, sweet potatoes were so prized that they became an item of trade. During the Revolutionary and Civil Wars it was a staple food. A popular legend describes how Francis Marion, known as the "Swamp Fox," met during the American Revolution with a British officer to discuss an exchange of prisoners. Following the negotiations, General Marion invited his guest for dinner. The menu consisted solely of sweet potatoes and water. The British officer was appalled and impressed at the same time. He reported, "I have seen an American general and his officers, without pay, and almost without clothes, living on roots and drinking water; and all for Liberty! What chance have we against such men?"

BOURBON SWEET POTATO CASSEROLE

FOR THE POTATOES:

2 cups of cooked, peeled, fresh sweet potatoes

¾ cup sugar

¼ teaspoon salt

4 tablespoons butter (½ stick)

2 eggs, well beaten

½ teaspoon freshly ground cinnamon

½ teaspoon freshly grated nutmeg

¼ cup milk

2 tablespoons good bourbon, the kind you wouldn't mind drinking

½ cup drained crushed pineapple

Preheat oven to 350 degrees. Grease an 8 x 8" ovenproof baking dish and set aside.

Into the cooked sweet potatoes, beat the sugar, salt, butter, eggs, spices, milk, bourbon and pineapple. Pour into the baking dish.

FOR THE TOPPING:

¾ cup light brown sugar, packed

⅓ cup flour

4 tablespoons butter (½ stick), melted

¾ cup chopped pecans

Mix brown sugar and flour together. Add melted butter and mix. Add pecans and mix again. Spread on top of sweet potato mixture.

Bake for about 30 minutes, or until slightly browned on top.

YIELD: *6 servings*

When I make this dish for holiday crowds, I usually double the recipe. I use the sweet potatoes of the season and same-year-crop pecans, and buy cinnamon sticks and grind them, and whole nutmegs and grate them.

7

Extras:
BEVERAGES, SAUCES,
CONDIMENTS AND OTHER
SPECIALTIES

DORI SANDERS,
PEACH FARMER

Amy Rogers

Spring had come early—too early, in fact. By February the peach trees were in bloom, by March the tiny fruit buds had appeared. Yes, it was beautiful to see, but farmer Dori Sanders was worried. If there was another cold snap, the young peaches could freeze and the crop would be lost. There would be no fruit to sell that summer at the family's farm stand in York County, South Carolina.

It happened. The peaches did not survive the early spring cold of 1997. What would Sanders do when the customers began arriving in June, looking for those wonderful peaches to put in pies, cobblers, and home-made ice cream?

That was the summer Dori Sanders sold rocks. Not just any old rocks, but 100% genuine FARM rocks, each with its own certificate of authenticity. She sold them to kids and she sold them to grown-ups. She carefully washed the peach-sized hunks of rosy quartz, polished them up to look pretty, set them out on the farm stand tables, and when people stopped to ask what she was doing, she told them, "We don't have any peaches, but we do have farm rocks that you can take home with you today."

Sound far-fetched? Not for the woman who has turned her memories of life on the family farm into two successful novels and a cookbook.

The youngest of ten children, Sanders grew up near Clover, South Carolina, where her father was principal of a two-room schoolhouse. Even though resources were often scarce in rural schools, Sanders is emphatic about the richness of her education, stating simply: "We had books."

As a child, she read Hawthorne and Homer, George Eliot and James Joyce (although she admits it was wasn't until many years later that she learned Eliot was a woman and Joyce wasn't). When her Daddy came home at the end of the day, she'd run to him, eager to tell him what was on

Despite the runaway success of her books, including her first novel, *Clover*, Dori Sanders still works as a peach farmer in South Carolina.

345

her mind. "He told me, 'Write it down,'" she says with a laugh. And so she did, beginning her letters to him, "Dear Mr. Sanders . . ."

"If you grow up on a farm," she says, "you learn by doing." Tall for her age, she taught herself to drive a tractor before she was ten. Soon the young girl grew into a woman. But instead of moving away and seeking a different kind of life, as many of her siblings did, she remained on the farm, where she still works today—with her brothers Jarvis and Orestus, and her sister Virginia Malone—to bring forth from the earth not only peaches, but sweet potatoes, greens, melons, okra, tomatoes, crowder peas and silver queen corn.

She rises early every day, before the sun, as farmers have for generations. "As soon as it's light enough to see, we start picking and gathering. We pick okra and pull corn," her strong hands demonstrate, "down and twist." When the sun moves higher in the sky and brightens up the day, it's time to pick the peaches, when you can see the perfect blush that signals the time is right.

"There is no electricity at the farm stand, so we must pick fresh every day," Sanders explains. For customers to drive from 20, 30, even 40 or more miles away, the produce and the place it comes from must be extra special.

Maybe it's the easy banter among the Sanders family and their customers. Or maybe it's a desire to remember a way of life that's becoming rare. But whatever it is, people come. Many sit under the tin-roofed "porch" and find that hours go by while they chat and feel the rhythms of life all around them: the cars pulling in and out, the hugs and hellos from friends, the breezes that blow gently through the leaves as the peaches slowly ripen.

And it was watching from this place, "looking at the landscape of my youth," that inspired the storyteller in Sanders. One day, she saw a funeral procession pass by, and in one car rode a little black girl who waved at her. Later that day, she saw a white woman drive past, sad in her own way, alone in her car. *What if I put them together,* Sanders asked herself, *that woman and that little girl?* The story of *Clover* was born.

Critics praised the book for its gentle humor, wisdom and freshness. They compared Sanders to Willa Cather, to Zora Neale Hurston, and to Maya Angelou. But the pull of success couldn't tug hard enough on Sanders to take her away from the farm, even after she wrote another novel, *Her Own Place.*

Her publisher had noticed that food cropped up often in Sanders' stories, and suggested she write a cookbook. *Dori Sanders' Country Cooking* was the result. "Food is a major topic of conversation," the author explains. "If it weren't for the weather, who died, and food, we wouldn't have any conversation!"

A farmer rarely rests, and Sanders is no exception, rambling around the farm in a 1974 Ford pick-up truck she calls Yellow Boy, and still driving her Massey Ferguson 235 tractor. "There is always something to do," she says.

When the summer growing season ends, it will be time for autumn greens, dark and leafy. There will be rows and rows of trees to prune, and seeds to buy for next year. And Sanders is at work on another writing project, a non-fiction work for which she is calling upon her own personal memories and recollections.

If next winter is too mild or spring is too harsh, the family will cope with quiet confidence. "The weather can be very crippling in its way, but the farmer can also in his own way become a little more resourceful," Sanders says. There are fish in nearby streams, wild berries, muscadine grapes. And what if the delicate peach blossoms should freeze again next year? What if there are no peaches to sell?

The author who remained on her family's land despite her successes in the literary world has a philosophy. "If you have survived up to that point you can surely survive what's ahead. We will survive because we are farmers."

WASTE NOT, WANT NOT
GOLDEN GLO PICKLES

DORI SANDERS

Day long during the summer peach season, the welcome mat is always spread. Customers, friends, and neighbors drop by—to buy or just to sit and visit.

And nearly always, the conversations turn to food and recipes. Safe talk, that makes even newcomers feel like comfortable old timers. The long 2002 summer drought and scorching heat burned fields of watermelons, cucumbers and okra to shades of golden yellow. When a customer learned the field of cucumbers was about to be plowed under, she screamed, "Wait! Don't let those big overripe yellow cukes go to waste!"

4 quarts bite-size chunks of over-ripe yellow cucumbers
3 medium onions, chopped
1 large green bell pepper, seeded and chopped
1 large red bell pepper, seeded and chopped
¼ cup salt
Water enough to cover
2 cups cider vinegar
15 whole cloves
3 cups sugar
⅓ cup mustard seed
2 teaspoons turmeric

Wash and peel cukes, cut into halves. Remove all seeds, slice halves lengthwise into quarters, and cut into bite-size chunks. Put into large lidded pot (approximately 6 quarts).

Put onions and peppers on top of cukes. Sprinkle with the salt. Cover and let stand overnight.

Drain and add just enough water to cover. Bring just to a boil, but DO NOT BOIL. Remove from heat and drain.

Add cider vinegar, whole cloves, sugar, mustard seed, and turmeric. Cook over medium heat 15 to 20 minutes. Pour into hot sterilized jars. Seal tightly and turn jars upside down on clean kitchen towels.

YIELD: 4 to 5 pints

LIB'S LIDLESS POPCORN

DIANA PINCKNEY

This recipe is a family secret. For grandchildren only. But my daughter relented and told me. When I was in a Charlotte hospital for a long spell, she stayed in Columbia with my mother. One night the two of them and Mother's little rat terrier were in the kitchen. Mother poured vegetable oil into a pot and turned on the flame. She dropped in a few kernels and when they popped, she poured in the rest. My daughter said the corn popped into the air, springing up out the pot, some of it bouncing off the ceiling, that it rained popcorn. The dog jumped, snapped and swallowed. My squealing daughter caught popcorn in her skirt, in her open mouth, hopped around crunching it under her feet and my mother, my mother sat in a wooden kitchen chair and laughed until she cried. And maybe the dog laughed at such sport. The dish didn't run away with the spoon, but my daughter was way over the moon.

I don't know why Mother left the pot's lid off. I wasn't there. Maybe she was distracted or had trouble reaching or grasping the top. She was no longer quick in the kitchen or anywhere else. By this time my mother had developed multiple sclerosis and carefully moved about by gripping furniture, pushing against walls. But I like to think she just wanted to give a weepy, homesick child some fun. My grandchildren will not be as fortunate. I have popcorn and popsicles, but I also have a newly renovated kitchen. If you're more adventurous than I, or maybe yearning to jazz up your kitchen, all you need is:

1 bag of corn kernels
1 deep pot
Oil, enough to cover the bottom of the pot
1 child or more, any age
1 dog or more, any age

CLARA BLISS'S CARAMEL CORN

LESLIE B. RINDOKS

When I'm feeling absolutely crummy—aching, coughing, running a fever—I think of my old college boyfriend, the aspiring thespian who kept a desk crammed with poems of undying love he'd written to some chick in Cleveland (I lived near Columbus); the sweetheart that proposed to my classmate at graduation; the guy whose silver Trans Am I wrecked. When I'm feeling my absolute worst, my thoughts turn to him. Actually, in my fever induced state, I conjure up his mother, Clara. But not for the reasons you might think.

A wild Pisces woman, Clara charted horoscopes, read palms and eyes, even strands of hair. She analyzed handwriting and dreams with uncanny insight, and in her spare time she cooked up a storm. Italian sausage and peppers, pot roast, cream puffs, éclairs and anything chocolate. She came to my wedding (no, I didn't marry her son, the actor) and was the star of the reception when she read the wedding guests' palms. But, why you might ask, do major head colds bring her to mind?

Two reasons: One, she could whip up an onion soup that had amazing curative powers. Forget what scientists have proven about chicken soup, they obviously never tasted Clara's onion soup. Two, Clara knew how to nurse a cold. An inveterate movie buff, she was the first in her neighborhood to subscribe to the Movie Channel and HBO. She knew every role that any actor of any note had ever played. After a bowl of spicy onion soup that cleared out the sinuses, it was time to settle down on the couch and turn on the movies. As an accompaniment to movies, what else would there be but popcorn, Clara style? Sadly, the secret to Clara's onion soup died with her, but her favorite popcorn recipe lives on.

Popped corn, enough to fill two 9 x 13" pans
2 cups brown sugar
2 sticks margarine
½ cup light corn syrup
1 teaspoon salt

1 teaspoon vanilla
1 teaspoon baking soda

Preheat oven to 200 degrees. Grease two 9 x 13" pans and set aside.

Put the popped corn in a big bowl. Combine the sugar, margarine, corn syrup and salt in a saucepan, bring to a boil and cook for 5 minutes. Stir occasionally. Remove from heat, add soda and vanilla; then stir. Pour over popped corn and stir to coat.

Divide the coated popped corn into the two pans. Bake for 1 hour, stirring every 15 minutes.

YIELD: About 8 servings

ARTILLERY PUNCH, OR "PUT SOME PUNCH IN YOUR PARTY"

ROBERT INMAN

Robert Inman's first novel, *Home Fires Burning,* became a Hallmark Hall of Fame movie.

I once built a bar. I was young, single, and full of foolishness, living in a Southern capital city and sharing a dilapidated old house with a male roommate (both of us were later rescued from complete decadence by marrying above ourselves). We decided one day that our down-at-the-heels dwelling needed a touch of class, and we hit upon the idea of turning a spare upstairs room into a lounge where we and our friends could relax in convivial good cheer, act irresponsibly without public embarrassment, and—most importantly—impress girls.

So, we built the bar. We made the mistake of building it outside the house. It was a sturdy thing, having the approximate heft and mass of a pocket battleship. It took six strapping young men to carry it up the stairs to the second-floor lounge. The house is still there today, and I dare say the bar is too, unless it has fallen through the ceiling in the ensuing years.

We painted the bar in gaudy colors, purchased bar stools, and decorated the room in 1960s Southern male chic. As I remember, the focal point of the room (besides the bar) was a neon Budweiser sign that someone had stolen from a roadhouse.

What automatically follows? A party, of course. We invited a few close friends to show up on a Saturday evening for a lounge-warming. What shall we serve? "Artillery Punch," my roommate said. I had never heard of the stuff—a gap in my cultural development—and so I left the concocting of it to him. He put a five-pound block of ice in a ten-gallon galvanized washtub, and proceeded to pour all manner of fermented spirits over the ice. I was astonished at the volume and variety of liquor.

"That stuff looks damn potent," I said.

"That's why they call it Artillery Punch," he averred.

Well, the word got out. The handful of close friends we invited swelled to a mighty crowd. There was no parking to speak of at our abode, so streets for blocks around were clogged with cars that had been abandoned by party-goers. The crowd spilled out of the house and onto the lawn and into a busy thoroughfare. Everyone was having a grand old time, drinking our Artillery Punch and congratulating us on our fine bar. The cops came. Several times. The neighbors finally gave up and moved to motels for the night. The entire ten-gallon washtub of Artillery Punch was consumed, and sometime in the wee small hours of the morning, when the punch gave out, the party died with a whimper. The next morning, we found several people sleeping in the bushes, including a couple of high-ranking state officials.

The party became legendary. And since then, I have been looking for a recipe for Artillery Punch. A bookseller friend finally gave me one, and I offer it herewith. I guarantee it will add punch to your party and make it legendary. My only advice: provide plenty of designated drivers, and check the bushes carefully the next morning.

¼ pound green tea
½ gallon cold water
Juice of 9 oranges
Juice of 9 lemons
1¼ pounds brown sugar
1 pint maraschino cherries
3 quarts Catawba or Rhine wine
1 quart St. Croix rum
1 quart brandy
1 quart rye whiskey
1 quart gin

Put tea in the water. Allow to stand overnight. Strain and add the orange and lemon juices. Add brown sugar, cherries, and all the liquor. Cover lightly and allow to stand for two to six weeks in a 5-gallon stone or glass crock. Strain off liquid into bottles.

To serve: Mix one gallon of liquid with one quart of champagne. Pour over large piece of ice in punch bowl.

YIELD: About 50

MOCK-RIDGEWOOD BARBECUE SAUCE

JOHN SHELTON REED

John Shelton Reed is a professor of sociology at the University of North Carolina. He and his wife, Dale, are the authors of *1001 Things Everyone Should Know About the South.*

Midway between Johnson City and Bristol in upper East Tennessee, not far from where my wife and I grew up in Kingsport, stands the small town of Bluff City. Just outside the town is a barbecue joint known simply as "The Ridgewood," a modest-looking place that since 1948 has served what *People* magazine has called the best barbecue in the country—and therefore, presumably, in the world.

But (I hear you say) what does *People* know about barbecue? O.K., try this: The Ridgewood is the only out-of-state establishment mentioned in Bob Garner's book, *North Carolina Barbecue: Flavored by Time.* Given Tar-Heel chauvinism in these matters (largely justifiable), that is testimonial indeed. Of course, Bluff City is only some 25 miles from the North Carolina line, though nearly twice that far by mountain roads.

People drive a long way to eat at the Ridgewood, despite its capricious hours and service that can range from brusque to surly, service almost as legendary as the food. The indispensable guide, *Real Barbecue*, by Greg Johnson and Kingsport boy Vince Staten, quotes one long-time customer who said that going to the Ridgewood was like going to the Don Rickles Restaurant, but people keep flocking to the Ridgewood for the barbecue: good pork, well smoked, served with an incomparable sauce.

Let me tell you about that sauce. Like most sauces west of the mountains, the Ridgewood's is sweet, thick, and red. But the flavor is marvelously complex—what catsup will taste like in heaven. This nectar is poured over the pork sandwiches before they are served, and the management has definite ideas about how much sauce to use: a lot. There are no squeeze bottles of sauce on the tables. You eat what's put before you.

Naturally the ingredients are a closely guarded secret, but a few years ago some ladies in Kingsport, no doubt tired of driving 30 miles to find the place closed, set out to duplicate the sauce. The recipe they came up with is a reasonable facsimile, and I will share it with you. And if you're ever in upper East Tennessee, stop by the source. Maybe it will be open.

24 ounces (by weight) catsup

¼ cup Worcestershire sauce

1 tablespoon good prepared mustard

¼ cup cider vinegar

½ cup oil

5 tablespoons white sugar

1 medium onion, finely chopped

1 large garlic clove, minced

3 tablespoons molasses

1 tablespoon Kitchen Bouquet brand seasoning

1 tablespoon Tabasco sauce

Salt and pepper to taste (start with ¼ teaspoon)

Mix these ingredients in a bowl, then blend the mix in a blender. Put the goop in a pot and heat it to the boiling point, then simmer it for 15 to 20 minutes.

YIELD: About a quart, and the sauce freezes well

HINT

You probably don't want to baste with this, because the sugar in it makes it turn black and ugly-looking (although it still tastes good). It makes a fine dipping sauce for ribs, and—don't tell anybody I told you this—it's also great on beef brisket, or chicken. Shoot, I've been known to eat it with a spoon. But it's best the way the Ridgewood serves it: Just pour it on some sliced or pulled pork, heaped on a big, warm, white-bread bun.

SLIGHTLY SANGRÍA

Amy Rogers

It was one of those last-minute things: a week-night Halloween party for folks who should have been too old to revel in such silliness. The menu? That part was easy—Snickers Bars, Gummy Worms and Peanut Butter Cups; plus chips, dips, salsa, cheese and crudités.

But what do you *drink* with such a menu? Sangría, of course. We mixed it up in a borrowed punch bowl, then set afloat into it an oval ice-blob someone had the foresight to freeze a few hours earlier. Guests ladled the punch into their cups and slurped up the fruit when they'd drunk down to the bottom.

Trick-or-treaters knocked on the door again and again, and we lavished upon the little Batmen, Spidermen and princesses a cornucopia of candy treats (although none of the kids accepted our enthusiastic offers of carrot sticks and broccoli stalks).

Before long, we'd used up all the leftover wine and poured in some more we'd otherwise have been too embarrassed to serve on its own. No one could find the recipe that listed the proportions. No matter. More fruit, more wine, a little sugar, fizzy water. The music and laughter got louder. This stuff was dangerous.

Is that why they call it "punch," because of what it does to you? In any case, the way it was going, there were going to be a lot of headaches afterward—or worse. My husband John and I quietly put away the wine, and for the rest of the evening, we doled out cups of punch that contained nothing stronger than black tea, berries and bubbles. No one even noticed.

Later that night, as guests drifted home, we cleaned up the candy wrappers and cracker crumbs. All in all, we'd used about five bottles of wine for twenty adults, not an exorbitant amount at all. The next day, friends

Sangría, a festive beverage with a deep red color, gets its name from the Spanish word for blood.

who'd awakened without hangovers or regrets called to say how much fun they'd had. Some asked for the Sangría recipe. Here it is:

PARTY SANGRÍA

Fresh fruit: cherries, grapes, tangerines; about 2 cups total
Peel from a fresh lemon, lime or orange; sliced
Sugar, if the fruit is too tart
1 cup brewed iced tea
1 bottle red wine
1 bottle sparkling water
Ice

Pit the cherries and peel the tangerines, if you are using them. Put the fruit (and sugar, if using) in a punch bowl or large pitcher. Add the tea and wine. Just before serving, pour in the sparkling water and add ice.

YIELD: About 2 quarts

HINT
This recipe can easily be doubled or even tripled. If you prefer, you can make white Sangría by substituting white wine for the red; or non-alcoholic punch by omitting the wine and combining the other ingredients to your taste.

BETTE'S RAISIN SAUCE

ANN H. HOWELL

My mother-in-law, Bette Burgin Howell Pryor, of Waynesville, North Carolina, was a good cook. It was her passion. She was intimidating for a new daughter-in-law. It might have been Sunday dinner or her Christmas feast when I first tasted her Raisin Sauce. I couldn't fathom how she made it, except I could spot raisins. Inwardly, I snarled up my nose, but to be polite, I ladled a small portion over my slice of ham. The mahogany color was a rich contrast to the ham, Harvard beets, green beans, yams and homemade yeast rolls. The taste was exotic, delightful. I was hooked. And it didn't hurt if a little bit happened to get on your roll, either.

Eventually, she gave me the recipe, one contrived in her head. She called it off on a Sunday when we were resting after one of her dinners while I wrote. Even if Bette consulted a recipe, she doctored it until it was uniquely her own. I'm grateful to have a few she handed down to me in the way of the mountains: oral tradition.

Now, if I could just duplicate her roast beef!

About a half-box of raisins, more or less
2 cups salted water
½ cup brown sugar
About 1 tablespoon flour, mixed with a little water until smooth
½ teaspoon vanilla
¼ stick of butter

Boil raisins in about 2 cups salted water approximately 15 minutes, or until plump. Add brown sugar and about half the flour-water mixture. You can add more if needed to thicken the sauce. Stir in the vanilla and butter. Heat through.

YIELD: About 2 cups

If you grew up doing it or learned a good while back, making gravy is no mystery. But if you've never tried—or if you have, only to wind up with a lumpy, salty mess—read on and learn the secrets to practically perfect gravy.

FOOLPROOF GRAVY

JOANNA VIRKLER

I'll never forget calling my mother from college my freshman year on Thanksgiving morning.

"Help! I'm making dinner for 24 friends and I don't have a clue how to make gravy," I said in a panic. "I think the turkey is O.K., but now what do I do?!?" Mom remained calm and somehow I must have turned out something resembling gravy.

Memories of Southern summers redolent of fried chicken and its even better partner, fried chicken gravy, may have factored in as well, but from that first-Thanksgiving-away-from-home on, I have considered it a personal challenge to create good gravies. And you know what? It's not hard if you know a few tricks.

A simple gravy is made from fat (such as butter, Crisco, chicken fat, bacon fat), flour, a liquid (such as milk, stock and even a little wine, port, sherry or cognac) and seasonings.

START WITH:

About two tablespoons of fat
About two tablespoons of flour
About 1 cup milk or broth (beef, chicken or vegetable)

In a heavy pan, melt the fat over low to medium heat. Add the flour. Now, very important, mix flour with fat and brown slowly for a *minimum* of three minutes. Stir frequently and make sure it does not burn.

Cooking the flour and fat together sufficiently binds the flavors and gets rid of the bland, uncooked flavor so many dull gravies have. The longer you cook the flour paste, the *roux*, the browner it will become and the more flavor and color it will impart to the gravy. For so much of the New Orleans-style cooking, the roux is cooked for 40 minutes or even more. For a simple, traditional gravy, though, 5 to 10 minutes is best. Just be sure not to burn it.

The second step is to add the liquid. It helps if the liquid is warm or hot, though not absolutely necessary. If you are using the two table-spoons each of fat and flour, begin by incorporating one cup of liquid. One cup of milk will make a mellow, richer tasting gravy; if you are us-ing broth, homemade is always best, but store-bought is fine. If you use unsalted or low sodium, you'll have more control over the amount of salt at the end of the process. Using water is fine in certain circumstances, such as when you are deglazing a pan you have used to brown meat, but usually you want a liquid that has some flavor.

Sometimes a spoon or spatula will be fine, but a wire whisk will al-ways do a great job. The whisk helps break up the roux and incorporate the liquid for a smooth gravy. The trick now is to watch the gravy care-fully as it begins to thicken. Keep the heat at low to medium. You can add more liquid if it thickens too quickly. Then, take off the heat, taste and add seasonings—salt, pepper, cayenne and/or any herbs. Put back on the heat for just another minute if you like. If gravy is too thick, again, just add some more liquid. If gravy is too thin, keep cooking.

Play with it—it won't break. Keep tasting until it's just what you want. Sometimes you want a thick gravy, sometimes thinner. Sometimes spicy, sometimes not.

Now, a butter/flour/milk gravy is pretty bland, a good base for a cheese sauce. Throw in a cup of grated cheddar or a combination of sev-eral cheeses, but please, *no* processed cheese of any kind.

A good chicken gravy needs chicken stock. If you use chicken fat or bacon fat, the flavor will be more intense. Or you can use part stock/part milk.

A word about fried chicken gravy: This is a gravy that belongs in a class by itself. If you are going to the trouble of frying chicken, please plan to make gravy with leftover oil and crispy bits. Pour off excess oil, leaving browned (though not burned!) bits. Add flour, cook, then thicken with milk only. Taste, add seasonings.

A good sausage and biscuit gravy is best made from the brown bits scraped up from the bottom of the pan the sausage was cooked in. And definitely use milk for this one. Or add some cooked sausage, some cayenne or hot sauce. Bacon fat is great with this, though butter will do fine, too.

If you are inclined to try a gravy with a little more sophistication, add a tablespoon or two of white or red wine, a sherry, port or cognac. Be sure to cook for a few minutes to incorporate well and burn off the alcohol taste. White wine will add the least aggressive taste and no sweetness. Red wine will certainly change the color and does add a touch of sweetness. Sherry and ports add lovely flavor. Cognac (a cheap brandy will often do just fine) is more aggressively sweet. Feel free to experiment, though err on the side of too little, not too much.

YIELD: About 1 cup

REDEYE GRAVY

GLORIA DAHL

My father told stories. From the time he got up in the morning until he went to bed at night, he had a story waiting to be told. Mealtime at our house always began the same. Daddy would say the blessing, fill his plate with food, and begin another tale.

Most were taken from his own life, the central characters his relatives and friends. He enjoyed humor, and was a master at embellishment, but there were serious stories as well. He dished out slice-of-life adventures to his children like potatoes from a stew. I often wondered how he managed to time the endings of his stories to coincide with the last morsel of meat and gravy that rested upon his fork or spoon.

At bedtime, after my siblings and I had settled down, a strong, clear voice drifted from the back part of the house. "Once upon a time. . . ." Then came the old familiar fables we loved so well. The rhythm of Daddy's words lulled us into sleep. He would live to tell his stories to his grandchildren and to his great-grandchildren.

Years after his death my mother reached into an old trunk and handed me a worn and tattered manila envelope. Inside lay a packet of photos and the yellowed pages of a story titled *Ol' Jack's Last Hunt.*

I'd never seen the photos, nor had I seen the story, but I'd heard about Ol' Jack many, many times. According to Daddy, Jack was the best hunting dog that ever lived.

The photos depicted a young, handsome man standing in an open field that led to a wood. Three hounds stood in the foreground as if waiting for a rabbit hunt to begin. The smart hunting outfit that Daddy wore gave him the appearance of a country gentleman instead of the sharecropper that he was.

We sat, my mother and I, and read the story that had been written before my birth. And we wept over the pages and photographs that had lain in a trunk for over forty years.

The aged envelope bore the address of a sportsman's magazine based in New York. There was no letter of rejection, only the story and the photos that spoke of a man's wish to share "a perfect day and a perfect hunt."

Although Daddy was well read, his formal education was limited. He'd given the manuscript to a teacher, who'd agreed to edit the story. His intent was that *Ol' Jack's Last Hunt* be a folksy little tale concerning a day of rabbit hunting. The story was genuine, written in the dialect of a man who wouldn't have known how to "put on airs" if he'd tried. The teacher, however, in her eagerness, polished the story right off the page. The flavor of the hunt was lost, and poor *Ol' Jack* was left out in the cold.

Had Daddy been able to obtain the services of a professional editor, who knows what could have happened? From beginning to middle to end, he knew how a story should be told. And now here am I, wishing with all my heart, that I'd listened more closely to the man who told stories.

HINT
Some people like to add $^1/_2$ to $^3/_4$ cup water to the ham in the final cooking stage. The steam tenderizes the ham and helps lessen the sometimes bitter taste if the coffee is too strong. This simple recipe may require a bit of experimenting to suit the taste.

1 large slice center-cut ham, or 1 pound ham slices
4 tablespoons butter or oil
¾ to 1 cup coffee
⅛ teaspoon salt
⅛ teaspoon pepper

In an iron skillet, allow the ham to cook slowly over low to medium heat in butter until thoroughly done. Remove from skillet and set aside.

Add coffee, salt and pepper to drippings. Stir well. Serve over grits, potatoes or rice.

YIELD: About 4 servings

CUTTING UP IN THE KITCHEN

Amy Rogers

Randy Snyder is a known purveyor of practical jokes. He'll tell you there's no water pressure in the drinking fountain, and when you lean in close, hoping to get a little sip, an icy geyser will douse you while Randy chuckles from a safe distance, over in the corner. Then he'll present you with a bowl of torn-up greens and you'll wonder if he's handing you a salad—or leftovers scraped from the compost bin.

So it was no wonder I hesitated when he offered me a taste of his homemade pickled corn. It looked fine, but how could I be sure that the cloudy liquid was, in fact, pickling juice and not dishwater?

I took a tiny taste. It was delicious! Firm kernels of fresh corn, a nice sharp bite from the pickling, and just the right balance of taste and texture.

When it comes to cooking, Randy doesn't kid around. He's a first-rate cook who's worked around in Carolina restaurant kitchens for years. These days, he's one of the staff at Wildacres Retreat Center in the North Carolina mountains, and he prepares meals for dozens of people at a time.

Randy kindly shared his recipe for pickled corn, and sent me home with a jar of my own. But the corn I found back in the city was pale and dry. I knew the results would be disappointing, so I filed away the recipe to try next year. In the meantime, here's another recipe from Randy. I thought he was joking when he told me to add chocolate to the milk gravy...

RANDY SNYDER'S CHOCOLATE GRAVY

2 tablespoons cocoa powder	2 tablespoons flour
½ cup sugar	1 cup milk

In a saucepan, combine the cocoa, sugar and flour. Over medium heat, slowly add milk then stir until thick. Serve over buttered biscuits.

YIELD: About 1 cup

HARVARD BARDWELL'S RED WHAMMABAMMA SAUCE

DAN HUNTLEY

Harvard Bardwell of Baton Rouge, Louisiana, has worked professionally in the restaurant and food business for over three decades. Presently, he's vice-president of research and development at Revere Foods in Paincourtville, Louisiana, in Ascension Parish. The company produces and ships frozen entrees such as crawfish étouffée, crab cakes, gumbo and lobster Thermidor for mail-order businesses such as Nieman-Marcus, Omaha Steaks, Ruth's Chris Steak House and Harry & David. One of seven children, Harvard learned to cook at his father's side.

"Daddy was a developer and he cooked at home and in hunt camps on the weekends. But once a year he would rent out Sardi's Restaurant in New York on a Sunday evening—when it was closed—to entertain his business clients. He'd fly some Louisiana chefs in, and they'd cook quail and other game on the grill with this demi-glace sauce made from the drippings. Man, you talk about eating. . . . At home on Sunday afternoons, he'd grill dove breasts with homemade sauce, sugar-coated sirloin steaks charred on the grill . . ."

*1 jar of raspberry jelly
2 heaping tablespoons of Tabasco Sauce
¾ stick unsalted butter
¼ cup good red wine, like a Merlot or Syrah

*You may substitute plum or blackberry. If you can only find jam, make sure you heat it and run it through a strainer to get rid of seeds.

Combine the ingredients and cook in a pan over low to medium heat until it bubbles and the water is beginning to draw out. The sweetness of the jelly accelerates the other seasonings and brings out the buttery flavor. It should still have the thick consistency of the jam. Remove from heat and use as a sauce or glaze to pour over grilled meats. It's a good complement to any grilled meat, particularly game like quail or grouse. I personally prefer it over deep-fried Cornish hens; let them set about 20 minutes. Debone the breast and remove the rest of the meat onto a platter. Pour the sauce over the meat and you will soon discover how this sauce got its name.

YIELD: About 1 ½ cups of sauce

NORTH CAROLINA VINEGAR SAUCE

ELIZABETH A. KARMEL

This sauce can be made in advance, but the longer it sits, the hotter it will become as the vinegar "leeches" out the heat of the red pepper flakes. Once you've made North Carolina-Style Pulled Pork (see Chapter 2), serve it warm on white buns and top it with coleslaw that has been dressed with this sauce—never mayonnaise-dressed slaw. Serve additional sauce on the side, if desired.

FOR THE SAUCE:

2 cups cider vinegar
1 tablespoon salt
1 tablespoon ground white pepper
1 tablespoon red pepper flakes
2 tablespoons white sugar
¼ cup brown sugar
½ teaspoon black pepper
½ cup ketchup

Mix all ingredients together and let sit 10 minutes. Add to chopped barbecue when the meat is still warm to season the meat and keep it from drying out.

YIELD: About 2½ cups

FOR NORTH CAROLINA COLESLAW:

1 medium head green cabbage, chopped

Mix sauce and cabbage together until well mixed but not floating in liquid. Refrigerate. Let sit at least 2 hours or overnight. Spoon on top of pulled pork and serve on a bun, or eat by itself with barbecue or grilled meat.

YIELD: About 8 servings

OKRA PICKLES

CAROLINE CASTLE HICKS

I am not a picky eater. My mother tells me that even as a child, I ate anything she put in front of me—anything, that is, except okra. I *hate* okra. Hate the sickly shade of gray-green, the tough stems, the coarse, furry pods. And I find it hard to trust anything that can make its own slime.

My younger brother, on the other hand, refuses to believe that there are people who don't like okra. Tell him you don't like okra and he'll tell you you're just eating bad okra, or worse yet, you are responsible for good okra gone bad. An electrician by trade, he earns his living within the overgrown madness of Atlanta, but his soul takes refuge in the small plot of land he owns well beyond the city. He's a would-be gentleman farmer and okra is his staff of life.

Fortunately, my brother grows a great many things besides okra and every summer, I make it a point to voice my enthusiasm for his other crops. His baby green beans rival those in any Parisian food stall and his tomatoes can bring me to tears. "Don't know about the tomatoes yet," he'll tell me when I start pestering him about them in May. "Tomatoes are unpredictable. Like women. But you take okra," he goes on, "now *that's* reliable. As soon as it gets good and hot, it'll be coming in like a house afire." (That's another thing; I'm at odds with any substance that can thrive with that much arrogance in a Georgia July.)

Ordinarily, our wildly divergent tastes in any one vegetable would be of little consequence, but over the years, I have unwittingly allowed a *situation* to develop. Although it is hard to admit, I must confess that I have never told my brother my true feelings for okra. Long ago, I passed the point of no return. To tell him I hate okra now would break his heart.

And so, every summer, I accept with a wan smile the sacks and sacks of pods he bestows upon me. "It's good for what ails ya," he's fond of saying as he loads me up at every visit. Indeed, our mother affirms that a daily dose of okra across America could put *Ex-Lax* out of business, but I remain blissfully ignorant of its therapeutic effects. That's because every year, a certain quantity of okra is martyred in the name of sibling harmony.

I try to give it away, but after a couple of bushels, even my okra-tolerant friends see me coming and cry, "Enough!" This year, however, operating under the delusion that vinegar might mask the taste and texture (as well as soften the fur), I bought a gallon-sized canning jar and followed my brother's prized recipe. After all, I thought, I *like* pickles. Alas, pickling does not a pickle make, and after biting into one briny pod, I knew it was a lost cause. A year later, it sits there still, taunting me from the back of my refrigerator, my Mason jar of shame.

No, I will never tell my brother my guilty secret because, thank God, I learned something before it was too late. From the beginning, the eight years between us set us on very different paths. It was our love of growing things, of feeding people, that taught us how to reconnect. Every summer, my brother shares with me some beans, some squash, and if I'm lucky, a few of the lush, perfect tomatoes the squirrels don't get. But with okra, from the heart of his garden, he fills me up.

3 pounds okra pods	4 cups white vinegar
6 small hot peppers, or more to taste	2 cups water
3 teaspoons mustard seed	¼ cup pickling salt
3 teaspoons dill seed	6 pint jars with lids
6 to 12 garlic cloves, peeled	

Wash okra thoroughly. Pierce each pod a couple of times with a fork and trim, leaving approximately ½" of stem on the pods.

Sterilize 6 pint jars. Place one pepper on the bottom of each jar, more if you want hotter okra. Then add ½ teaspoon mustard seed, ½ teaspoon dill seed, and 1 to 2 garlic cloves to each jar. Alternating stems up and down, pack the okra into the jars vertically.

Bring vinegar, water and salt to boil in saucepan. Pour hot solution into the jars, leaving headspace of ¼". Wipe rims and adjust the two-piece lids. In a boiling water canner, process jars for 15 minutes. Remove immediately. Let stand at least 2 weeks before serving.

YIELD: 6 pint jars

PLENTY TO GO AROUND

DON BOEKELHEIDE

If you're serious about cooking, then your kitchen door should lead straight into your vegetable garden.

Oh, I know, you can buy a big red tomato at the supermarket anytime you like, even in mid-January. They may look pretty, but if you want a tomato that really tastes like a tomato, the surest way to get one is to grow it yourself.

But, you don't have space? Your yard is too shady? Don't feel like working all by yourself? Don't think you have the know-how to grow vegetables and herbs?

A community garden might be the answer.

Ask Mary Ellen Nash and the other gardeners at Wilmore Community Garden, the oldest in Charlotte, North Carolina. She will tell you how the community garden puts tasty vegetables and fresh herbs on her table, and how gardeners make friends and assist each other with advice and a helping hand. All are especially proud that their community garden delivers delicious food even in hard times, providing what researchers call "food security."

In an America facing an obesity epidemic, who's worried about food security? Besides, don't Americans spend less for food per capita than citizens of other developed countries?

In spite of our overfed majority and competitive prices on fast food, America still has a long way to go before we reach food security—where everyone is able to obtain enough nutritious food at all times, without relying on emergency assistance. Based on USDA estimates, some 30 million Americans face "food insecurity" annually. Even in the midst of plenty, these Americans are not sure of having enough food to maintain active, healthy lives.

Establishing food security won't be easy. As Andy Fisher of The Community Food Security Coalition points out, while every city or county has departments of water, housing, health and transportation, nowhere can you find a "department of food." Instead, a welter of food-related policies and programs, unarticulated and disconnected, are tucked away within different government bureaucracies, making effective food system planning very difficult.

Ironically, agricultural "progress" may have contributed to the crisis. During the past century, technology and financial forces have completely restructured the American food system. Older people often tell stories about a time when families grew food in their backyards, and shopped and swapped for produce and eggs grown on local farms. Today, in contrast, a complex network of specialized food processors, refiners, manufacturers, wholesalers and retailers stretching around the world transforms output from vast factory farms into highly processed products that crowd supermarket shelves.

Though suburban consumers pay low prices, the costs are high. The system isn't sustainable. It is heavily reliant on petroleum and toxic chemicals, generates horrific mountains of waste, requires huge amounts of water, and is potentially vulnerable to disruption and contamination. Over the century past, America has lost countless family farms, and prime farmland is even now heedlessly covered with blacktop and strip malls. Little by little, most Americans, including policy makers, have completely lost touch with growing food, the most basic necessity of life.

The first step toward food security (and sustainable agriculture), experts agree, is to revitalize and support local community-based food production, processing and marketing. All of us can help, if we are willing to change our habits. We can buy locally at farmers' markets, join a community supported agriculture project (CSA), and buy local crops in season, adjusting our menus accordingly. In the Carolinas, we can replace part of our water-guzzling, time-consuming and chemically-dependent lawns with productive patches of vegetables and herbs.

And all of us, working with our neighbors, local government, churches and non-profits, can support community gardens. For those interested in cooking delicious foods, a community garden is one good way to supply gourmet fresh vegetables. In the process, community gardens can transform trash-filled empty lots into green community resources.

Compared to other kinds of food aid, community (and home) gardens offer special benefits in terms of food security. Food produced in community gardens tends to end up on the plates of those who need it most—children, the elderly and mothers. This unfortunately isn't always the case, especially with cash assistance. In a garden, a person can cultivate vegetables they want to consume, including "ethnic" crops rarely available in stores. And gardens are empowering. You work to grow that food. It isn't charity. Thoughtfully organized gardens that encourage grassroots leadership can make a huge positive difference in neighborhoods, and in the lives of youth and seniors.

As Mary Ellen Nash and her friends remind us, community gardens are as much about cultivating community as about cultivating tomatoes, as much about raising hope as raising turnips.

SQUASH PICKLES

MARY ELLEN NASH,
INTERVIEWED BY TE'QUILLA SHANTIA GRAHAM

I was born October 10th, 1931. I've lived in Mecklenburg County all my life. Where we lived was in the rural country. There was cotton fields, pastures, cows, dairy farms, and all of that. The house we lived in didn't have inside bathrooms. We had to get our water from a well out in the yard a couple of blocks away.

When I grew up, from a baby until around five years old, my father was farming, but he was farming for his own self. He used to work on the railroad but he still did patchwork. What you call patchwork, it's just like these gardens—see, over here you'd probably put corn in it, another place you put sweet potatoes. Whatever he planted was his own garden.

I learned to plant and grow stuff by tracking behind him in the field. My daddy used to plant cotton, too. My mom said she used to take me to the field and lay me on a pallet on the ground, and would go and hoe cotton and pick cotton to the end of the rows and come back and check on me. When I got up big enough to help, we had to pick it. It just killed my back to pick the cotton. But I had to do it anyway.

In the summer, we gathered berries for canning. And my daddy, I helped him in the garden, we had to gather the crop corn, had to pick the peas, and all that.

When I was growing up, my family raised animals. We raised pigs, chickens, and my daddy had cows. In the fall of the year we'd kill the hogs and preserve the meat. And we'd have them to eat all year. We didn't have refrigerators, we had what you call an icebox, a box that you put the block of ice in. To make sausages, my mother would make a sack and stuff those sausages in the sack. And hang them up. Or she would stuff them in corn shucks, you know, corn after it dries on the stalk. She would put the seasoning stuff in it, stuff them in the corn shuck and tie it up at the top.

All my life, I've been living beside people that were different. We've made it together all my life. Where we lived at, the neighbors, we played with their children. They'd come to our house, we ate at their house, they ate at my house. So that part is no different. But the only thing is in the time of segregation, we didn't like to ride the bus uptown; we couldn't stop at different counters to eat. You know, I remember that part.

Ever since I've been married, I've been planting seeds and setting out plants. I got married as a teenager and I married my husband that I have today. We've been married 54 years in January. I have seven children, I have 25 grandchildren, and I have about 17 or 18 great-grands.

At Thanksgiving, they gather at my house for dinner. I have like 35 to 40 people for Thanksgiving. And Christmas, they gather at Pauline's house, my daughter, for Christmas breakfast. Easter, they gather at my oldest daughter's house for dinner. And different days, we gather at my oldest son's house for cookouts. When we have family reunions, 200 or 300 people come.

I've lived in Wilmore for 32 years. My husband and I just fell in love with it and we moved in. And we still living in it. When the garden first started in Wilmore, I knew a lot where they had torn down the house. It was growed up with grass, and they had threw trash all in it. And I kept on telling Cissy, "Why don't we try to get this spot?" And she said, "We'll look into it." So then they looked into it, and they did get this spot.

In the community garden, it's like a fellowship with friends, neighbors, we all get together and talk and I just like doing it. I already knew about gardening, so I have helped a lot of the other ones that didn't know. Because usually, when we come to the garden to plant, I'm all the time doing somebody else's and I'll be the last one to do mine. I usually have my garden all year. When it's time to plant for the spring, I'll still be picking stuff out of my garden. And most everybody pulls all their stuff up, but I always keep something.

I like greens, all kind of greens, tomatoes, and what else? I'd grow cucumbers. Greens you can eat all year round. And tomatoes is good, you can eat them in the summer. Then you take the green tomatoes and make pickles. You can make chow-chow. Sometime I make pepper and tomato peppers, because I like hot peppers and the vinegar, to eat on your food.

You can make cucumber pickles, any kind, dill pickles, sweet pickles, all of that. Then you can eat it on a salad day.

Vegetables are fresher when you go out and pick it in your own yard. You can get a little bit. You don't have to buy this much, or you don't have to weigh it and see if you owe too much. If you don't have any money, you can just go out in your own yard and just pick your own little vegetables.

I learned how to take a small amount of food and make a big meal off of it. Sometimes people today, they think they can't cook unless they go to the store, but they have stuff in their pantries that they can go in and make a meal off of.

In my garden, I have sage and garlic, I got onion, got dill and some parsley, and some kind of basil, got little basil. I'm kind of like my father. I like to see stuff grow. I got mint in my backyard, and lemon balm, I think. But most of the gardeners laugh at me because I like the little things. I take little bitty things and put them out and, you know, most of the time they grow.

It is important to till your garden and lay out your garden. You make your rows and you build up the dirt piled up on top. Just like this garden here. But before we plant it you put fertilizer in it, and topsoil in it, or manure and cut it up in the dirt. Then you plant your seeds or set out your plants.

I learned to can from my pa, from my mother, and from neighbors and friends. And freezing, I don't do much freezing. I mostly put up soup mix and tomatoes. I love to do green beans. I usually freeze the greens at a spare moment. I froze lima beans, peas and okra. I freeze corn. With tomatoes, we usually eat them raw. Sometimes, I stew them. I have stewed them with zucchini, and some onions and seasoning. It tastes pretty good. What I season it with is a little bit of sugar, and a little bit of soul seasoning. I use a lot of carrots and a lot of onions, and that gives it a flavor. I use chicken bouillon seasoning sometimes. But I can't tell you how much to make because I don't cook off a recipe.

My seven children, I only got one likes to garden. I helped him to plant the summer garden, but the fall garden he planted by his self. So he just got collards, and he say he going to plant some greens. So when the summer time comes, this summer past, he had cucumbers and greens, okra, pepper, and some cabbage, some onions in his garden.

I think young people need to learn gardening so they learn how to survive themselves. Like if you don't have any money or you can't get out to go get what you need, you can harvest from your garden. All kind of beans, all kind of peas, all kind of greens, cabbage, white potatoes, sweet potatoes. I've planted all of that in my backyard. My advice to young people is to be interested in any garden. Go to school, get some more learning about it. Because I didn't go to school to get the learning about it, I just grew up doing it.

The biggest difference in today's garden is that you don't really have ground. Because the city has took the country, it has made developments, it has bought the land, put in shopping centers, business parks and all of that. Most of where you live, you got a little piece of yard and that's all. And some of that you can't plant in.

I like working in the garden because I'm an outside person. I love gardening, and it doesn't matter where it is or who I'm with. I'll work in the garden before I'll work in the house. I do my flowers, and I do my vegetables. Working with the neighbors, you get to know your neighbors. And the friendship, the fellowship, is what I like.

8 cups yellow "crooked neck" squash, sliced

2 cups onions, sliced

1 green pepper, sliced

1 tablespoon salt

1 cup cider vinegar

1 ¾ cup sugar

1 teaspoon celery seed

1 teaspoon mustard seed

Combine squash, onions, green pepper and salt in a large bowl and let stand for one hour. Rinse and drain. Set aside. In a large saucepan combine cider vinegar, sugar, celery seed and mustard seed. Bring mixture to a boil and add vegetables. Return to a boil. Pack in hot jars and let season for three weeks.

YIELD: About 5 pints

A RECIPE THAT CONTINUES TO FEED

VINCENT CALABRESE

My wife is Lynda Calabrese, the poet and artist. Years ago when she was in her first Creative Writing class at Central Piedmont Community College with Irene Honeycutt, she had an assignment to write a poem in the form of some kind of directions. She wrote "Marriage Muffins" and I can still remember her laughing at her keyboard while she was putting together the recipe.

Through the years, even though she says it's corny, we've included it in many wedding gift envelopes. Everyone gets a kick out of it because it's witty, but they pay attention because ours is such a great marriage. And that's what everyone wants: To be well fed by food for the soul and heart.

MARRIAGE MUFFINS, A RECIPE BY LYNDA CALABRESE

2 enriched souls
1 teaspoon time
1 pint self-rising love
1 teaspoon honesty
1 cup pure unsulphured commitment
1 cup friendship
2 teaspoons organic arousal
2 tablespoons unsaturated bliss
⅔ cup 10x conversation
fun, to taste

blend souls with self-rising love
slowly add unsulphured commitment
and organic arousal
sift time, friendship and honesty
add to love mixture
beat with mixer until firm peaks are formed
knead with friendship and unsaturated bliss
dust with fun
roll into any shape
no more than one inch apart
on slightly greased sheet
bake till golden

SNAPPING TURTLE STIR-FRY AND 'POSSUM GRADUATE STUDENT STYLE

DORIS A. DAVIS

My husband, Donald M. Davis, and I moved from Arizona to North Carolina in 1962. He was studying zoology at Duke University and received his Ph.D. in 1968. Graduate students are known for being poor; hence, our slightly different meals.

We moved to the island of Guam for a while, where my husband taught at the University of Guam, then back to Sylva, North Carolina, where he taught at Western Carolina University. We now spend the winters in the Florida Keys, but return to Sylva in the spring in time to enjoy the ramp festivals and the spring wildflowers. And we have held on to our graduate student recipes.

SNAPPING TURTLE STIR FRY

Our three boys couldn't stand this if they thought it was made with turtle; they licked the plates clean if they thought it was beef!

One turtle
2 tablespoons butter
1 or 2 onions, chopped fine
1 green pepper, sliced
1 carrot, sliced
3 to 4 tablespoons soy sauce
1 to 2 cups water
Arrowroot powder

Catch, kill and cut turtle into pieces, and freeze. Freezing tenderizes the meat. Remove from freezer and let thaw a little bit. Do not completely thaw or it is more difficult to cut into slivers. Put butter in a frying pan, brown the onions, add the slivered turtle meat and stir-fry over medium to high heat. Add the green pepper and carrot, then the soy sauce and water. Thicken the sauce with arrowroot. Serve with rice and salad.

YIELD: About 4 servings

'POSSUM GRADUATE STUDENT STYLE

Check along road. When you find a dead 'possum, stop the car. Feel the 'possum. It should still be warm, indicating it was freshly killed, not warm from the sun on a hot summer's day—this takes practice. Skin and clean, cut into portions. Cook with your favorite barbecue sauce. Invite other graduate students for special dinner. (For some reason, we haven't had any 'possum since my husband got his Ph.D.)

YIELD: Depends how hungry the students are!

GRAMMA'S BLACK SALVE

WENDY H. GILL

No drugstore medicines were allowed in our Christian Science household, so our parents provided us kids physical comfort in alternative ways: a six-ounce can of frozen orange juice concentrate rolled across a forehead to lower a fever; Mennen Aftershave splashed on poison ivy to cool a rash; and teaspoonfuls of honey swallowed to soothe a sore throat. And then there was Gramma's Black Salve. Its job was to draw infection from a laceration, an abrasion, or on one ugly occasion, a festering boil.

A family member, who shall remain unnamed, was unfortunate enough to have a large boil on one of her buttocks. It required lancing with a needle sterilized over the flame of our gas stove in a ceremony marked by equal shares of sympathy and suppressed laughter. My father performed the operation while my mother rifled through the bathroom junk drawer and pulled out a crusty-lidded baby food jar containing the miracle goo—Gramma's Black Salve. It looked like tar and smelled like sin. For the patient, it added insult to injury. But after several days on a soft pillow and salve, our unnamed family member was sitting pretty once again.

That single jar passed down from my father's mother lasted throughout our family's lifetime together. But my mother held on to the recipe, just in case:

> 1 pound mutton suet; melt down and take out the grit.
> Add 1 pound unsalted butter and melt;
> Add 1 pound beeswax and melt;
> Add 1 pound rosin; just until it melts.
> Remove quickly and pour in jars. It will set up quickly
>   (and last forever!).

YIELD: A lifetime supply

DAD'S COUGH SYRUP

SHERI MORETZ

My dad made this mountain cold remedy for me when the over-the-counter cough syrups just didn't seem to work. He said that his mom used to make it for him when he was younger, too. Warm your ingredients to mix them well, but be careful if you use the microwave. Any more than 10 or 12 seconds and your syrup is likely to boil – or worse, catch fire! When you go to bed, stay covered up. This remedy will make you sweat, and that's part of the cure; you're sweating the cold right out of you.

  2 tablespoons whiskey/bourbon (or White Lightning if you can get it)
  Splash of lemon juice
  1 teaspoon honey
  Dash of ginger

Mix whiskey, lemon juice, honey and ginger in a small glass. Fill a bowl with hot water (bowl must be big enough to hold the glass). Put the glass in the water and stir its contents until warm. Drink and go to bed.

YIELD: 1 serving

JOHNNY CAKES AND PEACHES OVER AN OPEN FIRE

DIANE RUGGIERO

A few years ago, I had the wonderful opportunity to work at Historic Latta Plantation, a beautiful living history site more than 200 years old in Huntersville, North Carolina.

Staff and volunteers were required to know how to perform various tasks that represented what the original families did every day in the 19th century. In an effort to learn more about historic interpretation, I went to Historic Brattonsville in York, South Carolina. There, I learned how to make things out of gourds, how to start a fire with flint and steel, and my favorite—cooking.

Cooking over an open flame, a big open flame, was a new experience. Dressed in period costume, in July, I wore my wool apron and my oven sleeves to keep from catching on fire. It turns out that wool doesn't catch on fire like the cotton in my dress. That's a good thing to know.

The tools were very different, and measuring was done by eye and feel. Heat was determined by how close something was to the fire. It took all morning for the group to make a full meal of string chicken (a trussed-up chicken that hangs down from a string and spins over the fire), greens and fat back, a layered dish with onions and spinach, johnny cakes and peaches for dessert.

Here is a variation of what we made:

FOR THE JOHNNY CAKES:

1 cup cornmeal
Pinch of salt
1 tablespoon of lard
Boiling water

Mix the cornmeal and salt together. Then add the lard and enough water to form flat patties about the size of your hand.

The Dutch oven is a large, iron cook pot with a heavy, fitted lid. It is believed to have been made popular by the Pennsylvania Dutch, back in the 18th century.

Place the patties under the ashes in the front of the fire. Cook until centers are done. Wipe off the ashes and enjoy!

YIELD: About 4

FOR THE PEACHES:

* Can substitute ²⁄₃ cup of brown sugar

8 peaches
*About ⅔ cup of sugar
*A little molasses
Large pinch of cinnamon
Pinch of nutmeg
Butter
Pound cake (optional)

You will need a cast iron Dutch oven with lid for this recipe.

Peel the peaches, remove pits and cut in half. Mix the sugar and molasses together (skip this step if you are using brown sugar), then add the cinnamon and nutmeg. Set aside.

Place enough melted butter to coat the bottom into the Dutch oven, then add the peaches, cut side down. Sprinkle the peaches with the brown sugar mixture.

Put the lid on the Dutch oven, then place it on the hearth with a few coals under and coals on the lid. Cook until the sugar is melted and the peaches are starting to soften. Then, turn the peaches over and spoon the melted sugar mixture on top of the peaches. Cook a few minutes more.

This is enjoyed either by itself or over a pound cake.

YIELD: 4 servings

ICED TEA

Amy Rogers

Leave it to Southerners. We drink gallons and gallons of tea poured over ice, and we can't decide whether to call it *iced* tea or *ice* tea. We slice up lemons into neat wedges that we perch on the rim of the glass, only to watch our guests discard the sour bits of fruit, almost every time. A family member of mine sweetens her pitchers of tea with sugar, then adds a generous amount of artificial sweetener, just in case the sugar doesn't do the trick. Then there are those who serve the chilled tea unsweetened and helpfully offer a sugar bowl, when everyone knows you could stir till next Tuesday and that sugar still wouldn't dissolve in your glass.

There are books about tea that will tell you its history. There are iced tea connoisseurs who shop for exotic leaves and use only purified water. But there are a few who admit to loathing the stuff. North Carolinian Fred Chappell, in his essay, "Iced Tea: A Contrarian's View," proclaims himself "one southerner who detests that dirty water the color of oak-leaf tannin and its insipid banality."

Making iced tea is a simple thing, really. Most of us have done it so often we never think about it. If you're a newcomer to the South, never fear. There's only one hard-and-fast rule you need to remember:

Never, ever use a mix!

One quart fresh, cold water, plus more to taste
3 "family size" tea bags, or 6 regular size
Pinch of baking soda
Sugar to taste (optional)
Lemon wedges or slices (optional)
Large (1 ½ to 2-quart) pitcher

In a pot, bring the water to a rolling boil. Remove the tags from the tea bags; you don't want to steep ink into your tea! Drop the tea bags into

HINT
Never heat water for tea in the microwave. The water will heat unevenly and produce a tasteless brew.

the water and remove from heat. Add a pinch of baking soda and let the tea steep about 5 minutes for regular, a little longer if you like it extra strong. Remove tea bags.

If you are using sugar, add it now to your taste, and stir until dissolved. Put 1 or 2 cups of cold water in the pitcher, then pour in the tea. Stir and serve over ice, with lemon if desired.

YIELD: 4 to 6 servings

THE ONE TRUE BARBECUE

JOHN ROGERS

Arguing about which kind of barbecue is best, or even what constitutes true 'cue is like arguing about the causes of the Civil War—everyone is sure his belief is the right one, and few are willing to keep an open mind on the matter. Whether your taste runs to the vinegary sauces of eastern North Carolina or the thicker red sauces of the Carolina foothills, we all have our favorites. Regardless of whether you take your sauce thin and red or thick and yellow, or if you prefer your pork chopped or pulled, there are some things about the experience of barbecue that are universal.

For many of us who were raised and fed in the Carolinas, our recollections center on places and occasions where we ate meat slow-cooked over an open fire, soaked and basted in a sauce that tasted better to us than wine. In this cowardly new world of fast and franchised food, it is the memory of these tastes against the backdrop of family reunions and church gatherings and political campaigns that we remember with the same feeling some reserve for the mythologized days of the Old South.

There is a band of South Carolina that runs a hundred miles or so inland and parallel to the coast. These sandhills are the vestige of the prehistoric coast of lower Carolina, and the source of one of the most vigorous arguments since the Nullification Crisis. That dispute is over who has the best mustard-based barbecue sauce, and it has literally pitted brother against brother.

The Bessinger family of South Carolina has within its ranks two generals in the sauce wars: the famous Maurice of West Columbia, who serves his chopped pork drenched in a sweetly spiced mustard sauce, along with a side order of far-right Southern politics and myth; and his brother Melvin of Charleston, who has both a spicier sauce and a milder view of his fellow man. Despite having been fed on both of their sauces, I have my own personal Old South myth, a fond memory that will always taste better in remembrance than it ever did on my tongue.

About 30 miles north of Columbia, firmly in the mustard belt of South

Carolina, there sat on an expanse of farmland a simple concrete-block building. This humble one-story structure resembled a social hall at any rural Carolina Protestant church. Inside, folding tables and chairs lined up in long stretches on a linoleum floor. The room was a rectangle broken only by a single serving window in one wall. There was no church adjoining this social hall, however—just a large open-sided shed with a tin roof and a chimney, and a large pile of seasoned oak. This was Ray Lever's, a simple home to the best meals I ever ate.

Ray Lever's offerings were always the same. Chopped pork was served with a tangy mustard sauce that I can still taste, more than a decade after the place closed with the passing of its namesake. The marvelously moist pig was accompanied by a minced hash over white rice. As you went down the line, you could take two or three slices of white bread from the loaves that lay inside their bakery wrappers slit down the top with a knife. I seem to vaguely recall green beans also being served, but to me they were merely something that took up room on the plate that could have been far better used as space for more of Ray's heavenly barbecue.

The point isn't whether this was the One True Barbecue, or even the best I ever ate. It was the total experience of Ray Lever's that I will always treasure. The drive with my family as a child, the high school road trips there that celebrated our fledgling freedom to travel and eat what we wanted, and the pleasure I had several times of introducing my graduate schoolmates to this little corner of Southern culture—these are part of the flavor I will never forget about Ray Lever's.

Perhaps that is the real significance of Southern barbecue. It isn't just the way it's cooked or served or sauced; it is its place in the culture of the South as a simple food served at important times, by a community of people gathering to share a meal in a manner that goes back generations.

Pork; allow about ½ pound per person
Sauce of your choosing, or your creation
Sweet tea (really sweet)
Cheap beer (long-necks are best)

Rice, fries and hushpuppies
Slaw
White bread

The best meat to use is pork shoulder; fresh is the best—if you can find a real butcher. The pork must be slow-roasted over a fire of charcoal or wood. The meat has to cook slowly and thoroughly, so a regular grill won't work, since it's not designed for adding fuel as the meat cooks. Baste the meat generously as it cooks.

Other than these basic instructions, the rest is up to you. Part of the joy of a true Southern barbecue is its similarity to the music form known as the Blues—the basics may be the same, but the piece of your soul you put into it makes it uniquely yours.

YIELD: Depends on who shows up and how hungry they are!

HINT
You can use traditional coleslaw made with mayonnaise, or instead you can dress the shredded cabbage with the same sauce used for the meat.

ACKNOWLEDGMENTS

I will always be grateful to Bob Cannon, the staff and Board of Trustees of the Public Library of Charlotte and Mecklenburg County. They and the Novello Festival Press Advisory Committee—Judith Abner, John Cleghorn, Charlie DiPerna, Fannie Flono, Bob Inman, Scott Jagow, Patsy Kinsey and Ashley Warlick—believed that publishing the work of regional writers would benefit the larger community, and they were right.

Irene Blair Honeycutt is a wonderful poet who works tirelessly on behalf of her fellow writers, and Bob Inman is a superb novelist of great generosity. Both spoke up in support of my work at a critical time, and I am deeply indebted to them.

I thank the Arts and Science Council for recognizing and rewarding non-fiction writing. The Creative Artist Fellowship they awarded me was the most wonderful affirmation of my work, and it directly supported me during the writing of this book.

The Wildacres Retreat Center provided me not only a residency, but the ideal setting in which to work, with the perfect balance of solitude and support. It was in the Wildacres kitchen that this book began to take shape, and I am grateful to everyone on staff at the center.

The North Carolina Arts Council supports Novello Festival Press, the publisher of this book. I appreciate their recognition, both for the press and for its individual projects.

John Egerton, author of *Southern Food*, is one of our finest writers. He has always said kind things about my work, and I am honored that he wrote the foreword to this book.

John T. Edge and everyone at the Southern Foodways Alliance at the University of Mississippi are doing the incredibly important work of documenting the culinary and cultural history of the American South. I thank them for their encouragement and support.

Carolyn Sakowski, Anne Waters, Ed Southern and the staff of John F. Blair, Publisher, continue to be an invaluable resource.

Thanks to Jerry Bledsoe, who in 1994 took a chance on a hungry writer who couldn't bake a biscuit but learned how.

Frye Gaillard, Carol Adams, Melinda Farbman and Leslie Rindoks are my NFP family. They always work hard and with good humor on behalf of our projects, and I'm fortunate to have them as my colleagues and my friends.

I thank David Wilgus for his imaginative cover illustration, and designer Bonnie Campbell for giving shape to the material that comprises this book.

Jayne Dowdy of the Mast Store in Valle Crucis shared staff recipes from the mountain regions of North Carolina. June Blotnick and Kristin Sherman directed me to storytellers who personify the cultural richness of our region.

My family couldn't believe it twenty years ago when I moved "South" from Florida to South Carolina, where finding fresh bagels or dim sum was far from a sure thing. They've finally come around and I'm glad they learned what I knew all along about living in the Carolinas.

Last and always, I thank John Rogers, who gave me a kitchen of my own and never once complained that during the time his wife was writing a food book, he rarely got a home-cooked meal.

ABOUT THE AUTHORS

Julie E. Adkisson, a Tennessee native and the daughter of a Baptist minister, moved around for much of her early life before her family finally settled in North Carolina. She makes her living writing advertising copy, but enjoys poetry and food writing on the side.

Cordelia B. Anderson is the public relations coordinator for the Public Library of Charlotte and Mecklenburg County. She is a native of Virginia, where she says she developed her love of writing in the shadow of Revolutionary and Civil War history.

Barbara Appling is a traditional North Carolina cook who grew up in a large family. Like her mother and grandmother, she doesn't measure ingredients and rarely uses recipes.

Scottie Karen Ash, a native of Allendale, S.C., is manager of the museum gift shop at the South Carolina State Museum in Columbia. Her interests in the kitchen are more than culinary; she is a collector of vintage Fiesta dinnerware.

Sherry Austin is a North Carolina writer who now lives in the mountain town of Flat Rock. She is the author of *Mariah of the Spirits and Other Southern Ghost Stories.*

Ellyn Bache, who lives in Wilmington, N.C., is the author of five novels, including *Safe Passage*, which became a film starring Susan Sarandon. She is also the author of a children's book, *Granddaddy Terry and the Pink Flash.*

Mignon F. Ballard is the author of twelve novels, including *The Angel Whispered Danger.* She is best-known for her mysteries, but is also the author of *The War in Sallie's Station*, a novel about growing up in World War II. She lives in Ft. Mill, S.C.

Carrie Barnes is a native of Duplin County, N.C., now living in Charlotte, where she works as a patient access representative at Presbyterian Orthopaedic Hospital. She has studied culinary arts, and her hobbies include cooking, reading and writing family stories.

Anne C. Barnhill is a writer living in Kernersville, N.C. She has published both fiction and non-fiction, including several articles in *Our State* magazine. She says she is happy to pass along a recipe made famous in her family by her 100-year-old grandfather.

Ingrid Bialas-Wilson was born and educated in Germany. She is a math and language teacher who came to America when she married Scott Wilson, a native of Fayetteville, N.C. The Wilsons have two children who are learning to speak English, German and Italian.

Janie W. Bird is a native of Greensboro, N.C., and a retired educator who received her undergraduate degree from the University of North Carolina and her Ph.D. from the University of South Carolina.

Wanda Stephens Birmingham is a native of Mecklenburg County, N.C., where her family has lived for more than 200 years. As a child, she lived for a time in Alaska before moving back to North Carolina. She learned to cook through the example of her parents, both of whom were gifted in the kitchen.

Jerry Bledsoe is an award-winning journalist and author whose books include the number one *New York Times* best-seller *Bitter Blood* and the recently published *Death By Journalism?* He is founder and editor in chief of Down Home Press in Asheboro, N.C.

Doe Boekelheide is a former Peace Corps agriculture volunteer in Togo, West Africa, and is now an avid gardener who lives near the University of North Carolina at Charlotte. He has written for *OG* Magazine (formerly Organic Gardening) and other publications.

Monty Branham and B.J. VanZant are Catawba Indians living on the reservation outside of Rock Hill, S.C. They are brother and sister, both active in cultural education programs for the tribe. Branham is a Catawba musician and potter. VanZant is the mother of two.

Janet Bright is a married grandmother of four, a former secretary now working part-time at the Mast General Store in Hendersonville, N.C. She lives near other members of her family in the Southern Appalachians, and like her mother is an avid collector of recipes.

Elizabeth C. Burgess, who now lives in Asheboro, N.C., has been a teacher and a leader in her Episcopal church, and has recently completed her first novel, *Prison Camp Road.*

Leah E. Burris is a lifelong resident of North Carolina who grew up in Concord and later attended Appalachian State University in Boone. She says her recipes reflect not only her Carolina roots, but her appreciation of how the region is becoming more diverse.

Lynda Calabrese is a poet, painter and playwright living in Charlotte. She has led writing workshops at Queens University, and her books of poetry include *The Sum of Our Breath* and *On the Cusp of Something Else.*

Vincent Calabrese is an illustrator, painter and web page designer and the cofounder of Manzanita Books. He has designed record albums and CD covers and has had showings of his acrylic and digital paintings.

Will D. Campbell, a graduate of Wake Forest University, is a writer and minister now living in Mt. Juliet, Tenn. His memoir, *Brother to a Dragonfly,* was a finalist for the National Book Award. His other books include *Forty Acres and a Goat,* and *Soul Among Lions.*

Marshall Chapman, a native of Spartanburg, S.C., is a singer-songwriter living in Nashville. She has released eight critically acclaimed albums, and her songs have been recorded by Emmylou Harris, Jimmy Buffett and others. She is the author of a memoir, *Good-bye Little Rock and Roller.*

Tricia Childress, who has lived in different locales around the U.S., is a food writer whose work often appears in *Creative Loafing.* She is married to Pierre Bader, who grew up in Lebanon and is the proprietor of Sonoma Bistro and Wine Bar. They live in Charlotte, N.C.

Stowe B. Cobb Jr. is a Kannapolis, N.C. native. He retired in 1992 after 25 years of service as a Cabarrus County deputy sheriff. Since surrendering his uniform and badge, he enjoys regular weekly rounds of golf and spending time with family and friends.

Karen S. Cobb is a native of Concord, N.C., whose passion for food led her to the Culinary Institute of America in Hyde Park, N.Y. When she isn't trying out new recipes in the kitchen, she works as a corporate communications manager for a home textiles manufacturer.

Cassandra King Conroy and Pat Conroy are husband-and-wife novelists living on Fripp Island, S.C. King's most recent novel is *The Sunday Wife.* Conroy's books include *The Great Santini, The Prince of Tides,* and the recently published memoir *My Losing Season.*

Leslie Stanton Couick lives in Rock Hill, S.C. She grew up with stories of her grandmother, Eliza Faries Stanton, who raised twelve children and managed the family farm after the death of her husband. Couick is happy to preserve that legacy in the form of one of her grandmother's recipes.

Campbell and Meredith Coxe live in Darlington County, S.C. Both are outdoor enthusiasts, and they began growing rice on family land along the Pee Dee River in the 1990s. They are the proprietors of Carolina Plantation Rice.

Lynda F. Crisp was raised in Kannapolis, N.C., by her grandmother, Mary McBride, a mill worker and gardener who was legendary for her cooking. Crisp, who now lives in York, S.C., raised four children and enjoys spending time with her ten grandchildren.

Jackie Denise Cureton is a graduate of the University of North Carolina at Charlotte and the mother of two children. She began cooking for her whole family when she was twelve, and still enjoys her artistic experimentations in the kitchen.

Deborah Cutshall is a native of Newport News, Virginia, who moved with her husband to Madison County, N.C. There, she says, she learned how to can food, raise a garden, and cook the kind of good Southern food that her husband was raised on.

Gloria Dahl is a writer, musician and artist who lives in Piedmont, S.C. She wrote her first story at the age of ten and has been writing professionally for 18 years. Her articles have appeared in *The Journal,* a weekly newspaper in Williamston, S.C.

Ahmad Daniels is a writer, educator and activist who has championed the cause of African liberation. He recently played an active role in the United Nations World Conference on Racism, Racial Discrimination, Xenophobia and Related Intolerance in Durban, South Africa. He is the author of the book, *To Your Journey.*

Liane Crowe Davenport is a resident of Greensboro, N.C., and a graduate of the University of North Carolina. She says she has been cooking "practically since I was able to reach the counter." She is a full-time homemaker and a part-time kitchen assistant for a gourmet store in Greensboro.

Doris A. Davis is a zoologist's wife who divides her time between the mountain town of Sylva, N.C., and Summerland Key, Fla. She says she learned to be resourceful in her cooking during her family's graduate student years when money was scarce.

Eva L. Dawkins is a poet, single mother and community activist. She is a recent graduate of the University of North Carolina in Chapel Hill, where she majored in political science. Her poetry has appeared in two anthologies, *Out of the Rough* and *Celebrating Life.*

Gina Jones DeLisle is a database specialist for the Public Library of Charlotte and Mecklenburg County. She lives in Midland, N.C., with her husband, four cats, a cockatiel and a dog. She says she has been cooking, especially baking, for as long as she can remember.

Kathleen H. Falin is a full-time homemaker transplanted from Maryland to North Carolina in 1983. She lives in Clemmons with her husband of 35 years, and enjoys spending time with two grown sons and a grandson.

Melinda Farbman, a native of Albany, N.Y., is a teacher and children's author. A graduate of Yale University, she is the author of *Spacechimp: NASA's Ape in Space* and *Bridges*. She is a regular contributor to *Charlotte Jewish News*.

Lauren Faulkenberry is a writer and artist who grew up in Kershaw, S.C. She is a graduate of Washington University in St. Louis, and is the author of the nationally acclaimed children's book *What Do Animals Do on the Weekend?*

Heidi Flick is a graduate of Virginia Tech. She grew up near Richmond, Va., but a newspaper job brought her to North Carolina. She is a versatile and innovative cook who is married to newspaper editor Will MacDonald. They live in Gastonia.

Edna L. Foust has won blue ribbons for her baking at the North Carolina State Fair. Now retired after working for 56 years in the field of nursing, she lives in Durham, N.C. She says she is looking forward to future competitions at the fair.

Sheila Freeze moved to North Carolina in 1997 "as a mid-life career changer in search of new meaning." In 2002, she graduated with honors from Guilford College, where she discovered the pleasures of creative writing. She lives in Summerfield, N.C.

Rebecca Adams Fry is a grandmother living in Valle Crucis, N.C., where she works at the Mast General Store. She says her recipe for Old South Fruitcake has been handed down in her family since the time of the Civil War.

Frye Gaillard is a journalist and author of 19 works of non-fiction, including the national award-winner *If I Were A Carpenter*. He is a founder and executive editor of Novello Festival Press and lives in Indian Trail, N.C.

Nancy Gaillard, a native of Greenville, S.C., is a principal in the Charlotte-Mecklenburg Schools and co-author of the book, *Mobile and the Eastern Shore*. She lives in Indian Trail, N.C.

Irene Gammon describes herself as a "Southerner by default." She was raised in New Jersey, attended college in Virginia and later moved to North Carolina. She offers a recipe that she first made at the age of seven—a great one, she says, for "kids to cut their culinary teeth on."

Jeff Ganoung is a Florida native; his wife, Janet, grew up in Hickory, N.C. After careers in food science and nutrition in Illinois, they moved to Janet's home state where they now own Charlotte's Great Harvest Bakery.

Gayle Kelly Garrison is a native of Whiteville, N.C., who now makes her home in northern California. Over the years, she and her husband have made frequent trips back to North Carolina, driven in part by the need for barbecue.

Karen A. Geiger is a native of New Jersey who loves living in the South. She is an educator at the McColl Graduate School of Business. She and her husband, Damon Rumsch, have two wonderful teenage sons and three dogs.

Wendy H. Gill is a teacher and freelance writer who lives in Matthews, N.C. Her essays have appeared in *Tis the Season: The Gift of Holiday Memories, Skirt!* magazine and *Writer's Digest On-Line Chronicle.*

Devorah Leah Gordon is from Brooklyn, New York. She is a graduate of Bais Chaya Mushka Seminary and a Judaica teacher at the Jewish Preschool on Sardis in Charlotte. She is the mother of four children.

Jessica Graham is a Director of Community Relations for Time-Warner Cable. She lives near the town of Indian Trail with her husband and two cats.

Maureen Ryan Griffin is the award-winning author of *When The Leaves Are In The Water,* a collection of poetry. She offers writing classes and critiques through her business, WordPlay, and through Queens University.

Janeth Guzman is a native of Ibarra, Ecuador. She came to North Carolina to study English and culinary arts, and dreams of someday opening her own restaurant where she can serve the cuisine of her home country.

Debra Long Hampton, who grew up in Concord, N.C., is now the director of book design and production for John F. Blair, Publisher, in Winston-Salem. She is married and the mother of a six-year-old daughter.

Rose Hampton has won blue ribbons and accolades for her baking. She inherited her love of cooking from her mother, Pearl Jackson, and has passed it along to her daughter, daughter-in-law and stepdaughter. Rose and her husband, Danny, live in Raleigh, N.C.

Emmylou Harris is a Grammy Award-winning singer and songwriter who is widely regarded as one of country music's most important artists. She grew up in Alabama, lives in Nashville and attended undergraduate school at the University of North Carolina at Greensboro.

Noushin Heidari is a native of Tehran, Iran, and came to the U.S. as a student in 1983. She lives in Columbia, S.C., where she is married and the mother of three. She writes children's stories in her spare time.

Dene Hellman is a writer and former corporate newsletter editor who lives in Fletcher, N.C. She and her late husband Werner Hellman were partners in a Wisconsin advertising agency before moving to North Carolina, where they both retired.

Caroline Castle Hicks is a free-lance writer living in Huntersville, N.C. Her work has appeared in several anthologies, including *Chicken Soup for the Woman's Soul* and *' Tis the Season: The Gift of Holiday Memories.*

Pamela K. Hildebran, a former college instructor now living in Hildebran, N.C., offers her pumpkin pie recipe as a tribute to her mother, Agnes Hallman Hildebran. The recipe is a reminder, she says, of the wisdom and values passed from one generation to the next.

Linda Whitney Hobson, former executive director of the N.C. Writer's Network, grew up in the suburbs of Cleveland, Ohio, and moved south to attend Duke University. She is the author of *Understanding Walker Percy,* published by the University of South Carolina Press, and lives in Durham, N.C.

Ann H. Howell is a native North Carolinian now living in Asheville with her husband, two sons and a 15-year-old cat. She is the author of one published short story, "My Eight O'-Clock and Me."

Josephine Humphreys is an award-winning novelist living at Sullivan's Island, S.C. Her books include *Rich in Love, Dreams of Sleep, The Fireman's Fair,* and the recently published and nationally acclaimed *Nowhere Else on Earth.*

Dan Huntley is a *Charlotte Observer* columnist who lives in York, S.C. His fiction was published in the regional anthology *No Hiding Place* and his poetry has appeared nationally in *Rolling Stone* magazine. He is also a competitive barbecue chef.

Nadine Carriker Hyatt, who lives in Monroe, N.C., recently coordinated the publication of a cookbook at her church, Antioch Baptist. A native of Mint Hill, N.C., she is the mother of four, grandmother of ten and most recently the great-grandmother of one.

Robert Inman, a television news anchor turned screenwriter and novelist, divides his time between Charlotte and Boone, N.C. He is the author *Home Fires Burning, Old Dogs and Children, Coming Home* and *Captain Saturday,* among other books.

Dot Jackson, a former columnist for the *Charlotte Observer,* is a now a free-lance writer living near Pickens, S.C. She is the co-author of *The Catawba River* and *Keowee,* and a contributor to the anthology *No Hiding Place.*

Virginia H. Jackson is a prize-winning biscuit-maker who lives in Kenly, N.C. Among her other jobs through the years, she has baked biscuits for nearby restaurants, and her own recipe has won a blue ribbon at the N.C. State Fair.

Scott Jagow is a public radio reporter for WFAE, Charlotte's NPR news station. He is a three-time N.C. Radio Journalist of the Year, who has won numerous awards for reporting. He is married to Amy Quinton, who is also a public radio reporter.

Roxane Maria Javid is a Charlotte writer whose non-fiction has appeared in *The Charlotte Observer* and whose poetry has appeared in *Main Street Rag* and *Wellspring.*

Debe Jones is a native of Silverstone, N.C., in the Appalachian Mountains. At a young age, she learned to cook "good ole Southern country meals," a skill passed on to her by her mother. She lives in Boone and contributed to the cookbook, *Mast Store Cooks.*

Karyn Joyner, who lives in Hendersonville, N.C., says her recipe for mango bread was given to her by the 97-year-old mother of a friend—a priceless gift on a faded scrap of paper, reminding her that fragile traditions need to be preserved.

Vassilios Karamitros is a native of Greece. After serving in the Air Force, he attended culinary school where he learned how to prepare traditional dishes of his home country, France, Italy, and the U.S. He and his family live now in North Carolina.

Elizabeth A. Karmel grew up in Greensboro, N.C., and now lives in Chicago. Recognized as the nation's female authority on backyard barbecue, she teaches grilling in cooking schools and was a contributor to *The Barbecue Bible.* A coleslaw recipe included here belongs to her mother, Lynn Karmel, a counselor in private practice and a native of Rich Square, N.C.

Patsy B. Kinsey learned to cook "out of necessity—I had three children to feed." Known for her involvement in civic activities, she served two terms on the Mecklenburg Board of County Commissioners. Currently, she is Director of Business Development for Pease Associates Architects-Engineers.

Lisa Williams Kline is a writer living in Mooresville, N.C. She is the author of two novels for young readers, *Eleanor Hill* and *The Princesses of Atlantis,* and her stories for adults have appeared in *The Plum Review, Peregrine* and the anthology *'Tis the Season.*

Phyllis H. Lambert lives in Robbins, N.C., where she is a career counselor for the Moore County Schools. She is author of the book *Turning Every Stone: Autism With Love,* and she has won accolades for her fiction and poetry.

Brad LeGrone is a freelance video director in North Carolina, and a long-time lover of Krispy Kreme doughnuts. He says he read about a restaurant that was serving Krispy Kreme bread pudding, and was determined to create a concoction of his own.

Lori LeRoy is a wife and mother of two small children, now living in Charlotte. She says she was inspired in her love of good food by the "delicious" example of her grandmother's cooking.

Sylvia Little-Sweat is a teacher of English at Wingate University. In 2001, she chaired the school's Fine Arts of Being Southern Symposium, which helped her discover that "in the South creative cooking and creative writing go hand in hand."

Marianne London is a writer who lives in Matthews, N.C. Her work has appeared in *The Charlotte Merchandiser* and in the poetry anthology, *Celebrating Life,* and her commentaries have aired on WFAE public radio.

Shirley Maddalon holds a B.S. degree in Sociology from N.C. State University. She looks forward to passing along recipes from her grandmother, "Mama Sarah," who is 90 years old and still cooks for the family.

Amanda Dew Manning grew up on a South Carolina farm. She has worked for the Department of Education, the C.D.C., and the U.S.D.A's Food and Nutrition Service. She lives in coastal South Carolina, where she works to promote regional agricultural products.

Allen Mast was born and raised in the town of Valle Crucis, N.C., and works there today at his family's business, the Mast General Store. "I can think of no other place I would rather be," he says, and cooking is a part of his family's tradition.

Jill McCorkle is the award-winning author of five novels, including *Tending to Virginia* and *Carolina Moon,* and a collection of short stories, *Crash Diet.* She is a native of North Carolina, now living near Boston.

Rick McDaniel writes about food and cooking for four North Carolina newspapers from his home in Asheville. A Kings Mountain native, he learned his love of Southern food at his grandmother's knee. He is a member of the Southern Foodways Alliance.

Caren McNelly McCormack is a Charlotte writer who holds a B.A. degree in journalism from Texas Tech University and a Master's degree from the Medill School of Journalism at Northwestern University.

Joan Medlicott lives and writes in the mountains of western North Carolina. She is the author of the popular Ladies of Covington series of novels, including *The Ladies of Covington Send Their Love, The Gardens of Covington* and *From the Heart of Covington.*

Patti Frye Meredith is a North Carolina native and public television producer who has worked in Chapel Hill, N.C., Charlotte, N.C., and Columbia, S.C. She now lives in Huntsville, Ala., where she is at work on a series of short stories.

Peter Meyer, who lives in Wilmington, N.C., is the author of four books, including *Nature Guide to the Carolina Coast: Common Birds, Crabs, Shells, Fish and other Entities of the Coastal Environment,* and *Blue Crabs: Catch 'em, Cook 'em, Eat 'em.*

Helen Lloyd Montgomery was a resident of North Carolina before moving to St. Paul, Minn., in 1998. She serves as moderator for SouthSide Writers, a St. Paul critique group, and says she enjoys serving Southern cornbread to her new friends in the North.

Helen S. Moore is a long-time food columnist for both *The Charlotte Observer* and *The News & Observer* in Raleigh. In the course of a career spanning more than three decades she has judged hundreds of cooking contests in North Carolina and the South.

Virginia Moore has always loved the adventure of cooking. "I take liberties with recipes," she explains, "not always successfully." After living in Kansas City, Dallas, New Orleans and Memphis, she moved to North Carolina in 1984, where she enjoys spending time with her family.

Sheri Moretz lives in Boone, N.C., the town where she was born and attended college at Appalachian State University. She works at the Mast General Store in Valle Crucis where she combines her degree in public relations with her passion for history and heritage.

Mary Ellen Nash was raised in a farm family in Mecklenburg County, N.C., and is now a leader of the community gardening project in the inner-city Wilmore neighborhood. She was interviewed for the story in this book by Te'Quilla Shantia Graham, a junior at Charlotte's Myers Park High School where her favorite subject is theater.

Joy Nettles is a native of Columbia, S.C., who now lives in Rock Hill. She says she learned to cook by "osmosis," mostly through the example of her mother and grandmother, both of whom were cafeteria cooks.

Sally Olin describes herself as a "transplanted Yankee" from upstate New York who developed her appreciation of good food when her extended family of aunts, uncles and cousins would congregate on weekends. She is now a registered nurse in Charlotte.

Joan Osborne, who lives in Boomer, N.C., has long been an avid collector of cookbooks. "I love reading them like some people read novels," she says. She comes from a distinguished line of family cooks and is eager to see some of their recipes preserved in this book.

Katharine W. Osborne is a writer in Salisbury, N.C. Her personal essays appear regularly in the *Salisbury Post,* and she is the author of a book of poems, *She Done What She Could.*

Sarita Osborne was raised in western North Carolina and is currently studying psychology at Salem College in Winston-Salem. She says she has been helping her mother and grandmother in the kitchen since she was two years old.

Janet Culley Oyler is a native of South Carolina, a graduate of Winthrop University, and an Air Force wife who now lives in Fletcher, N.C. She says she developed "a keen interest in foods of many kinds" in the course of her travels with her husband.

Nancy Pate is a North Carolina native now working as book critic for the *Orlando Sentinel.* She is one third of the mystery writing team of Caroline Cousins, author of *Fiddle Dee Death,* published by John F. Blair in 2003.

Diana Pinckney grew up in South Carolina but now lives in North Carolina. She is the author of two books of poetry, *Fishing With Tall Women* and *White Linen,* and her work has appeared in several anthologies, including *Word and Witness: 100 Years of North Carolina Poetry.*

Crissy Harrison Pitman is food service manager at the Wildacres Retreat Center in Little Switzerland, N.C. She is a native of the town of Spruce Pine, and grew up watching her grandmother cook "absolutely wonderful meals." She has sought to build on that family tradition.

Michael Platnik is a native of Washington, D.C., who moved to Charlotte with his family in 1992. He says food is a reminder of family gatherings and holidays spent around his grandmother's table, traditions he wants to pass on to his children.

Marilyn Meacham Price lives in Fort Mill, S.C. She learned to cook at her widowed grandmother's side in the town of Statesville, N.C. "Those were exciting times for a little girl," she says, as she watched her grandmother feed her family with the help of a garden, a cow and an orchard.

Karen Proctor is a medical transcriptionist, writer and self-described "jack of all trades" who lives in Chapel Hill, N.C. Her writing has been published in the *North Carolina Writers Network News.*

Dee Pufpaff, who was raised in the Cajun country of Louisiana, moved to North Carolina in 1972 after coming to the state to visit a friend. She has traveled the world, sampling the food wherever she has gone, and now lives in Raleigh where she makes quilts, wreaths and other folk crafts.

Kathleen Purvis is the food editor of *The Charlotte Observer.* She is a member of the Association of Food Journalists, The James Beard Foundation and the Southern Foodways Alliance. She lives in Charlotte with her husband and their son.

Ron Rash is a novelist, poet and short story writer living in Clemson, S.C. He is the author of seven books, including his debut novel, *One Foot in Eden,* which was a national best-seller and the winner of the Novello Literary Award for 2002.

John Shelton Reed is William Rand Kenan Jr. Professor Emeritus of Sociology at the University of North Carolina in Chapel Hill. He is the author of more than a dozen books, including *1001 Things Everyone Should Know About the South*, co-authored with his wife, Dale Volberg Reed.

Gretchen Rhodes is a retired educator who lives in Madison, N.C. She enjoys cooking, reading and camping with her grandchildren, and in recent years she and her husband have been spending their time restoring a 150-year-old log house.

Peggy J. Riddle is a retiree living in Advance, N.C., whose favorite pastimes, in addition to cooking, are basket-making and knitting. She is a member of the Macedonia Moravian Church and the North Carolina Basket Association.

Leslie B. Rindoks is an artist, writer and book designer who lives in Davidson, N.C. She was a contributor to the anthology *'Tis the Season: The Gift of Holiday Memories* and is the author of *The Origins of Tradition*.

Amy Rogers, a native of Detroit, is an award-winning writer and editor. Her books include *Red Pepper Fudge and Blue Ribbon Biscuits*, and she is a contributor to *Cornbread Nation I: The Best of Southern Food Writing*. She is a frequent public radio commentator, and is a founding editor of Novello Festival Press.

John Rogers grew up in Columbia, S.C., a city known for its mustard-based barbecue. Rogers now lives in North Carolina, where he is a preservation planner and historian. With his wife, Amy, he co-authored the book *Charlotte: Its Historic Neighborhoods*.

Mary Ann Rogers lives in Columbia, S.C. She is working on a novel based on her memories of growing up in a mill village. She is a mother of three and grandmother of five. She enjoys cooking large holiday meals.

Marisa Rosenfeld, a native of Brazil, is a free-lance writer now living in Charlotte. Her columns have appeared in *The Charlotte Observer* and her poetry was published in the anthology *Celebrating Life*.

Jenny Rosenthal is a reference librarian at the Public Library of Charlotte and Mecklenburg County. Her interests include reading, movies, art, gardening, foreign languages and cooking. She says she steals all her best recipes from family and friends.

Cissie Darr Roth is the daughter of a gourmet cook. She was born in Winston-Salem and now lives in Elkin, N.C., where she is the mother of five and owns a bookstore with her daughter.

Diane Ruggiero grew up on New York's Long Island. She has always enjoyed being in the kitchen, but learned a challenging way to cook—over an open fire—when she worked as a cultural interpreter at Historic Latta Plantation in North Carolina.

Lynn Veach Sadler, a former college president with her Ph.D. from the University of Illinois, is a native of Duplin County, N.C. She is the author of five academic books and some 68 articles, and most recently, a chapbook of poetry entitled *Poet Geography*.

Dori Sanders is a South Carolina peach farmer turned novelist. Despite the runaway success of her first novel, *Clover,* followed by her cookbook, *Dori Sanders' Country Cooking,* she continues to work the family farm, selling her peaches by the side of the road near Filbert, S.C.

Sean A. Scapellato is a teacher and novelist living in Charleston, South Carolina. Though his culinary skills are limited, his mother and his wife, Sara, know no bounds in the kitchen. The Scapellatos enjoy the dishes of Sara's Lowcountry heritage and Sean's Italian relatives.

Rebecca Schenck is a native and current resident of Charlotte, former president of the Charlotte Writers Club and co-author of *Maryland's Historic Restaurants,* published by John F. Blair.

S.J. Sebellin-Ross is a free-lance writer specializing in corporate communications for *Fortune* 500 corporations such as McDonald's Restaurants. She has also written for international magazines and newspapers, including *The New York Times,* and is author of the book *Small Marketing on a Small Budget.*

Bland Simpson is author of five books, including *Ghost Ship of Diamond Shoals* and has collaborated on several musicals, including *Diamond Studs* and *Kudzu.* A member of the Tony Award-winning Red Clay Ramblers, he directs the creative writing program at UNC Chapel Hill. For his musical recipe in this book, he collaborated with singer-songwriter Jim Wann, whose latest composition is called "Catfish."

Alice E. Sink of Kernersville, N.C., is a writer and teacher who received her MFA from the University of North Carolina at Greensboro. She is the author of *The Grit Behind the Miracle,* and her articles have appeared in magazines from North Carolina to California.

Gay R. Small, who lives in Chapel Hill, N.C., is a free-lance writer who loves to cook. She offers her recipe in this book as a tribute to her Aunt Eva Grace who brought "magic" and a sense of family history to her childhood.

Lee Smith, winner of both the O. Henry Prize and the Robert Penn Warren Prize for Fiction, is the author of more than ten books, including the national best-seller *The Last Girls.* She lives in Hillsborough, N.C., with her husband and fellow writer Hal Crowther.

Randy Snyder lives in Mitchell County, N.C. He began his cooking career as a carhop at a local diner where he went on to cook for 25 years. He now works at Wildacres Retreat Center near Little Switzerland, N.C., where staff and visitors enjoy his culinary creations.

Cheryl Spainhour teaches journalism and communications at the University of North Carolina at Charlotte. She is a graduate of the University of Georgia and has her Master's degree from Wake Forest University. She lives with her family in Gaston County, N.C.

Amy Stallings is a public librarian living in Charlotte. Now the assistant manager of the Myers Park branch of the library, she is a graduate of Pfeiffer College in Misenheimer, N.C., where she earned a degree in English.

Lorraine Stark lives in Matthews, N.C., with her husband, having moved to the South from Monroe, N.Y. Before the move, she wrote a human interest column for her local newspaper, and still enjoys writing, gardening, cooking and crafts.

Linda Stroupe grew up in a large, extended family in Gaston County, N.C., where reunions featured recipes handed down from one generation to the next. She's especially proud of her mother's prize-winning macaroni and cheese, included in this book.

Karen M. Sullivan is a native of St. Louis and former resident of Washington, D.C., who moved to North Carolina more than 15 years ago. She says she learned about life, as well as food, in the hours she spent in her mother's kitchen.

Gilda Morina Syverson is a writer and artist who lives in Cornelius, N.C. She was raised in Syracuse, N.Y., in a large Italian family where cooking played a significant role. Her work has appeared in *Today's Charlotte Woman*, and her commentaries have aired on WFAE public radio.

James Taylor is a singer-songwriter who spent a part of his life in Chapel Hill, N.C., and was a popular figure in the folk-rock movement of the 1970s. He is best-known for such songs as "Fire & Rain," "You've Got A Friend," and "Carolina In My Mind."

Betty Baker Terres is a native of Cramerton, N.C., and now lives in Gastonia. She has been a wife and mother and a collector of cookbooks (she now owns about 50), and enjoys passing along family recipes to her children.

Meredith Brady Trunk, who is married and lives in Charlotte, has worked as a Wall Street corporate lawyer, a stable hand at a horseback riding establishment, a substitute librarian, a cafeteria monitor and a fifth grade literacy assistant. She has two daughters.

Joanna Virkler, who grew up in Chicago, moved to North Carolina more than 14 years ago. For seven years, she wrote the column "About Town" for the weekly newspaper, *The Leader,* and now moderates a half-hour interview program for WDAV radio.

Huy and Kim Vu are refugees from Vietnam who settled in Charlotte. They are the parents of two children, and own a dry cleaning business which has been consistently recognized as one of the area's best.

Ashley Warlick is a novelist who was born in North Carolina and now lives in South Carolina. She is the author of *The Distance from the Heart of Things*, winner of the Houghton-Mifflin Literary Prize, and *The Summer After June.*

Cydne Horrocks Watterson is a native of Utah who has lived in North Carolina for 18 years. She is the mother of three sons, a former editor at large for *Shape* magazine, and author of a Christmas story published in *The Charlotte Observer.*

Vicki White-Lawrence is a stay-at-home mother living in Stokesdale, N.C. She volunteers in both of her sons' schools and writes for her local newspaper, *The Northwest Observer.*

Ann Wicker is a graduate of Davidson College. A journalist for 20 years, she also writes mysteries, and is now pursuing her MFA in creative writing. She is married to producer and recording engineer Mark Williams.

Annelle Frye Williams is a native of Moore County, N.C., a graduate of the University of North Carolina and a resident of Martinsville, Va. She says her love of cooking began with her grandmother's Southern recipes, and her greatest pleasure is cooking for family and friends.

Becki Nell Williams graduated from the College of William and Mary in 2002 with a degree in Southern Studies. She now lives in Raleigh, N.C., where she is an administrative assistant for *Metro Magazine*.

Betty T. Williams is a prize-winning cook who lives in Monroe, N.C., and owns a business in nearby Polkton with her husband and two sons. She is a proud winner of a first-place prize for her egg custard pie from the North Carolina Egg Association.

Connie Williams is a native North Carolinian, the second of eleven children, who received her undergraduate degree from California State University at Northridge. She is a writer of both poetry and prose and the author of a novel, *Emily's Blues*.

Ellen Williams, a mother of three who lives in West Columbia, S.C., describes herself as "a Southern cook, born and raised, with international influences." She loves to experiment with recipes, and says it helps to have a husband with a culinary sense of adventure.

Tammy Wilson is a native of rural Illinois, now living in Catawba County, N.C. She is a member of the Charlotte Writers Club, and has written for the *North Carolina Literary Review, Emrys Journal, Thought Magazine* and *The MacGuffin*.

Alyssa Wood is an artist and teacher living in Davidson, N.C. She is a North Carolina native who grew up in Indiana and Virginia before returning recently to her home state.

Rachel R. Wright is a resident of Eden, N.C. She is a retired teacher who writes short stories and poems. Her work has appeared in the *Greensboro News & Record* and *The Greensboro Review*.

Lee Zacharias teaches writing and literature at the University of North Carolina Greensboro, and has won both the College and U.N.C. Board of Governors awards for excellence in teaching. Zacharias' books include *Lessons* and *Helping Muriel Make It Through the Night*.

Terrance Zepke is a Carolina writer who divides her time between North Myrtle Beach, S.C. and Greensboro, N.C. She is the author of *Lighthouses of the Carolinas: A Short History and Guide* and *Pirates of the Carolinas*, among other books.

Company Sweet Potato Casserole copyright © 2003 by Sheila Freeze. Used by permission of the author.

Cooked Coleslaw (Barbecued Coleslaw) copyright © 2003 by Elizabeth Karmel and Girls at the Grill™. Used by permission of the author.

Corn Chowder copyright © 2001 by Allen Mast. First published in *Mast Store Cooks: From Potluck Dinners to the Potbelly Stove*, published by New River Press, Boone, N.C. Reprinted by permission of the author.

Cotta Badertscher's Mule Ear Cookies copyright © 2003 by Leslie B. Rindoks. Used by permission of the author.

Crab Meltaways copyright © 2003 by Kathleen Falin. Used by permission of the author.

Crackling Cornbread copyright © 2001 by Debe Jones. First published in *Mast Store Cooks: From Potluck Dinners to the Potbelly Stove*, published by New River Press, Boone, N.C. Reprinted by permission of the author.

Cranberry Relish copyright © 2003 by Irene Gammon. Used by permission of the author.

Cream of Tomato Soup copyright © 2003 by Joan Osborne. Used by permission of the author.

Crissy Pitman's Broccoli Salad recipe copyright © 2001 by Crissy Harrison Pitman. First published in *Creative Loafing* magazine. Reprinted by permission of the author.

Crystal's Oatmeal Friendship Cookies copyright © 2003 by Amy Stallings. Used by permission of the author.

Dad's Cough Syrup copyright © 2001 by Sheri Moretz. First published in *Mast Store Cooks: From Potluck Dinners to the Potbelly Stove*, published by New River Press, Boone, N.C. Reprinted by permission of the author.

Divinity Under the Starlit Moon copyright © 2003 by Cydne Horrocks Watterson. Used by permission of the author.

Edna's Old Fashioned Pound Cake recipe copyright © 1995 by Edna L. Foust. First published in *Red Pepper Fudge and Blue Ribbon Biscuits: Favorite Recipes and Stories from North Carolina State Fair Winners* by Amy Rogers (Down Home Press, 1995). Reprinted by permission of the author.

Effie's Lemon Pie copyright © 2003 by Marianne London. Used by permission of the author.

Egg Custard Pie copyright © 2003 by Betty T. Williams. Used by permission of the author.

Ernie's Pound Cake copyright © 2003 by Anne C. Barnhill. First published in the *Winston-Salem Journal*, reprinted by permission of the author.

Favorite Congealed Salad copyright © 2003 by Mignon F. Ballard. Used by permission of the author.

Floye Long's Angel Biscuits copyright © 2003 by Debra Long Hampton. Used by permission of the author.

Foolproof Gravy copyright © 2003 by Joanna Virkler. Used by permission of the author.

Fried Apple Pies copyright © 2003 by Jill McCorkle. Used by permission of the author.

"Fried" Green Tomatoes copyright © 2003 by Joanna Virkler. Used by permission of the author.

Fudgy Chocolate Pie ("PMS Pie") copyright © 2003 by Gayle Kelly Garrison. Used by permission of the author.

Fuzzy Navel Cheesecake copyright © 2003 by Sylvia Little-Sweat. Used by permission of the author.

Garlicky Crab Claws copyright © 2003 by Josephine Humphreys. Used by permission of the author.

Gertrude's Rolls copyright © 2003 by Alice Sink. Used by permission of the author.

Gracie's Orange Fudge copyright © 2003 by Gay R. Small. Used by permission of the author.

Gramma Butner's Stuffed Peppers copyright © 2003 by Sherry Austin. Used by permission of the author.

Gramma's Black Salve copyright © 2003 by Wendy H. Gill. Used by permission of the author.

Gran Rice copyright © 2003 by Nancy Gaillard. Used by permission of the author.

Grandma Sadie's Marble Cake copyright © 2003 by Michael Platnick. Used by permission of the author.

Grandma Stanton's Applesauce Cake and Brown Sugar Frosting copyright © 2003 by Leslie Stanton Couick. Used by permission of the author.

Grandma Stephens' Chess Pie copyright © 2003 by Wanda Stephens Birmingham. Used by permission of the author.

Grandma's Cream Pie copyright © 2003 by Sheila Freeze. Used by permission of the author.

Grandma's Flapjacks copyright © 2003 by Carrie Barnes. Used by permission of the author.

Grandma's Persimmon Pudding copyright © 2000 by Peggy J. Riddle. First published in the *Dixie Classic Fair* cookbook. Reprinted by permission of the author.

Grandmommy's Chicken and Dumplings copyright © 2003 by Julie E. Adkisson. Used by permission of the author.

Granny's Apple Stack Cake copyright © 2003 by Ann H. Howell. Used by permission of the author.

Great Harvest Low-Fat Whole-Wheat Bran Muffins copyright © 2003 by Jeff and Janet Ganoung. Used by permission of the authors.

Grilled Tomatoes copyright © 2003 by S.J. Sebellin-Ross. Used by permission of the author.

Groundnut Stew with Corn Porridge (Azi Detsi with Akoume) copyright © 2003 by Don Boekelheide. Used by permission of the author.

Hamantaschen (A Dairy Dish) copyright © 2003 by Melinda Farbman. Used by permission of the author.

NOVELLO FESTIVAL PRESS

Novello Festival Press, under the auspices of the Public Library of Charlotte and Mecklenburg County and through the publication of books of literary excellence, enhances the awareness of the literary arts, helps discover and nurture new literary talent, celebrates the rich diversity of the human experience, and expands the opportunities for writers and readers from within our community and its surrounding geographic region. Proceeds from NFP books benefit the library.

THE PUBLIC LIBRARY OF CHARLOTTE AND MECKLENBURG COUNTY

For more than a century, the Public Library of Charlotte and Mecklenburg County has provided essential community service and outreach to the citizens of the Charlotte area. Today, it is one of the premier libraries in the country—named "Library of the Year" and "Library of the Future" in the 1990s—with 23 branches, 1.6 million volumes, 20,000 videos and DVDs, 9,000 maps and 8,000 compact discs. The Library also sponsors a number of community-based programs, from the award-winning Novello Festival of Reading, a celebration that accentuates the fun of reading and learning, to branch programs for young people and adults.

Award-winning writer and editor Amy Rogers is a food essayist for public radio and a founding editor of Novello Festival Press. Her books include *Red Pepper Fudge and Blue Ribbon Biscuits,* and she is a contributor to *Cornbread Nation I: The Best of Southern Food Writing* and *The North Carolina Century: Tar Heels Who Made a Difference, 1900–2000.* Her work has also appeared in the *Charlotte Observer, Oxford American* magazine and other publications. She and her husband, John, live in Charlotte, North Carolina.

INDEX